Laboratory Exercises in Physiological Psychology

FOURTH EDITION

prepared by

Paul J. Wellman
Texas A&M University

ALLYN AND BACON
BOSTON • LONDON • TORONTO • SYDNEY • TOKYO • SINGAPORE

Copyright © 1994, 1986 by Allyn and Bacon
A Division of Paramount Publishing
160 Gould Street
Needham Heights, Massachusetts 02194

All rights reserved. No part of the material protected by this copyright notice may be reproduced or utilized in any form or by any means, electronic or mechanical, including photocopying, recording, or by any information storage and retrieval system, without the written permission of the copyright owner.

ISBN 0-205-15966-4

Printed in the United States of America

10 9 8 7 6 5 4 3 2 1   98 97 96 95 94 93

TABLE OF CONTENTS

Preface

BASIC METHODS:

		Page:
Chapter 1:	Principles of Animal Care and Ethical Use	1
Chapter 2:	Anesthesia Procedures	19
Chapter 3:	Surgical Instruments, Aseptic Techniques and Procedures	33
Chapter 4:	Stereotaxic Surgery	53
Chapter 5:	Histology	75

LABORATORY EXERCISES:

Exercise 1:	Human Psychophysiology	91
Exercise 2:	Adrenergic Control of Brown Adipose Thermogenesis in Rats	97
Exercise 3:	Gross Anatomy of the Sheep Brain	103
Exercise 4:	Electrical Stimulation of Rat Motor Cortex	113
Exercise 5:	Apomorphine-induced Stereotypy in Rats	119
Exercise 6:	Morphine-Induced Analgesia in Rats	125
Exercise 7:	Pain Perception in Humans	131
Exercise 8:	Sexual Receptivity in the Rat after Ovariectomy	135
Exercise 9:	Thirst induced by Intraventricular Angiotensin II in Rats	141
Exercise 10:	Hypothalamic Adrenergic Receptors and Feeding in Rats	149
Exercise 11:	Effects of Bombesin on Feeding and Drinking	161
Exercise 12:	Emotional Behavior in the Septal Rat	167
Exercise 13:	Rewarding Brain Stimulation	177
Exercise 14:	Peripheral Catecholamines and Memory	185

APPENDICES

Appendix A:	Commercial Sources for Equipment and Materials	189
Appendix B:	Common Laboratory Drugs and Sources	195
Appendix C:	Stereotaxic Atlas	197

PREFACE

Physiological psychology refers to the area of psychology that studies how physiological mechanisms mediate behavior. Physiological psychology has as its chief goal a complete understanding of the neural underpinnings of behavior. Its focus is experimental in nature and usually involves some manipulation of brain function. Examples of manipulations in this manual include both chemical and electrical stimulation of the brain, and a variety of techniques that cause lesions or destroy a circumscribed brain area. Our goal is to determine which of these techniques produces a change in behavior. However, physiological psychology does not focus solely on neurons within the brain. The peripheral nervous system as well as the peripheral endocrine systems impact behavior. For example, rats treated with the adrenal hormone epinephrine exhibit dramatic changes in memory while hormones such as angiotensin induce drinking in rats. Thus, physiological psychology, in general as well as in this manual, focuses on both the peripheral and central nervous systems.

This manual is written for upper-class undergraduate students. It assumes that you have either completed a course in physiological psychology or are concurrently enrolled in that course. This manual will provide you with laboratory exercises that complement and extend the concepts that you are learning in your course. Many, but not all, of the exercises involve projects using rats as subjects. This presents two special issues. The first is how to care for and work with these animals; thus, the first 5 chapters cover material on (1) the care and use of lab animals , (2) anesthesia, (3) basic surgical techniques, (4) stereotaxic surgery techniques, and (5) histology. The second issue relates to research ethics. When the first edition of this manual was written in 1985, there was only slight concern surrounding the use of animals for teaching purposes. The ascent of animal rights to the forefront of the national consciousness has resulted in the adoption of rules and guidelines which significantly limit procedures which might cause pain and distress in animals. Chapter 1 describes the current animal use guidelines and provides a discussion of the ethical issues surrounding using animals in a teaching environment. Chapter 1 also provides a discussion of how local animal use committees consider and approve animal use protocols. An actual animal use protocol form is provided at the end of Chapter 1.

The exercises of this manual represent a diverse group of topics and methods of physiological psychology. They were selected to illustrate points connected to major chapter topics. One of the first topics covered in most physiological courses is the physiology of nerve cells and how their electrical potentials transmit information. An added exercise in this edition relates to electrophysiology in humans. In Exercise 1, students learn about physiological instruments and how to record human electrical potentials such as skin resistance. The concept of transmitter release and of receptors is also covered early in most physiological psychology courses. Exercise 2 deals with a peripheral tissue in the rat termed brown fat and how various transmitters activate specific receptors to cause this type of fat to release heat. Neuroanatomy is covered in

Preface

Exercise 3, and deals with dissection of the sheep brain. Later course topics related to motivation and to memory are covered in subsequent exercises. It is unlikely that you will attempt all of these exercises; rather, your instructor will choose a number that will fit your particular lab interests.

In each exercise, you will be provided with a background description and rationale for the project. Each exercise is self-contained. You are provided with a list of materials required to complete the exercise, a summary of the experimental procedures and information on data summary and interpretation. The background and rationale serve to briefly introduce the lab concept to be discussed and the literature that provides the background to the exercise. Where possible, you should read some or all of the citations for each exercise prior to completing the exercise. In addition, these references can serve as a starting point for a literature review that will aid you if your instructor asks that you write a formal paper on an exercise. The list of materials given in each exercise is tentative in that your laboratory instructor may provide alternative materials, depending on availability and cost. For each exercise, I provide a description of the type, sex and number of animals along with the procedures and apparatus required to complete the exercise. In addition, I have provided surgery sheets for your use in those exercises that entail stereotaxic surgery of the rat brain. You should carefully collect the data for each exercise as instructed in each data summary and interpretation section. For each exercise, I have provided one or more graphic axes that you should use to depict the data of the experiment. Finally, you should write up each laboratory section that you complete and should address the interpretation questions that are provided at the end of each exercise. A summary of the laboratory report is provided at the end of this section.

LABORATORY REPORTS

During the semester or quarter term, your laboratory instructor will expect you to complete some number of the laboratory exercises described in this laboratory manual. As you complete an exercise, your instructor is likely to require that you provide a formal written report of the exercise and its results. Although the laboratory report is often viewed by students as either an exercise in masochism or futility, the true purpose of the laboratory report is to provide you with an opportunity to practice the art of scientific communication. That is, in writing the laboratory report you will have to provide a rationale for the experiment, a description of the methods and procedures and results, and will have to interpret the results with regard to the prior literature. Each exercise will be an opportunity for you to learn the art of concise communication.

The laboratory report should be written in the style dictated by the Publication Manual of the American Psychological Association (1983). The report consists of the following sections: Title, Author and Affiliation, Abstract, Introduction, Methods, Results, Discussion and References. Consult the Publication Manual for specific guidelines on format and style. Christensen (1994) also provides a concise example of an APA-style report. The following sections are designed to introduce each of the components of the laboratory report.

Title.
The title and the author lines form the basis for the cover page on the laboratory report. The purpose of the title is to briefly, yet accurately, convey to the reader what the report is about. You should attempt to provide an understanding of the independent (IV) and dependent (DV) variables of the report and of the species that served as subjects. If you were to write a laboratory report on Exercise 2 of this manual a title such as "Effects of phenylpropanolamine on brown adipose tissue thermogenesis in the adult rat" would be appropriate. Titles such as "Thermogenesis" (too narrow, no indication of IV or DV or the species) or "Male rats injected with a pinch of an over-the-counter drug exhibit increases in brown fat thermogenesis" (too long, too specific, what is the IV drug?) are not appropriate.

Author and Affiliation.
The author citation gives you credit for the report and identifies your departmental and University (or other) affiliation.

Abstract.
The abstract begins on a new page following the cover page. The abstract serves as a brief summary of the laboratory report. The typical abstract is 70-100 words in length. The abstract should communicate to the reader a sense of the rationale for the project, a brief description of the methods, a summary of the results, and your interpretation of the data.

Introduction.
The introduction is not labeled as such and begins on a new page. The introduction of a laboratory report can be viewed as composed of 2 components. The first component serves to briefly introduce and describe the general research area and is typically 1-2 paragraphs in length. As you refer to research papers in the published literature, you must provide citations for each (see the APA Publication Manual, 1983, pages 107-116). The second component of the introduction serves to identify the purpose and rationale of your paper. In this section, you should explicitly identify the independent and dependent variables, the subjects, and the expected results (hypotheses).

Method.
The method section serves to provide specific details as to the materials and procedures that were required to carry out the research project. The method is broken down into sub-headings as follows:

Animals. This section should detail the source (supplier), age, sex and strain of the subjects. This section provides details on how the animals were housed (e.g. individually or in groups), the lighting and temperature of the colony room, and the type of food and water (and how delivered) given the animals.

Preface

Drugs. If drug treatments (other than anesthesia) are used in an exercise, you should describe the source of the drug and how the solution was prepared. You should detail whether the solution was prepared prior to injection and whether the drug solution was calculated as the weight of the drug base or the weight of the drug base and salt per unit volume (see Chapter 2). Also indicate whether the drug was dissolved or suspended and describe the drug vehicle (e.g. distilled water or saline). Indicate the dose of drug administered in mg/kg.

Surgery. Any surgical procedures used in an exercise are described in this section. You should indicate that suitable anesthesia was used during the procedure and indicate the type and doses(s) of anesthetic. Also indicate whether atropine was used to reduce respiratory problems. After describing how the surgical groups were prepared (e.g. "the sham-rats were anesthetized and were treated as were the surgical group except that no current was passed through the intracranial electrode.") Finally, the post-operative care procedures and the length of the post-operative recovery period should be described in the surgery section.

Procedure. The purpose of the procedure section is to provide the reader with an accurate accounting of the chronological events of the laboratory project and with details describing the methods of the exercise. Specifics as to the procedures will vary with the project but will in general resemble the procedure section of the laboratory exercise (hint, hint...).

Results. The results section serves to summarize the findings of the exercise. Here you should present data summaries (tables or figures) rather than a listing of the individual data points. If you present the data in figures or tables, these should be numbered consecutively and placed at the end of the report. For each figure, provide a caption that describes the axes of the graph, the groups and the units of measurement, as illustrated below:

Figure 1.   Mean group interscapular brown adipose tissue temperature (degrees C) in rats treated with either 0.9% saline or 10 mg/kg phenylpropanolamine.

Another aspect of the results section is presentation of the statistical analyses of the group data. Your instructor will provide information on the computational procedures used to evaluate any group differences that emerge from the laboratory exercise. As you refer to a difference between groups, you should indicate whether the difference is statistically significant and provide information (in parentheses) as to the type of statistical test used to evaluate the difference between groups. For example, "rats treated with apomorphine exhibited significant increases in activity over a 5 minute period ($\underline{t}$ (6) = 2.6, $\underline{p}$ < .04)", would indicate that a comparison of activity prior to and after apomorphine was significant, that a $\underline{t}$ test was used, the degrees of freedom were 6, and that the probability that this difference resulted by chance was less than 4 out of one hundred. If the laboratory exercise included stereotaxic manipulation of the brain, then the results of the histological examination of the subject brains must be described in the results section (See Chapter 5).

<u>Discussion</u>. The discussion section serves several functions. First, you should describe the general results of the exercise. You may wish to relate your results to those of the literature and note any similarities or differences. You should comment on the significance of your data for the literature and perhaps speculate as to what the next research step might be in this area. In addition, if you encountered problems in conducting the exercise, describe those problems in the discussion section and speculate about potential solutions (if any).

<u>References</u>.
The references serve to document the literature papers that you have cited in the body of the laboratory report. The references begin on a new page and should be organized alphabetically. Only include those citations that are necessary; do not cite all reports that you read in preparation for the laboratory exercise. For details as to the proper format for references, consult the APA Publication Manual (1983, pages 111-116). The general format is:

Author, I.M.N. (1984) Hypothetical publications that illustrate the art of creating laboratory reports. <u>Journal of Experimenting Psychologists</u>, <u>1</u>, 101-124.

<u>Tips on writing laboratory reports</u>.
After you complete the first draft of each report, put it in a folder for several days and then re-read the draft. You will frequently find that obvious errors in composition, spelling and punctuation become apparent on a second reading. Also, bribe a friend to read the draft and suggest changes. Finally, you might even be so daring as to ask your instructor to preview the draft prior to the due date of the report.

REFERENCES

Author. (1983). <u>Publication Manual</u>, Washington, D.C.: American Psychological Association.

Christensen, L.C. (1994). <u>Experimental Methodology</u>, Boston: Allyn and Bacon.

Chapter 1
Principles of Animal Care and Ethical Use

Although rats are only used in 7% of experiments conducted by researchers in psychology, the small size and excellent health of this species have led it to be used by many investigators in physiological psychology. Consequently, a considerable database exists as to the physiology and the behavioral patterns of this mammal. The chapters and exercises of this manual reflect that tradition in that most of the experiments and demonstrations of this manual use rats as subjects. This chapter presents information about the anatomy and general physiology of the rat that will be useful to students in physiological psychology. In addition, information about general care, breeding and euthanasia techniques are discussed, as well as ethical issues related to the use of animals in physiological research and in teaching laboratories.

Anatomy

Many texts of rat anatomy are presently available. These range from early line drawings of gross anatomy and morphology (Wells, 1964; Smith and Calhoun, 1968) to a color plate atlas of rat gross anatomy (Olds and Olds, 1979). The latter text is a particularly useful atlas of the peripheral anatomy of the rat. In addition, several atlases describe the central nervous system of the rat in stereotaxic coordinates (see Chapter 4 and Appendix C). These include the early line-drawn atlas of deGroot (1959) and the photographically enlarged plates of König and Klippel (1963), Pellegrino and Cushman (1967), Skinner (1971), Thompson (1978) and Paxinos and Watson (1986).

Physiological Data For the Rat

Table 1.1 presents average values for several physiological variables of the adult rat. These average values are intended as general information about the rat; most important among these are the values for body weight, food intake, sexual maturity and body temperature.

Housing

Several organizations have developed explicit guidelines to regulate the care and housing of rodents used in the physiological psychology laboratory (Author, 1978; NIH Guidelines, 1986; Animal Welfare Act, 1989). According to the current standards, rats should be housed in spacious, well-ventilated, and dry cages constructed of either plastic or stainless steel. Bedding (wood shavings, sawdust or commercial litter such as Beta-Chip) should be changed frequently (2-3 times weekly) to minimize odor and to reduce the possibility of disease in the colony. After a changeout, each cage should be sterilized using either hot water or steam (at least 180° F) or a chemical disinfectant. Humidity within the colony room should be maintained between 40 and 60 percent whereas the room temperature should be kept between 70 and 74 degrees F. Lighting should be diffuse throughout the colony and of an intensity (75-125 foot-candles) sufficient to allow laboratory procedures to be carried out. Light schedules should be diurnal (i.e. 12 hr/12 hr day/night schedule) because continuous lighting schedules may produce partial retinal

Chapter 1: Animal Care

degeneration in rats. Tap water and nutritionally complete feed such as Purina Rat & Mouse Diet should be freely available from water bottles and feeders suspended outside of the cage except where inconsistent with the experimental procedures. While it is recognized that not all rat facilities can meet these stringent guidelines, you should be aware of their existence and strive to meet this standard of care.

Table 1.1: Typical physiological values for the rat.

Adult Weight:	
Male	300-400 grams
Female	250-300 grams
Body Temperature	35.9-37.5 ° C)
Ingestion:	
Food	10 gm/100 g/day
Water	10-12 ml/ 100 g/day
Life Span	2.5-3 years
Surface Area:	130-325 cm^2
Birth Weight	5-6 gm
Breeding Onset	65-100 days
Gestation	21-23 days
Litter Size	6-14 pups
Puberty	50 $\pm$ 10 days
Weaning	21 days
Heart Rate	250-420 beats/min
Blood Pressure	
Systolic	88-184 mm Hg
Diastolic	58-145 mm Hg
Cardiac Output	50 ml/min
Oxygen use:	0.7-1.1 ml/g/hr
Respiration Rate	70-120 min
Urine ph	7.3-8.5

Handling

Rodents that are individually housed (isolation) over a long period often display increased emotionality (urination, defecation and, perhaps, aggression) upon handling. Each rat should be weighed to the nearest gram on a balance (scale) daily to assess its general health and to provide daily handling. You should be aware that rapid weight losses (e.g. 10-20 grams overnight) are frequently the first indicator of illness. To remove a rat from it's cage, grasp the rat with your thumb and forefinger around the neck to

Chapter 1: Animal Care

preventing the rat from biting your hand. If the rat grasps the cage floor with its paws as you attempt to remove it, do not exert excessive pull to remove the rat from the cage as this may tear a toenail. Practice picking the rat up, holding it and then replacing it into the home cage. Body handling is the preferred method of handling rats. If tail handling is done at all, you should pick up the rat by the base of the tail (that part of the tail closest to the body). This method is not recommended for novices, however, as grasping the tip of the tail may shear off the flesh surrounding the tail tip.

Animal Identification

Rats are frequently group housed (i.e. 2-3 per cage) for reasons related to available space and expense. Yet, as an experimenter, you must keep track of individual animal data. Some method, therefore, must be used to reliably identify individual rats. The simplest technique is to place a small numbered metal tag in the ear (Fisher Scientific: Appendix B). Another technique used to identify each rat involves a system in which a metal punch is used to place a small notch at the edge of the ear (see Figure 1.1). In this system, one ear is used to represent single digits whereas the other ear is used to represent 10's. A particular number is represented by the location on the ear of a notch.

Dyes may be used to identify individual rats. These include India ink on the palmar surface or the inner surface of the ear. In addition, either picric acid (yellow: Sigma Chemical) or carbolfuchsin (red: Sigma Chemical) can be used to stain the fur on the rat's back. The dyes are typically prepared as 1-5% solutions in 70% alcohol and are applied to the fur using dye-soaked cotton tips. These dyes, however, quickly fade and will require reapplication of the dye to maintain the numbering system. Our lab has had some success in numbering rats using indelible markers to write numbers in block format on the base of the tail of each rat.

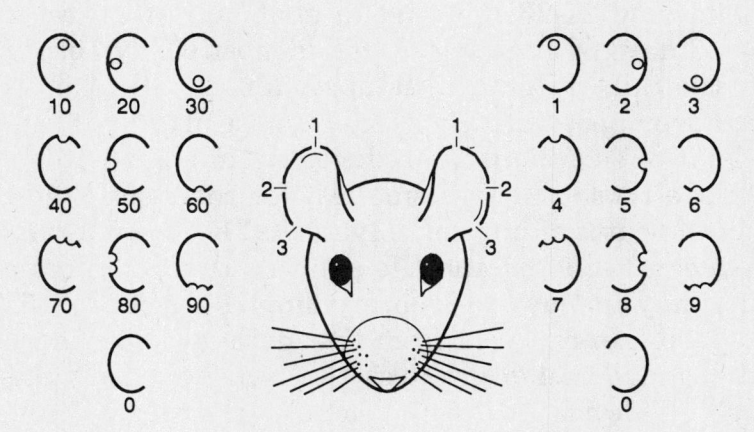

Figure 1.1. An ear notch system used to identify individual rats. The left ear is notched to represent single digits whereas the right ear is notched to indicate 10's.

Chapter 1: Animal Care

<u>Breeding</u>

The classic work of Long (1922) described the clinical characteristics of the estrous cycle of the female rat. The rodent estrous cycle is approximately 4 days in length and consists of 4 states: proestrus, estrus, metestrus and diestrus (refer to Figure 1.2). Maximal sexual receptivity of the female accompanies estrus, which in the rat occurs 24 hours into the cycle and is indicated by a dry vagina and a swollen vulva. Because the estrus cycle is associated with regular changes in the cell types found within the vaginal fluids, cervical smears can be taken daily to determine the onset of estrus. To do so, insert the blunt tip of a disposable pipette containing 1.0 ml of saline into the vagina of the female to be examined. Expel the saline and then a few minutes later, reinsert the pipette and withdraw 0.25 ml of vaginal fluid. This sample can be smeared onto a microscope slide, dipped into 100% alcohol, air-dried and then stained by dipping into a 5% solution of Fiemsa stain (Sigma Chemical). Clear the slide by dipping into distilled water, air-dry and then examine the cells on the slide using a light microscope. Using this method, estrus is indicated by the presence of large cornified cells in the vaginal smear (see Figure 1.2). Other clinical signs of estrus include an ear quiver response induced by stroking the head and back (Farris and Griffith, 1949) or the lordosis response (arched back) induced by manual stimulation of the vulva using a cotton swab.

Placement of an adult female rat into a cage with one or more adult male rats for a 6 day period will result in detection of sperm in the vaginal tract and eventual pregnancy (Baker, 1980). Sperm can be detected in the vaginal smear (using the technique described above without staining the vaginal smear) or one can examine the bedding of the rat cage in search of the so-called vaginal plug (a dried mass of sperm and vaginal secretions) that is dislodged from the vagina after successful copulation. To prevent cannibalism of the offspring by the male, the pregnant female should be isolated in a large cage provided with adequate amounts of food, water, and bedding. Gestation in the rat is approximately 21-23 days. The abdomen of a pregnant female rat is distinctly swollen at 13 days of gestation. This is most easily observed by suspending the rat vertically by the tail. Litter size is approximately 6-14 pups. The number of male and female pups are approximately equal in most litters. If the litter size is large (12 or more pups), the litter size should be reduced or culled to 8-10 pups. The pups that are to be euthanized are those that are smallest for their sex. One can use the ano-genital distance as an indicator of pup sex (Myers, 1971). In general, male pups exhibit a larger distance between the anus and the genitals than do females (see Table 1.2). Moreover, female pups may display rudimentary nipples at about 9-15 days post-partum. Litters should be weaned (i.e. removed from the mother) at 23 days post-partum with pups placed into either individual or group cages with chow and water freely available. If facilities are not available for breeding, commercial breeders (see Appendix A) can supply rodents of either sex and of a given weight range. Moreover, special surgical procedures (i.e. ovariectomy, hypophysectomy etc.) are often available from the breeder for a charge ranging from nominal to exorbitant.

Chapter 1: Animal Care

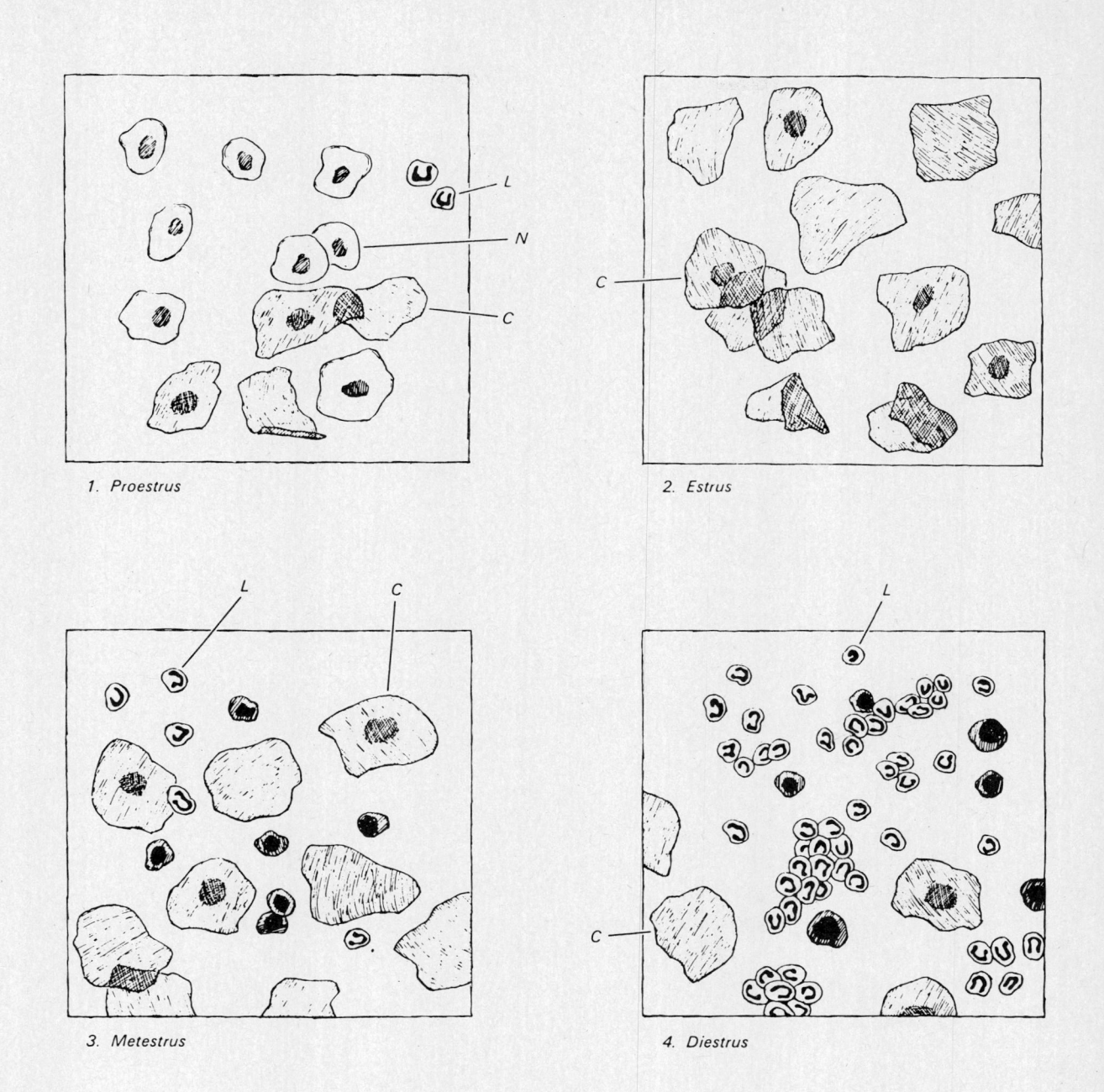

Figure 1.2 Cell types (C: cornified epithelial cells; L: leucocytes; N: nucleated epithelial cells) associated with various stages of the estrus cycle. (Reprinted with permission from: Adler, N.T. (1976). Induction of pregnancy in female rats by external stimulation. In: Hart, B.L. (Ed) <u>Experimental Psychobiology</u>, San Francisco: W.H. Freeman Co.)

Chapter 1: Animal Care

Table 1.2. Average ano-genital distance (mm's) in rat pups of different ages and sexes.

Age:	Male:	Female:
Newborn	2.8	1.2
7 Days	5.2	2.7
14 Days	8.2	4.9
20 Days	12.0	7.0
42-50 Days	21.0	13.0

Rat Diseases

Great advances in the production of disease-free laboratory rats have been made in the last two decades. Commercial breeders often derive their stock using barrier techniques in which a litter is delivered by caesarian section and raised in a germ-free environment. Such rats are remarkably free from diseases of the respiratory and digestive tracts. Upon arrival in your laboratory, however, rats obtained from a commercial supplier should be placed in quarantine for a 7 day period. If skin sores indicating lice or mites are observed, commercially available powders can be used to control lice and mites. Viral or mycoplasmal infections may produce upper respiratory difficulties in rats, often indicated by a chattering or wheezing sound. Such infections are highly contagious. Because antibiotic treatments do not readily reverse these conditions, infected animals (or whole colonies) should be euthanized (killed) and the colony housing cages should be disinfected with steam or chemical disinfectant. Another common disease observed in rats is labyrinthitis, a bacterial infection of the middle ear. Infected rats display a marked twisting of the body when suspended by the tail. No therapy is available for this disease; infected animals should be euthanized and the colony disinfected. If you are concerned about the health of animals in your care, you should alert your laboratory instructor.

Ethical Issues in Animal Use

As mentioned at the beginning of this chapter, animals are used in only a small percentage of the research projects conducted in Psychology. These projects have provided a considerable data base of information about sensory physiology, learning, the central nervous system and the governance of behavior. Concerns have been expressed by animal rights activists that animals in Psychology research projects suffer great amounts of pain at the hands of callous researchers who have little concern for their animal subjects. Another concern relates to duplication of research efforts that give us little new information. For example, hundreds of projects have examined the dramatic

Chapter 1: Animal Care

overeating that follows placement of lesions within the ventromedial hypothalamus of the rat. One issue raised by these studies is how many of these were simple duplications of research design that did not yield new information about the neural controls of feeding. Some of these specific issues raised by animal studies in psychology have been addressed by Neal Miller in his 1986 review article.

During the last 20 years, many different forces have marshalled to provide some degree of protection to animals used in research. In the 1960's there were widespread reports of pet dogs and cats being taken off the street for use in medical and other research projects. Those reports of abuse led to the Pet Protection Act of 1966 which was subsequently renamed as the Animal Welfare Act. This legislation and its amendments provide a legal basis for mandated standards of animal care and a provision for review of research involving animals.

Most Universities and Colleges which receive grant funding from the Public Health Service follow the guidelines of the Animal Welfare Act (1989). The Act specifies that each unit that uses animals must carry out the following:

1. Appoint a Veterinarian who is responsible for all aspects of animal use and care in the unit.

2. Appoint a committee which approves and monitors animal usage. The committee is usually composed of a veterinarian, at least one scientist, a non-scientist and one person not affiliated with the institution. The committee reviews animal use protocols submitted for research and for teaching purposes. Approval of an animal use protocol requires consideration by the committee of the following issues:

- Does the project have the appropriate facilities to house the animals? This chapter has discussed some of the issues of housing laboratory rats for research and teaching purposes.

- Is the project justified by its rationale? Is there a strong reason to conduct this particular project or is the project driven more by curiosity than science?

- How many animals are required to conduct the project? One goal of the Animal Use Committee is to reduce to a minimum the number of animals used for research and teaching purposes.

- Does the project duplicate earlier projects? Will we learn anything new from this project? Another goal is to minimize unnecessary duplication of animal research projects. This issue is particularly cogent for students enrolled in teaching labs since these labs necessarily involve some degree of duplication. Your instructor will have to seek approval for each of the labs that are described in this manual and will have to justify the use of animals to teach you the basic

Chapter 1: Animal Care

skills involved in physiological research and the specific concepts illustrated by the laboratory exercises of this manual.

☼ Has there been an effort to minimize pain and discomfort for animal subjects? Experimenters must recognize the signs of pain and discomfort in their subjects. Projects that involve pain and discomfort must be justified. Some projects of this manual involve surgical manipulation. Such surgery must always be carried out under suitable anesthesia (described in Chapter 2). If post-surgery complications develop, surgically manipulated animals may require injections of analgesics to minimize pain and distress. These complications are rare, but you should monitor animals closely after surgery. Some exercises involve assessment of pain to demonstrate the effects of analgesics such as morphine. Exposure to these stimuli must be kept to a minimum and should be justified.

☼ If surgery is involved in a project, that surgery must be carried out by trained personnel and aseptic technique must be used. Because surgeries involve trauma to subjects, which can cumulate with multiple surgeries, most instances of multiple survival surgeries are prohibited and are allowable only with strong justification. Your instructor has been trained in these stereotaxic techniques and will provide oversight as you learn the techniques.

☼ Finally, after a procedure has been finished, what happens to the animals? In some procedures such as stereotaxic surgery, you will have to euthanize each rat to remove the brain for histological inspection. Chapter 5 describes the process of histology. In the section below, we consider various techniques for the painless and rapid euthanasia of rats.

<u>Animal Euthanasia</u>

Care should be taken during the course of an experiment that animals are not subjected to unnecessary pain or discomfort. This principle especially applies to procedures which aim to sacrifice animal subjects at the end of a study or project. The term euthanasia means "good death". The 1993 Report of the AVMA Panel on Euthanasia suggests that each method of euthanasia should have the following characteristics:

"Each method should have the ability to induce loss of consciousness and death without causing pain; each method should require minimal time to induce unconsciousness; each method should be reliable; each method should be safe to personnel; each method should be irreversible; each method should be considered for its impact on human observers and each method should be evaluated as to whether it is appropriate for each species and for each age of a species."

Chapter 1: Animal Care

Euthanasia methods can be divided into categories of chemical methods, physical methods and inhalant methods.

An accepted and widely used chemical technique of euthanasia for rats involves lethal injection of sodium pentobarbital (80 mg/ml/kg, intraperitoneal; see Chapter 2 for complete descriptions of injection techniques). Such injections rapidly produce unconsciousness and then death. The technique is easily mastered, involves minimal pain and distress to the rat, is irreversible and is appropriate for all ages of rats. Although this technique may not be suitable for experiments in which biochemical samples are to be collected after death, it is the most humane technique for routine euthanasia of rats.

There are several physical methods of euthanasia approved for use in rats. Cervical dislocation can be used to euthanize small rats (< 200 grams) but not for larger rats (which would normally be encountered in physiological psychology laboratories). Cervical dislocation involves the rapid breaking and separation of the spinal cord between the head and trunk. Another physical euthanasia procedure is that of decapitation using one of several commercially available guillotines (Harvard Apparatus, Appendix B). The rat's head is carefully introduced between the guillotine blades and is then separated from the trunk using a rapid downward movement of the guillotine arm. This procedure may be used to collect large (approximately 5 ml) blood samples or to collect tissue samples in a way that is not compromised by chemically-induced euthanasia. It should be noted, however, that decapitation is not a routine euthanasia technique and would not be used for any laboratory exercise described in this manual. The technique has been considered problematic because of its effects on observers and because of concerns that consciousness may continue for some number of seconds after decapitation (Mikeska and Klemm, 1975; Vanderwolf et al., 1988).

Hypoxia can also provide a humane means of euthanasia. Placement of rats into a chamber containing highly concentrated carbon dioxide will result in unconsciousness and then death. This technique is often used to euthanize large numbers of rats and is thought to be more humane than decapitation. Inexpensive carbon dioxide euthanasia chambers are described in the literature (Myers, 1971; Kraus, 1980). Ether, chloroform, halothane and metofane have been used in high concentrations to euthanize rats. Ether and chloroform, although inexpensive, are rather caustic to the lungs of the rat and may result in a painful death. In contrast, halothane and metofane are not caustic, are somewhat rapid but can be prohibitively expensive. Moreover, these gases may be harmful to hepatic function in laboratory personnel that are repeatedly exposed to these gases.

Death should be verified (absence of heart rate, cool body and rigidity of the body) in any euthanized animal prior to its disposal. Again, if you are in doubt, consult your instructor. Each carcass should be double-wrapped in plastic bags and tagged as to its source. Disposal of carcasses should be carried out according to local Institutional Animal Care Committee practice.

Chapter 1: Animal Care

<u>Completion of An Animal Use Protocol</u>

Often times, discussing ethical use of animals occurs in the abstract when we speak of rights, freedom from pain and discomfort, and a comfortable life for subjects. Yet, as scientists and as presumed future scientists, we must act within an objective reality in which our terms are operationally defined. One simple means by which to move from the abstract to the concrete is to consider how one might justify using animals for a teaching lab. To further that goal, the present manual provides at the end of this chapter an example of an Animal Use Protocol. This form is presently in use at my University. Please look over the protocol form as you conduct each exercise assigned by your lab instructor. S/he may assign your lab group the task of completing a form like this for one of the exercises of this manual.

REFERENCES AND SUGGESTED READINGS

Adler, N.T. (1976). Induction of "pregnancy" in female rats by external stimulation. In: Hart, B.L. <u>Experimental Psychobiology</u>, San Francisco: W.H. Freeman.

Author. (1986). Guide for the care and use of laboratory animals. U.S. Department of HEW publication (NIH).

Authors. (1989). Animal Welfare Act. <u>Federal Register</u>, <u>54</u>, number 168, 36151-36155.

Authors. (1993). Report of the AVMA Panel on Euthanasia. <u>Journal of the American Veterinary Medical Association</u>, <u>202</u>, 229-249.

Baker, H.J. (1980). Reproduction and Breeding. In: Baker, H.J., Lindsey, J.R. and S.H. Weisbroth (Eds). <u>The Laboratory Rat</u>, Volume 2: Research Applications. New York: Academic Press.

deGroot, J. (1959). A brain atlas. <u>Journal of Comparative Neurology</u>, <u>113</u>, 389.

Farris, E.J. (1950). <u>The Care and Breeding of Laboratory Animals</u>. New York: Wiley & Sons, 515 pps.

Farris, E.J. and J.Q. Griffith. (1949). <u>The Rat in Laboratory Investigation</u>. Philadelphia: Lippincott.

König, J.F.R. and R.A. Klippel. (1963). <u>The Rat Brain</u>. Baltimore: Williams and Wilkins.

Kraus, A.L. (1980). Research Methodology. In: <u>The Laboratory Rat</u>, Edited by H.J. Baker, J.L. Lindsey and S.H. Weisbroth. New York: Academic Press.

Long, J.A. (1922). The oestrus cycle of the rat and its associated phenomena. <u>Mem.Univ.Calif.</u>, <u>6</u>, 1-148.

Chapter 1: Animal Care

Mikeska, J.A. and W.R. Klemm. (1975). EEG evaluation of humaneness of asphyxia and decapitation euthanasia in the laboratory rat. Laboratory Animal Science, 25, 175-179.

Miller, N.E. (1985). The value of behavioral research on animals. American Psychologist, 40, 423-440.

Myers, R.D. (1971). General laboratory procedures. In: R.D. Myers (Ed), Methods of Psychobiology, Volume 1, New York: Academic Press, p.30.

National Academy of Sciences, National Research Council, Agricultural Board, Committee on Animal Nutrition. (1972) Nutritional requirements of laboratory animals. (2nd Rev.) No. 10. Cat, Guinea Pig, Hamster, Monkey, Mouse, Rat. Washington, D.C.: National Academy of Sciences, 117 pps.

Olds, R.J. and J.R. Olds. (1979). A Color Atlas of the Rat - A Dissection Guide. New York: John Wiley & Sons.

Paxinos, G. and C. Watson. (1986). The Rat Brain in Stereotaxic Coordinates, 2nd edition. New York: Academic Press.

Pellegrino, L.J. and C.J. Cushman. (1967). A Stereotaxic Atlas of the Rat Brain. New York: Appleton-Century-Crofts.

Skinner, J.E. (1971). Neuroscience: A Laboratory Manual. Philadelphia: W.B. Saunders.

Smith, E.M. and M.L. Calhoun. (1968). The Microscopic Anatomy of the White Rat. Ames: Iowa State University Press.

Thompson, R. (1978). A Behavioral Atlas of the Rat Brain. New York: Oxford University Press.

Vanderwolf, C.H., D.P. Buzak and R.K. Cain (1988). Neocortical and hippocampal electrical activity following decapitation in the rat. Brain Research, 451, 340-344.

Wells, T.A.G. (1964). The Rat. New York: Dover Publications.

Chapter 1: Animal Care

SAMPLE ANIMAL USE PROTOCOL
(for institutional use only)

NOTE: ANSWER ALL QUESTIONS, ENTERING NOT APPLICABLE (NA) WHERE APPROPRIATE. ALL ENTRIES ARE TO BE TYPEWRITTEN.

SECTION I. PROJECT IDENTIFICATION

A. Investigator Name: _____   Dept.:_____
    Work Phone #: _____   Emergency Phone #: _____

B. Title of Project: _____.

C. Project Animal-Care Contact Person [*Who is to be contacted in case of an animal emergency*]:

    Work Phone:_____   Emergency Phone: _____.

D. Abstract: Please provide a brief statement, IN LAY TERMINOLOGY, outlining the purpose of the experimental procedures of this protocol [*Provide a rationale for the experiments you wish to conduct.*]

E. Animal Procedures: Describe in narrative form, using LAY TERMINOLOGY, the experimental procedures and manipulations that will be performed on the animals. [*Be brief and specific (e.g. cannulae will be surgically positioned within the brain ventricles of rats to administer opiates and determine effects on feeding behavior.*]

F. Justify why you chose to use this(these) species in your research. [*Describe characteristics of the animal model that make it appropriate for use in your studies. This might include considerations of body size, comparative data from prior studies or unique physiological features. Cost alone is not an acceptable justification for selection of the animal model.*]

G. Describe the number of animals per experiment with a breakdown within experiments of animals per treatment condition (include number of replications and relevant controls). Explain why you chose a certain number of animals per treatment condition (taking into account known variation of the dependent variable, subject losses, etc).

Chapter 1: Animal Care

SECTION II. ANIMAL PROCUREMENT/MAINTENANCE INFORMATION

A. Describe the total number of animals used per year, by species: If animals are carried over from one year to another show this by drawing a line from one year to the next.

Number of Animals Used per Year of the Research Protocol

Species	Yr. 1	Yr. 2	Yr. 3	Yr. 4	Yr. 5

B. Where will you obtain the animals? [*If wild caught by you, please describe applicable permits, method of capture, evaluation of health risks to personnel*]. Does the project involve you breeding your animals. If so, how many breeder stock will be required and how many offspring will be used for the studies?

C. In which of the approved animal housing sites of the University will you house your animals? [*List Bldg*].

D. Describe any special housing, diet, environment or other requirements necessary for this study:

E. What will happen to the animals after you complete the experiment? [*If you plan to transfer the animals at the end of your study, please complete an animal transfer form prior to such a transfer. If the animals are to be euthanized, please describe the method to be employed including the agent/method employed. For injectable agents, describe the drug and dose (i.e. mg/kg) as well as route of administration (i.e. IV). Decapitation without anesthesia requires written justification below.*]
_____ Animal transfer
_____ Euthanasia [*Complete the section below*].
        Method: _____
        Agent: _____
            Dose: _____ Route: _____ .
Justification of decapitation without anesthesia:

F. Name (s) individual(s) administering euthanasia. [*Note: only the persons listed below will be authorized to perform the euthanasia procedure*].

Chapter 1: Animal Care

G.   Specify the education, training or experience which qualifies each of the persons named in Section IIF above to perform euthanasia.

SECTION III. ANIMAL PROCEDURES

A.   Where will you conduct the animal procedural work [*List Bldg. and Room #*].

B.   Briefly indicate below any <u>nonsurgical</u> procedures to be used. Identify each species involved [*If more than one*]:

    1.   Method of obtaining blood or other tissues: [*Indicate below the technique to be used, the volume to be collected, the frequency of collection and the interval between collections. Terminal blood collections require use of a suitable anesthetic*].

    2.   Other agents to be administered, including dose, volume, route, & frequency:

    3.   Method & duration of restraint:

    4.   Other procedures such as food or water deprivation, administration of noxious stimuli or substances/procedures which might induce clinical illness.

C.   Anesthesia/Analgesia.

    1.   If anesthesia is necessary, please describe the agent to be used, dosage and route of administration for each species. [*Also indicate any other preanesthetic procedures, such as fasting from food and water*].

          Preanesthetic: _____
          Anesthetic: _____.
          Analgesics :_____

    2.   Name (s) and qualifications [*include education, training and experience*] of individual(s) who will administer/monitor anesthesia:

Chapter 1: Animal Care

D.   Assessment of Pain and Distress

1. Does the project involve the use of painful procedures or paralytic drugs without the benefit of anesthetics or analgesics? Yes___ ; No ____ ; [If yes, justify below why anesthesia/analgesics are inappropriate for your experiments]:

2. Will the procedures of your studies cause animal subjects to experience more than momentary or slight pain or distress? Yes: ___ ; No: ____. [If yes, describe the methods and sources you used to determine that alternatives to these procedures are not available. These might include computerized database searches (Medline).]

3. If the procedures of this experiment are expected to produce signs of clinical illness in the animals, describe those effects and explain at what point (and by what criteria) the animals may be euthanized. Also describe the frequency per day that the animals will be observed (and by whom) after treatment administration.

5. Is death (without euthanasia) an endpoint of the study? Yes: _____; No: _____. [If yes, justify why an earlier end point is not acceptable].

Chapter 1: Animal Care

ATTACHMENT 1: SURGERY PROCEDURES

NOTE: FILL OUT ONE COPY OF THIS PAGE FOR EACH DIFFERENT SURGICAL PROCEDURE. PLEASE MAKE AN ENTRY FOR EACH CATEGORY. CAREFULLY LIST THE PERSONNEL NAMES FOR THOSE WHO WILL MONITOR ANESTHESIA, CONDUCT THE SURGERY AND MONITOR RECOVERY. ONLY THOSE PERSONS LISTED BELOW WILL BE AUTHORIZED TO PERFORM THESE FUNCTIONS. ALL SURVIVAL SURGICAL PROCEDURES REQUIRE USE OF ASEPTIC TECHNIQUE. THIS INCLUDES USE OF STERILE SURGICAL GLOVES AND INSTRUMENTS AND ASEPTIC PREPARATION OF THE SURGICAL FIELD.

S1. Where will the surgery be performed? [List Bldg, Room. #]:_____.

S2. Indicate the nature of the surgical procedure [check one]:
___ Non-Survival
___ Survival
___ Multiple Major Survival [Provide justification below.]

S3. Provide a brief description of the surgical procedure [Include relevant details from initial incision to wound closure].

S4. Identify each person who is authorized to perform the surgical procedure. Indicate the qualification of of each person to conduct the surgical procedure [Indicate previous experience, education, and specific training for performing the procedure. A listing of academic degrees is not an adequate response to this question.]

Post Operative Care:

POC1. Where will the animals recover from surgery? [List Bldg, Room #]:

POC2 Indicate what post-surgery complications might be anticipated.

POC3. List the names of the individual(s) who will monitor post-operative recovery:

POC4. Describe the post-operative medication(s) to be given. [List each agent, the dosage (i.e. mg/kg), route (e.g. IP) and the frequency of administration]:
___ Analgesics: _____
___ Antibiotics:_____
___ Other: _____

Chapter 1: Animal Care

SECTION IV. INVESTIGATOR'S ASSURANCE.

Federal regulations hold this University responsible for the conduct of animal research on this campus and specific associated facilities. In response to this requirement, the university has established the following procedures:

1. Approval of an Animal Use Protocol, by either the University Laboratory Animal Care Committee (ULAC) or Institutional Agricultural Animal Care and Use Committee (IAACUC), is required for all vertebrate animal use. <u>In addition, each protocol must be reviewed on an annual basis</u>. ULAC/IAACUC is empowered to stop any objectionable procedures or projects. Investigators may appeal such action to the Provost as appropriate.

2. Any proposed change in personnel, species usage, animal procedures, anesthesia, post-operative care or biohazards procedures that would significantly impact upon the animal portion of a study must be reported <u>in writing</u> to ULAC or IAACUC as appropriate. <u>Committee approval of the proposed changes is required prior to proceeding with the revised animal procedures</u>.

3. Unannounced inspections and observations of animal quarters and/or experimental procedures may be performed by the attending veterinary staff. Where procedures are causing severe distress to an animal and the pain cannot be relieved, veterinarians are authorized to humanely destroy that animal. (Note: institutional veterinarians will always make a concerted effort to discuss such situations with investigators prior to initiating such drastic action.)

4. Use of biohazardous materials in animal subjects mandates compliance with the protocols approved by the appropriate Biohazards Committee. Failure to follow the approved biohazard protocol could result in withdrawal of authorization to continue the research.

I HAVE READ THE ABOVE STATEMENTS AND AGREE TO ABIDE BY THE INSTITUTIONAL POLICIES GOVERNING ANIMAL USAGE. THE ATTACHED PROPOSAL (WHERE APPLICABLE) CONTAINS THE FINAL VERSION OF THE ANIMAL CARE SECTION WHICH IS TO BE FORWARDED TO THE GRANTING AGENCY. I FURTHER CERTIFY THAT THE PROPOSED WORK DOES NOT UNNECESSARILY DUPLICATE PREVIOUS EXPERIMENTS.

_____   _____
Signature of Investigator   Date

Chapter 1: Animal Care

Chapter 2
Anesthesia Procedures

Anesthesia

Animals, like humans, possess specialized nerve endings which signal tissue destruction to the brain resulting in a sensory condition known as pain. Experimental and surgical procedures involving animals must be accomplished in a manner calculated not to inflict pain, discomfort or suffering. If pain or discomfort is inherent to the procedure, the Principles for the Use of Animals (National Institutes of Health, 1986) state:

> ... the animals must first be rendered incapable of perceiving pain and be maintained in that condition until the experiment or the procedure is ended. The only exception to this guideline should be in those cases where anesthesia would defeat the purpose of the experiment and the data cannot be obtained by any other humane procedure."

The intent of this chapter is to provide an overview of anesthesia methods, to provide specific procedures to induce and monitor anesthesia and to provide an overview of procedures to be followed after recovery from anesthesia. Additional information on anesthesia can be found in Flecknell (1987) and Lumb (1963).

Pre-anesthetic Care

In general, rats should be weighed daily prior to anesthesia to verify good health via constancy of body weight. During the 15 hour period prior to surgery, each rat can be deprived of food and water so as to reduce anesthetic complications that arise from problems with anesthesia absorption and distribution. Several anesthetic agents are irritants and provoke secretion. Atropine treatment (given 10 minutes before anesthesia; 0.05-0.3 mg/kg, IP) will reduce respiratory complications often associated with anesthesia in the rat. These secretions can build up in the lungs and can eventually lead to respiratory failure.

Stages of Anesthesia

The surgical procedures described in this manual assume that each rat is maintained in a state of anesthesia during surgery. Depth of anesthesia can vary from a light state in which little pain is felt and the animal has some ability to move to deeper stages where no pain is felt and the animal is incapable of movement (see Table 2.1 below). In Stage 1, the rat does not experience pain (a condition termed "analgesia") but is capable of movement. In anesthesia stage 3, pain reflexes and muscle movements are absent. Ideally, surgical procedures in the rat are carried out in plane 3 of stage 3. Here the rat shows reduced muscle tone, no spontaneous movement, no reaction to painful stimuli (a pinch of either the tail, a toe or an ear) and does not blink when the eyelid is touched. Respiration should be regular during stage 3 anesthesia.

Chapter 2: Anesthesia

Animals placed under anesthesia require constant monitoring as the duration and level of anesthesia can vary between and within animals. The critical aspect is to keep the animal in stage 3 of anesthesia so that pain perception and movement are blocked. One aspect of anesthesia to be monitored during a procedure is the state of over-anesthesia. Clinical signs of over-anesthesia include slow and shallow (light) breathing, no reaction to touching the cornea and a cyanotic (bluish) tint observed in the skin of the paws. Measures to be taken during over-anesthesia are discussed below. The other aspect of anesthesia relates to under-anesthesia. For example, an animal may begin to display evidence of pain perception during a procedure. This situation will require that you administer supplemental anesthesia. Your instructor will provide you with specifics as to how much additional anesthetic to deliver to maintain a constant stage 3 level of anesthesia.

Table 2.1 Clinical Stages and Planes of Anesthesia

Anesthesia Stage:	Plane:	Membrane Color:	Respiration:	Lid:	Pedal:	Pain:	Comments:
I (Analgesia)		Normal	Rapid, irregular	Yes	Yes	No	
II		Flushed	Erratic	Yes	Yes	No	
III (Surgical)	1	Flushed	Slow, regular	Varies	No	No	
	2	Normal	Slow, regular	No	No	No	
	3	Pale	Abdominal			No	Reduced smooth muscle
	4	Pale	Light abdominal			No	Anal reflex absent
IV (Death)		Bluish	None	No	No	No	Bladder relaxation

INJECTION METHODS OF ANESTHESIA

Anesthesia in the rat can be easily and rapidly induced by injection of a variety of substances in solution. Injectable anesthetic agents offer a variety of induction times (i.e. how long after an injection before stage 3 anesthesia is reached), duration of anesthesia (ketamine and some barbiturates are very short-acting whereas pentobarbital anesthesia has a long duration), and margin of safety (relative danger of overdosing the rat). Curare derivatives (d-tubocurarine or succinylcholine) are not anesthetics; these drugs paralyse the neuromuscular junction but have no effect on pain perception or consciousness. If these drugs are used to block muscle movements, the rat will require artificial respiration (via a tracheotomy tube attached to a respirator) and will additionally require administration of a drug that blocks pain perception.

Anesthetics are routinely injected as the weight of drug in solution per unit body weight (i.e. milligrams of drug per milliliter of solvent expressed per kilogram of body weight). A convenient method for calculating drug dosage for rats is to inject all solutions (where possible) as 1.0 ml per kg of body weight. For example, if you wish to deliver 50 mg of pentobarbital per kg of rat body weight (typically expressed as 50 mg/kg), then your solution should contain 50 mg of pentobarbital per ml of vehicle. When drug solutions are injected in a volume of 1.0 ml/kg, you simply round the body weight, expressed as kg, to 2 decimal places. Thus, a rat that weighs 257 grams or 0.26 kg would receive an injection of 0.26 ml while a rat that weighs 212 grams or 0.21 kg would receive an injection of 0.21 ml of drug solution. Additional information regarding solution preparation can be found in Campbell and Campbell (1984) and in Flecknell (1987).

The most common vehicle used to prepare drug solutions is a saline solution (0.9% w/v) consisting of 9 gm sodium chloride dissolved in 1000 mls sterile distilled water. An alternate saline solution is a phosphate buffered saline solution (pH 7.4) consisting of:

potassium chloride	0.2 gm
sodium chloride	8.0 gm
disodium hydrogen phosphate	1.2 gm
potassium dihydrogen phosphate	0.2 gm
calcium chloride	0.0005 gm
magnesium chloride	0.0005 gm
sterile distilled water	1000 ml

Other vehicle solutions can be prepared to aid in dissolving certain drugs into solution for injection. Some drugs easily dissolve in a 10% (v/v) ethanol solution. Still other drugs may dissolve in up to 60% propylene glycol (v/v). You may have to experiment and use physical stirring and some degree of heat (using a magnetic stirrer/hot plate) to get some compounds into solution. Some drugs will not go into solution, so you will have to prepare a suspension often in an oil for injection. Other drugs are easily suspended in 10% Tween-80 (v/v). In addition, there are commercially available compounds that can used to prepare vehicle solutions (cyclodextrin: RBI, Appendix B).

Commercially prepared drug solutions are normally sterile. Solutions prepared in the lab require some degree of care to ensure sterility. Vials in which you will store drug solutions should be thoroughly washed and then either boiled or autoclaved. Place a small amount of aluminum foil over the drug vial mouth or store drug vials in autoclave bags. Use sterile distilled water whenever possible to prepare solutions. If not possible, filter the solution in order to provide some degree of sterility. Commercially available in-line filter units containing 0.2 micron filter material can be mounted on the end of a syringe. Push the solution through the filter into a sterilized injection vial. Such filters can be used to safely filter about 50 mls before a new filter is required.

After preparation, check the pH of the drug solution and adjust accordingly if it is not within the range of 4.5-8.0 pH. Moreover, you may wish to consider the degree to which the solution oxidizes. Either add 0.1% (w/v) sodium metabisulfite to preserve the solution or prepare immediately prior to use. Certain photoreactive solutions may

Chapter 2: Anesthesia

require storage in dark vials and most should be refrigerated during storage. Also, drug solutions, if refrigerated, should be warmed to room temperature prior to injection so that cooling of capillaries around the injection site does not produce local vasoconstriction and therefore slow drug absorption. Each vial should be labelled as to the date of preparation of the solution.

Each vial should be sealed with a rubber septum or stopper through which a needle can be pushed to withdraw the drug solution into a syringe. Sterile 1 cc tuberculin syringes can be fitted with disposable 25 or 27 gauge (half-inch) needles. Draw an amount of air into the syringe equal to that volume of solution you will withdraw from the drug vial. Push the tip of needle through the septum of the vial and turn the vial and syringe upside-down. Expel the air into the vial using the syringe plunger and then withdraw more than the volume of drug solution required. Now tap the shaft of the syringe to force any air bubbles to rise to the tip of the needle. Withdraw the needle from the vial and expel any air bubbles along with the excess drug solution. Inject the solution and then discard the needle into a Sharps container. When not in use, syringe needles should be stored in their protective cap or immediately discarded in a Sharps container. <u>Never leave bare needles on the counter or discard any needle into a trashcan.</u>

Injection Considerations

A number of factors must be considered when choosing a particular anesthetic for a surgical procedure. Obviously, the length of the procedure is an important factor. If you are doing a brief surgical procedure such as an ovariectomy, then a short-acting anesthetic is preferred. Surgeries which involve implanting intra-cranial electrodes may require a long duration anesthetic, particularly as you are learning these surgical procedures. In addition, you must always consider the potential influence of the anesthetic on the data you wish to collect. Anesthesia induced by the drug urethane, for example, is acceptable for some acute experiments but not for studies in which data are to be collected postoperatively. Urethane is slowly excreted from the body and is toxic to the liver; thus rats anesthetized with urethane are very ill after recovery from the anesthetic. Pentobarbital anesthesia is known to influence liver enzymes; this may affect psychopharmacology studies by altering the absorption and excretion of drugs.

Another important variable to be considered with regard to anesthesia is that of route of injection (cf. Gilman et al., 1990). The primary variable associated with route of exposure is the degree to which each route has ready access to the blood supply. The route by which a drug is delivered into the body will influence how rapidly the drug is absorbed into the vascular system and therefore how quickly anesthesia is induced. For example, intravenous (IV) injections produce more rapid effects than do intraperitoneal (IP) or intramuscular (IM) or subcutaneous (SC, below the skin) injections. Moreover, the route of injection chosen will require different restraint techniques and involve different volumes of solutions. Owing to the nature of certain drugs, certain routes of administration may be required while others may be contraindicated. Certain anesthetics can be injected into muscle but not into the peritoneal (gut) cavity or the venous system.

Chapter 2: Anesthesia

One truism in anesthesia is is variability of effectivenness in an animal. You cannot count on a specific dose and route to uniformly produce a fixed duration (e.g. 30 minutes) of anesthesia. A large number of variables may interact to influence onset and duration of anesthesia (Lumb, 1963; Flecknell, 1987; Waynforth and Flecknell, 1992). Different strains of rats may exhibit differential sensitivity to an anesthetic agent. We have recently noticed differences between anesthetic doses required in viral-free rats versus ordinary (i.e. viral-laden) rats. Obese rats may require less anesthetic than do lean rats. Female rats may require less anesthetic than do male rats. Because of their high metabolic rate, very young rats require a greater dose per unit body weight, whereas older rats exhibit a diminished metabolism and are more sensitive to anesthesia. General health influences anesthesia in that fatigued or diseased rats are more sensitive to anesthesia. You should realize that injection of a fixed dose will not always produce satisfactory anesthesia in all rats. Given the variability observed in anesthetic response, it is well worth the time to experiment with anesthesia dosages before attempting any surgical procedure.

A final issue to consider is whether you can easily alter the degree of anesthesia during the surgical procedure. For example, if the animal begins to show signs of distress, can you give a supplementary dose? If the drug used is potent, then the effective dose may be very close to the lethal dose and you may not easily give supplementary injections without killing the animal. Alternatively, if you detect that the rat is having difficulty breathing and its skin is bluish, can you reverse the anesthesia (or at least stimulate respiration)?

Routes of Injection:

Subcutaneous (SC). For a subcutaneous injection, the drug solution is delivered into the space between the skin and the underlying body wall, typically in the region behind the neck. Place the rat on a flat surface (Figure 2.1a). The skin on the neck is grasped with one hand while the other hand directs the tip of a 25 gauge needle at an angle into the subcutaneous space. If the needle is positioned properly, you should be able to freely inject the solution into the subcutaneous space. If, however, the needle tip is in the skin or the underlying body wall, considerable resistance will be felt as you try to depress the syringe plunger. If so, withdraw the needle and correctly reposition for injection. After injection, the bubble or depot of solution under the skin can be gently massaged to evenly distribute the injected solution. The subcutaneous route yields a very slow drug effect and is appropriate for drug volumes up to 5 mls. You may wish to slow the onset of drug effect even further by suspending the drug in a peanut oil vehicle. Drugs such as the barbiturates that irritate tissue should not be delivered via the subcutaneous route.

Intramuscular (IM). Injection of a drug solution into muscle will result in rapid onset of the drug effect. For an intramuscular injection, the rat can be restrained by placing your left palm over the head and shoulder of the rat as the rat is placed on your thigh facing down. Use the thumb of your left hand to lift the rat's left leg up and out so as to expose the flank muscles. Insert the needle into the flank muscle and slowly inject

Chapter 2: Anesthesia

the solution. After injection, gently massage the muscle to speed drug distribution and absorption. Another restraint technique for an IM injection is depicted in Figure 2.1b. The intramuscular route can be used for drug volumes up to 1.0 ml by splitting the dose (i.e. 0.5 ml per side) between the left and right flank muscles. Do not inject more than 0.25 ml into any one muscle site.

Intraperitoneal (IP). The intraperitoneal route is the most convenient route for drug injection in rats. In this procedure, the drug solution is injected directly into the peritoneal cavity. Because of the vascularization of the organs within the peritoneal cavity, injected drugs are absorbed rapidly. Restraint for intraperitoneal injections may be accomplished using either the procedure described for intramuscular injections or the restraint procedure illustrated in Figure 2.1c. Here, place your hand around the rat's neck and use your thumb and forefinger to restrain the rat's forepaws. The rat's hindpaws can be placed against a table top so as to expose and tighten the muscles of the abdomen. The injection site should be 1-2 cm to the right or left of the midline at a point midway between the diaphragm and the genitals. Take care not to puncture or inject drug solutions into hollow organs (bladder) or into solid organs (spleen, liver). This precaution can be accomplished by using a short needle (1/2 inch) to inject drug solutions. Quickly push the needle through the abdominal wall and at an angle perpendicular to the abdomen. Always pull the plunger out slightly after insertion and prior to injection to check for blood or urine in the needle. If either are present, reposition the needle and check again; if clear, then inject into the peritoneum. If blood were to be present, then your injection would be into the vascular system whereas if urine were to be present, then your injection would be into the bladder, a site that yields poor drug absorption (moreover, the rat would likely void the bladder contents including part of your drug solution). Finally, the IP route is appropriate for drug volumes up to 10 mls.

Intravenous (IV). The injection of a drug solution directly into the venous system produces the most rapid onset of drug effect and is therefore the most dangerous with regard to over-anesthetizing the rat if you are injecting the drug in a single bolus. Several sites are available for injection into the venous system of the rat. These include the lateral marginal vein, the jugular vein, the lingual vein, the tail vein and the dorsal metatarsal vein. Because of the difficulty involved in mastering the intravenous injection techniques (several require surgery to expose the vein), they are not discussed in this manual. The interested reader should consult Krauss (1980) and Waynforth and Flecknell (1992) for a thorough discussion of intravenous injection techniques.

<u>Miscellaneous Drug Administration Routes</u>

Other routes of administration encountered in certain laboratory procedures include oral (per oral or PO), intragastric (IG), topical, vaginal and rectal. The oral route of drug administration is used infrequently because taste factors (e.g. morphine and the barbiturates are very bitter) may reduce consumption of the drug and because of difficulty in controlling the precise dose delivered (i.e. the animal may not consume the complete drug dose). The other routes may offer some advantages (i.e. rectal and vaginal

Chapter 2: Anesthesia

routes can be used for drugs that disturb the gastrointestinal tract) but are less frequently used in physiological psychology.

Injectable Anesthetic Agents

Table 2.2 depicts the variety of injectable agents currently available to anesthetize the rat. The typical route of injection and the typical dose level given (these are for male rats) are also listed. These doses are only approximate; the actual doses that will induce suitable anesthesia will depend on the individual characteristics of your subject. The table also presents typical values for duration of anesthesia. Again, you should be prepared to experiment with the anesthetic dose required for your purpose.

Many of the injectable anesthetic agents are controlled substances and, as such, their possession and use is controlled by the Federal Government. Use of these drugs in the physiological laboratory can be prescribed by a veterinarian or the faculty member in charge of the lab can apply for a Controlled Substances Registration Certificate from the Drug Enforcement Administration, P.O. Box 28083, Central Station, Washington, DC 20005. This certificate allows the laboratory director to purchase and use controlled substances (anesthetics) for teaching and research purposes. In addition, your state may require an additional license to hold and use controlled substances in the laboratory.

The following discussion of various injectable agents is organized around their duration of anesthesia. Here, duration refers to brief (about 10-20 minutes), moderate (30 minutes to 60 minutes) and long (greater than 2 hours). Issues relating to side effects of these agents are also presented.

Chapter 2: Anesthesia

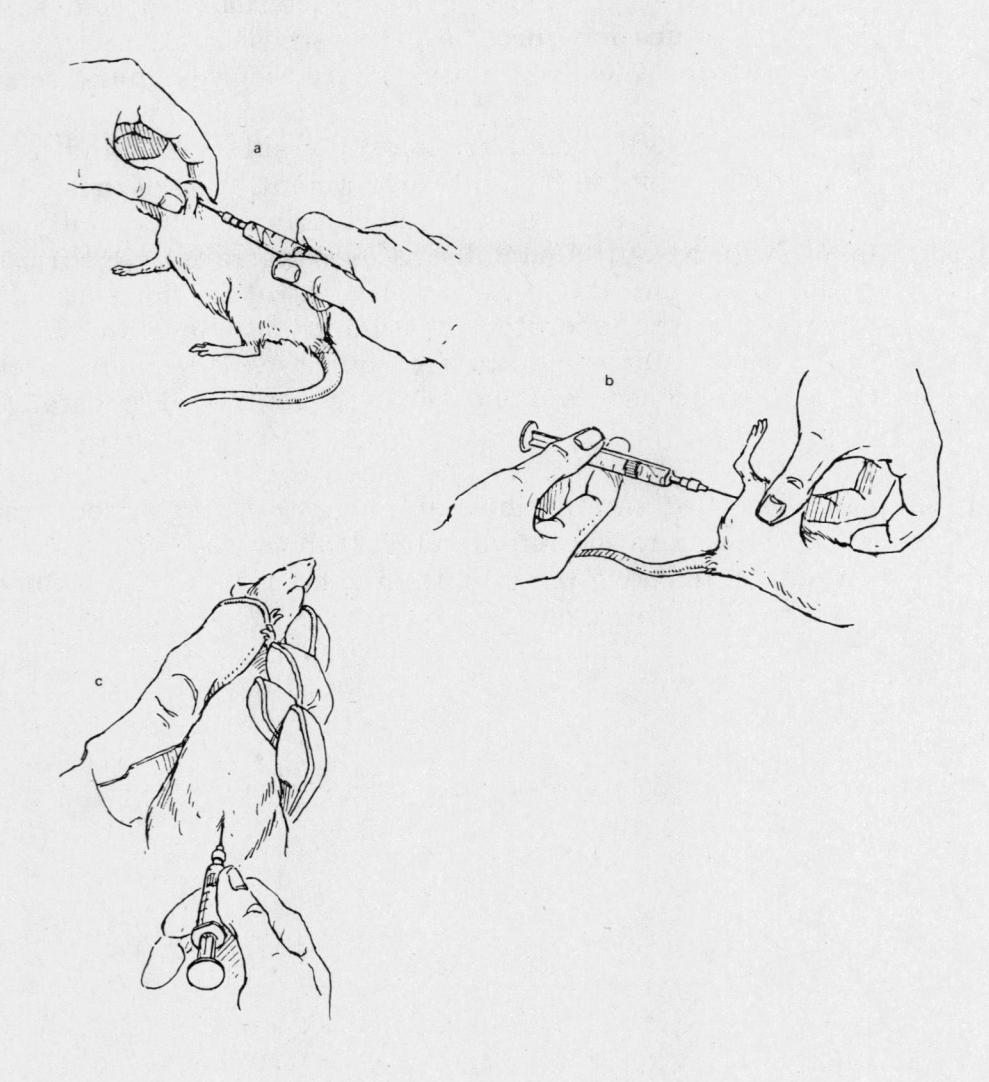

Figure 2.1 Restraint and injection procedures for the rat. a: Subcutaneous route (SC); b: Intramuscular route (IM); c: Intraperitoneal route (IP). (Reprinted with permission from: Hart, B.L. (1976). <u>Experimental Psychobiology</u>, San Francisco: W.H.Freeman Co.)

Chapter 2: Anesthesia

Table 2.2: Common Injectable Anesthetic Agents

Drug:	Category:	Dose:	Route:	Duration:
Ketamine/ Xylazine	Short	90 mg/kg 10 mg/kg	IP IP	20-30 min
Pentobarbital (NA)	Short/Moderate	30-50 mg/kg	IP	15-60 min
Thiopental	Short	30 mg/kg	IV	10 min
Innovar-Vet	Moderate	0.4 mg/kg	IM	20-30 min
Inactin	Moderate/Long	80-160 mg/kg	IP	1-4 hours
Equithesin	Moderate	4 mls/kg	IP	1-2 hours
Ketamine/ NA Pentobarbital	Moderate	60 mg/kg 20 mg/kg	IM IP	60 minutes
Alpha-chloralose	Long	55 mg/kg	IP	8-10 hours
Chloral hydrate	Long	300-400 mg/kg	IP	1-2 hours
Urethane	Long	1.2 g/kg	IP	6-8 hours

Brief Acting Anesthetics

Barbiturates. A variety of injectable drugs are available for very brief surgical procedures. Thiopental affords anesthesia at a dose of 30 mg/kg but often requires the IV route of administration. Sodium pentobarbital (30 mg/kg, intraperitoneal) will induce surgical anesthesia that is of moderate duration (15 to 60 minutes), but the effective dose of this drug is very close to its lethal dose. Thus, sodium pentobarbital alone is apt to produce over-anesthesia, particularly in female rats. In practice, it is not wise to give an additional or supplemental dose of pentobarbital to a rat that is not sufficiently anesthetized by the initial injection. Supplemental doses of the barbiturates often result in death due to over-anesthesia. Because the barbiturates induce mucous secretion, atropine is required to block mucous secretion. Atropine pretreatment (0.05-0.3 mg/kg, IP) should be given 10 minutes prior to injection of a barbiturate. The barbiturates can be given via intramuscular injection with some alteration of dose levels (Hughes, 1981).

Chapter 2: Anesthesia

If over-anesthesia is induced by the barbiturates, respiration can be stimulated using the procedures described below. Moreover, injections of Doxapram (5-10 mg/kg, IM) or Begimide (10 mg/kg, IP) or Mikedimide (1 mg Mikedimide per mg of pentobarbital administered) can be used to stimulate respiration (refer to Table 2.3).

Moderate-Duration Anesthetics

Fentanyl/droperidol. A combination of fentanyl citrate (0.3 mg/ml), an analgesic and droperidol (20 mg/ml), a tranquilizer can be used to anesthetize rats. Supplied under the trade name Innovar Vet, this combination requires 0.01 to 0.05 ml/100 gram body weight (IM) (comparable to 0.4 mg/kg). If over-anesthesia occurs, the effect of fentanyl citrate can be reversed by injection of levellorphan (6 mg/kg, SC) or naloxone (1.0 mg/kg, IP). Naloxone is a short-acting agent, so you should be prepared to monitor the progress of recovery of animals over-anesthetized with Innovar-Vet.

Ketamine mixtures. Whereas the barbiturates depress the action of the cortex and the lower brain stem to produce analgesia and anesthesia, ketamine, a member of the phencyclidine class, produces "dissociative" anesthesia by blocking the association areas of the brain with minimal effects on the lower brain stem or the somesthetic sensory pathways. When given alone in doses up to 100 mg/kg (IM), ketamine will produce sedation but not anesthesia. This drug is commonly mixed with other anesthetic agents to provide a moderate duration of anesthesia. Stickrod (1979) described a suitable anesthetic state induced in pregnant rats by a combination of ketamine (90 mg/kg) and xylazine (Rompum: Cutter Labs; 10 mg/kg). A combination of ketamine and pentobarbital will also yield rapid and safe short-moderate duration anesthesia (about 60 minutes). First, an injection of ketamine (60 mg/kg, IM) is given, followed five minutes later by an injection of sodium pentobarbital (20 mg/kg, IP). Because ketamine and the barbiturates are chemically incompatible, never mix them in the same syringe. Moreover, ketamine has a wide safety range (rats can tolerate doses in excess of 100 mg/kg) and supplemental doses can be safely given to prolong anesthesia. Thus ketamine is ideal for short-moderate duration surgical procedures. Atropine (0.05-0.3 mg/kg, IP) pretreatment should be used to reduce ketamine-stimulated salivation.

Equithesin. This commonly used solution is a mixture of chloral hydrate and sodium pentobarbital. The anesthetic dose is 4 mls/kg (IP). The solution is composed of:

4.25	g	chloral hydrate
2.13	g	magnesium sulfate
0.972	g	sodium pentobarbital
42	ml	propylene glycol
11.5	ml	ethanol
46.5	ml	distilled water

Long-Acting Anesthetic Agents

Chloral hydrate. At a concentration of 300-400 mg/kg (IP), chloral hydrate will induce surgical anesthesia. The duration of anesthesia induced by chloral hydrate is very long.

Chapter 2: Anesthesia

Because the margin of safety for chloral hydrate is large, supplemental injections can be given. An important issue for this drug is the frequent and fatal induction of paralysis of the ileus in some number of rats. In this condition, the intestines no longer operate correctly such that faecal material builds up leading to eventual death.

Urethane. This drug will induce anesthesia in rats when administered at a concentration of 1.2 grams/10 ml/kg, intraperitoneal. You should note that a 300 gram rat would receive 3 cc's of this solution. Urethane is a carcinogen, so you should be careful in handling this drug solution. Moreover, urethane is toxic to the liver and therefore this drug should only be used in terminal procedures (where the rat is euthanized after data collection).

Table 2.3: Treatments To Reverse Over-anesthesia

Drug:	Dose:	Route:	Comments:
Begimide	10 mg/kg	IP	
Doxapram	5-10 mg/kg	IM	For all anesthetic agents: general respiratory stimulant
Levellorphan	6 mg/kg	SC	For Innovar-Vet
Mikedimide	1 mg per mg of pentobarbital injected	IP	For pentobarbital anesthesia
Naloxone	1 mg/kg	IP	For Innovar-Vet
Yohimbine	2 mg/kg	IP	

INHALATION ANESTHETIC METHODS

Volatile gases can be used to safely anesthetize rats. Anesthesia induced by inhalation of gases such as halothane is preferable to the anesthesia induced by injectables such as the barbiturates because the depth and duration of inhalation anesthesia is easily controlled. Moreover, because gas anesthetics are exhaled via the lungs, recovery from anesthesia is rapid. A variety of delivery systems, varying in complexity and cost are available for gas anesthesia. These range from inexpensive and inefficient desiccator systems to very expensive, but efficient, closed-circuit systems. The desiccator system involves placing the rat in a desiccator containing cotton balls soaked with the anesthetic to be used. In a closed circuit delivery system, an endotracheal tube is connected to a regulator that delivers both anesthetic and oxygen and removes expired carbon dioxide. For a review of these systems, consult Kraus (1980), Myers (1971) and Waynforth and Flecknell (1992).

Chapter 2: Anesthesia

Ether

Ether is an inexpensive gas that can be used in a cotton-lined desiccator to anesthetize the rat for brief periods. Rats to be etherized should be pretreated with atropine (0.05-0.3 mg/kg, intraperitoneal) because ether produces excessive salivation. Care should be taken to prevent the rat from directly contacting ether-soaked cotton as ether is an irritant. To avoid this problem, place a wire-mesh floor over the cotton on floor of the desiccator. You should be very careful with ether as it is very flammable and explosive. Do not allow open flames in the lab when ether is used and do not dispose of ether-soaked cotton into waste cans. Most laboratories do not allow this hazardous material to be used for anesthesia. Others may allow it to be used only under an explosion-proof hood.

Halothane

Halothane (also termed fluothane) is a potent non-explosive anesthetic gas that rapidly induces surgical anesthesia. Halothane should be used in a closed circuit system because this agent rapidly saturates the atmosphere (and any personnel therein) when used in an open system. An open system is one in which the expired gas is vented into the room rather than recirculated. Moreover, halothane can be prohibitively expensive for use as a routine general anesthetic.

Methoxyflurane

This clear liquid can be used as an anesthetic when delivered in a desiccator. Methoxyflurane (also termed Metofane) does not rapidly induce anesthesia and requires longer induction times (5-10 minutes of continuous exposure to induce suitable anesthesia). This inhalant is relatively long-acting, safe and inexpensive.

POST-ANESTHETIC CARE

Following a surgical procedure, each rat should be placed into a clean dry cage positioned near a heat source. Never place the rat directly on sawdust bedding but rather use paper towels or other towel material. It is important that respiration be monitored in all rats recovering from surgery. If respiration is shallow and slow, resuscitation procedures, described below, should be initiated. A frequent cause of post-surgical death is hypothermia. Rectal temperature (measured 3 cm into the rectum) should be monitored frequently using a mercury bulb thermometer (calibrated to 0.1 degrees Centigrade). If rectal temperature drops below 33 degrees Centigrade (normal is approximately 37.5), external heating sources (heat pad or heat lamp) should be used to raise body temperature. Do not apply too much heat as overheating can cause death. Care should be taken to prevent burns, particularly when using heating pads. Placing the rat on a 35 degree incline (nose down) will allow fluids to drain from the respiratory tract. Pedal and corneal reflexes should be checked frequently to determine the extent of recovery from anesthesia. Do not place a rat back into it's home cage until that rat is capable of spontaneous movement.

Chapter 2: Anesthesia

Aspiration

Aspiration (withdrawing phlegm) from the lungs of a rat can be accomplished by inserting a rubber tube connected to a 5 cc syringe about 3 centimeters into the rat's throat. Do not force the aspiration tube down the throat; rather, twist the tube sideways as you maneuver the tube down the rat's throat. Slowly withdraw the plunger of the syringe as you withdraw the tube from the throat. This will induce negative pressure in the lungs and will withdraw the phlegm into the tube. This can be repeated several times until respiration is regular.

Resuscitation

If breathing fails during recovery from anesthesia, a resuscitator can be used to sustain breathing until respiratory stimulants can be administered and take effect. For example, Myers (1971) described an inexpensive resuscitator constructed from a one-ounce infant rectal syringe and a rubber atomizer bulb. The syringe is placed over the airway of the rat and the atomizer bulb squeezed once per second to maintain inspiration and expiration.

Post-surgical Pain

After a surgical procedure and recovery from anesthesia, you should frequently monitor the health and status of each rat. Body weight and food intake can be recorded daily to give a first hint of post-surgical complications. Signs of distress include a hunched posture, failure to groom, reduced body weight and food intake and extreme vocalization to being handled. You should consult with your local veterinarian who will initiate appropriate treatment. This may include administration of analgesics such as morphine (2-5 mg/kg, SC), meperidine (2 mg/kg, IM), or buprenorphine (0.02-0.05 mg/kg, SC). The latter is preferable owing to its long duration of action (8-12 hours).

Chapter 2: Anesthesia

REFERENCES AND SUGGESTED READINGS

Author. (1986). Guide for the care and use of laboratory animals. U.S. Department of HEW publication (NIH).

Authors. (1989). Animal Welfare Act. *Federal Register*, 54, number 168, 36151-36155.

Authors. (1993). Report of the AVMA Panel on Euthanasia. *Journal of the American Veterinary Medical Association*, 202, 229-249.

Barnes, C.D. and L.G. Eltherington. (1973). *Drug Dosage in Laboratory Animals*, London, England: University of California Press.

Campbell, J.M. and J.B. Campbell. (1984). *Laboratory Mathematics* (3rd Edition). St. Louis: C.V. Mosby Company.

Flecknell, P.A. (1987). *Laboratory Animal Anesthesia*, London: Academic Press.

Gilman, A.G., T.W. Rall, A.S. Nies and P. Taylor. (1990). *Goodman and Gilman's The Pharmacological Basis of Therapeutics*. New York: Macmillan.

Hughes, H.C. (1981). Anesthesia of laboratory animals. *Laboratory Animal*, September, 30-56.

Kraus, A.L. (1980). Research Methodology. In: *The Laboratory Rat* H.J. Baker, J.L.Lindsey and S.H. Weisbroth (Eds). New York: Academic Press.

Lumb, W.V. (1963). *Small Animal Anesthesia*. Philadelphia: Lea and Fibiger.

Myers, R.D. (1971). General laboratory procedures. In: R.D. Myers (Ed) *Methods in Psychobiology*, volume 1, New York: Academic Press.

Stickrod, G. (1979). Ketamine/xylazine anesthesia in the pregnant rat. *Journal of the American Veterinary Medical Association*, 175, 952-953.

Waynforth, H.B. and P.A. Flecknell. (1992). *Experimental and Surgical Techniques in the Rat*, (2nd Edition). London: Academic Press.

Chapter 3
Surgical Instruments, Aseptic Techniques and Procedures

<u>Aseptic Surgery</u>

The intent of surgery in physiological psychology is often to provide a manipulation of some organ in the periphery or to alter activity in a brain region. The further intent is to determine whether the specific manipulation altered some aspect of physiology and eventually provoked a change in behavior. The fact that many of the exercises in this manual involve assessment of behavior after surgical manipulation predetermines that your animals must be healthy before the surgery and that they remain healthy after the surgery. Assessment of behavior of health-compromised animals is unlikely to yield much information of value. The purpose of the present chapter is to review surgical practices that will skillfully accomplish the surgical procedure while at the same time minimizing infections that might compromise the health of a surgically-prepared rat.

There is a folklore in the physiology community that rats are hardy organisms that are extraordinarily resistant to infections. This view has led to many surgical procedures being carried out under "clean" conditions. No particular procedures were used to sterilize the surgical instruments and the surgeon often worked bare-handed. Whether such clean procedures produced evidence of infection is unclear. This lack of clarity resulted from experimental surgeons either not being trained to detect infections or not looking for evidence of surgically-induced infections. Yet, recent studies suggest that sub-acute infections can result in behavioral changes as well as physiological changes (Bradfield, Schachtman, McLaughlin and Steffen, 1992). These results reinforce the concept that surgery must be accomplished under conditions that do not lead to infection.

Aseptic surgical technique is presently mandated for use in rats. The term aseptic means "without infection". Briefly, aseptic technique means that the incision site is cleaned on the rat, sterile instruments are used to accomplish the surgical procedure, and the surgeon's hands are covered with sterile gloves.

The standards under which rodent surgery are carried out are slightly less stringent than the standards for dogs and primates. Surgery involving rats can be carried out in a lab area as opposed to a dedicated surgical suite. The surgery table should be located away from doors and windows and air vents. A good location for the surgery table would be out of the flow of traffic in the room. The table surface should be non-porous so that you can disinfect it prior to the start of surgery. On an adjacent table, you can locate the surgical recovery area. This is simply a table onto which are placed rat cages which can be warmed (usually by overhead heat lamps). After the surgical procedure, you will place the rats in these cages until they recover sufficiently from the anesthetic so that they can be returned to the general colony room.

Each surgery technique will require that the rat be placed on its stomach or on its back. In the stereotaxic techniques described in chapter 4, the rat will be placed on its

Chapter 3: Surgery Techniques

stomach and the head mounted in a stereotaxic instrument. We normally place a clean towel on the base of the stereotaxic instrument onto which the rat lies during the procedure. In some surgical procedures, the rat might be on its back and this may require that some restraints be used to keep the limbs in position. Surgery boards are commercially available to accomplish this stabilization of the limbs.

Some effort will be required to prepare the surgery area for aseptic surgery. If you are doing stereotaxic surgery, the stereotaxic instrument should be sprayed with a disinfectant such as Nolvasan and then rinsed with sterile saline. Prior to surgery, you will have to collect all of the surgical instruments and the ancillary materials (screws, drivers, glue, etc.) that are required to carry out the surgery. Sterilization of these materials can be accomplished using either heat or chemical treatments. Metal instruments can be sterilized using heat in a pressure cooker. If steam is used to sterilize metal instruments, as in a small pressure cooker, sterilized instruments should be "cooked" for at least 30 minutes. Also you should be aware that steam may not kill all microorganisms. Certain materials (e.g. plastic) will have to be gas sterilized. Chemical sterilants are more likely to kill fungi, germs and viruses. These include solutions of glutaraldehyde in which instruments are soaked overnight. These solutions are rather caustic to skin: both yours and that of the rat. Always rinse chemically disinfected instruments with sterile distilled water prior to use. Alcohol solutions alone will not provide sterilization. Your instructor will provide you with sterilization details suited to your lab and institution. After sterilization, maintain the instruments in the sterile pack until just prior to use.

Surgical Instruments

A small number of surgical instruments are used in physiological surgeries. These include scalpels to divide tissue, scissors to dissect or cut tissue, forceps to grasp tissue, hemostats to stop tissue bleeding, and either suture or metal clips to join tissue together. This chapter briefly describes each instrument and its proper use and care and then describes a number of common procedures that can be used to manipulate the autonomic nervous system and selected aspects of the glandular system.

Scalpel.

A scalpel (refer to Figure 3.1) consists of a sharp knife blade mounted onto a handle. The Bard-Parker #3 handle and a #10 scalpel blade are typically used in surgery on rats. A scalpel blade must always be sharp and sterile. When the blade becomes dull, replace it with a sharp blade. Unless you wish to learn the fine art of suturing by practicing on your own hands, never use your fingers to remove and replace a scalpel blade. Rather, use a hemostat forcep or blunt tweezers to grasp the blade during replacement. If you must use a scalpel for other purposes in the lab (such as cutting electrode wire), use an old scalpel and maintain it away from your instrument tray. The scalpel handle should be held between the thumb and the second finger with your forefinger on top of the scalpel handle to provide both control and gentle pressure. Use the curve of the scalpel blade rather than the blade tip to cut tissue. Always make clean, smooth incisions as ragged incisions are difficult to suture and usually heal poorly.

Chapter 3: Surgery Techniques

Scissors.
    Several different varieties of scissors are used in the lab to cut and dissect tissue and to cut suture material. Small iris scissors are useful in dissection where you use the tips of the scissors to divide tissue. Iris scissors are also useful for cutting the skull in the "hinge" technique for removing the brain from the skull (refer to Chapter 5). Both blunt and sharp tips are available for scissors. Sharp-sharp scissors (both tips are sharp) can be used to cut coarse tissue such as the abdominal wall but should not be used for tissue dissection as these tend to tear the tissue and induce bleeding whereas blunt-blunt scissors are useful for tissue dissection and for removing sutures from incisions that are healed. Never use surgical scissors to cut paper or metal unless you plan to replace them immediately (cutting wire will ruin the scissors). Keep surgical scissors clean by wiping with 80% isopropyl alcohol and lightly oil the scissors with gauze soaked with sewing machine oil.

Forceps.
    Forceps are used to grasp and hold tissue during surgery. Numerous types of forceps are available for a variety of applications. Tissue forceps (refer to Figure 3.1) have sharp teeth at the inside of the forcep tips; these serve to tightly hold tissue. Such forceps can be used to retract skin from the area in which you will be working. Never use tissue forceps to grasp hollow organs (stomach, intestine) as these forceps will puncture hollow organs. Dressing forceps (refer to Figure 3.1) are designed to grasp most tissues, including hollow organs. Dressing forceps have fine serrations at the inside tip that serve to hold tissue. Hemostatic forceps, unlike other forceps, are constructed so that the handles can be mechanically attached, one against the other, so as to exert tremendous pressure at the tip of the forceps. Hemostatic forceps (hemostats) are used to control bleeding by clamping the bleeding tissue between the tips of the forceps.

Rongeurs.
    Rongeurs (Figure 3.1) are used in the physiological laboratory to cut and chip bone as when the brain is removed from the skull. Rongeurs should be kept clean and lightly oiled. As is the case with scissors, rongeurs can be ruined by cutting material such as wire.

Preparation of the Surgical Site
    An aseptic surgical procedure in the rat requires the incision site be free of hair and cleaned prior to making an incision through the skin. Preparation of the site should be be done by a person who assists the surgeon. After the rat is anesthetized, surgical hair clippers (Oster Model A5: with #40 clipper blade) should be used to throughly remove the hair around the incision site. Next, clean the incision site using a disinfectant such as Povidone (or Betadyne). Lightly soak a 2X2 cotton swab in Povidone and clean the skin. Start in the center of the incision site and work out. Use several cotton swabs to clean the scalp. Then clean the incision site using 70% alcohol. Use sterile 2X2 swabs to dry the incision site.

Chapter 3: Surgery Techniques

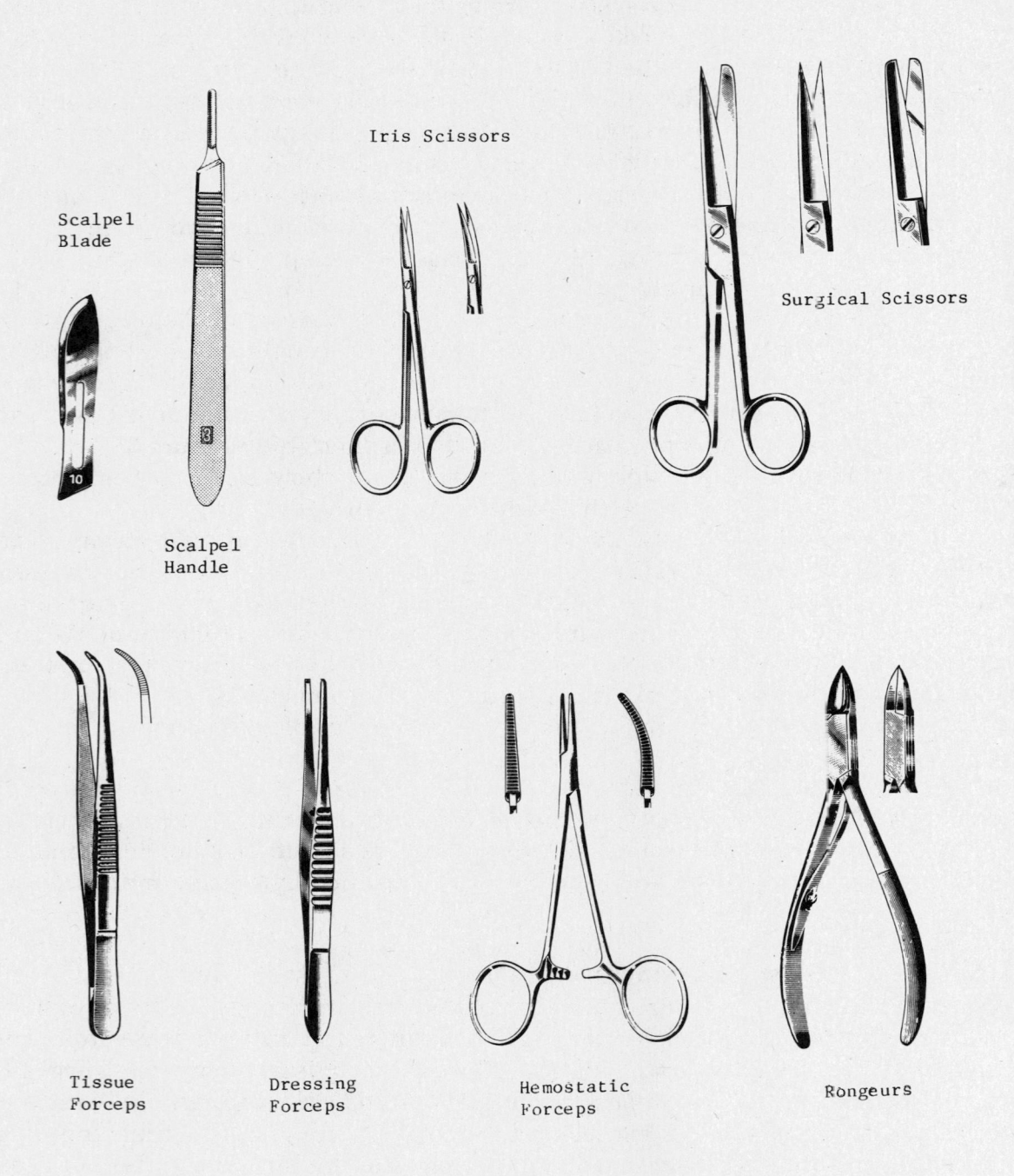

Figure 3.1. Surgical instruments commonly used in the physiological psychology laboratory. (Figure is reprinted with permission from Roboz Surgical Instruments, Washington, DC.).

Chapter 3: Surgery Techniques

The assistant can place the rat in its surgical position and then carefully cover the rat with sterile surgical drapes. These can be of the commercial variety or can be lab counterpaper which has been sterilized (usually with a sterilization gas). For stereotaxic surgery, the drape would be placed over the back of the body and would cover the tail. After draping the rat, one or more drapes should be placed near the surgery board. The assistant should use a sterile hold to place these drapes (in this technique, one side of a piece of towel which contacts their hands is non-sterile while the surface used to handle the drapes is sterile). These drapes on the table will form a sterile field onto which your sterile surgical instruments will be placed. Have the assistant place the sterile instruments on the sterile field. A beaker filled with 70% alcohol can be used to store the instruments in between uses.

The surgeon should don a lab coat and roll the sleeves past the elbows. The surgeon should use a Betadyne-type soap and a scrub brush to throughly wash their hands and their arms (to the elbow). Have a sterile cloth laid out by the sink prior to washing; this is used to dry the hands and arms after cleaning. The surgeon should then don sterile gloves. Keep your hands in the air and away from other objects (such as your face or pockets). Procede to the surgery room to initiate the surgery.

It is important that the surgical instruments be kept sterile within and between surgeries. As noted earlier, surgical instruments must be sterilized prior to surgery. During the course of the surgery, sterility can be maintained by storing the instruments in 70% ethanol. You should probably have a second set of sterile instruments on hand if you carry out more than 5 surgeries in a series or if you break sterilization (i.e. drop the instrument on the floor).

Incisions and Hemostasis

The term incise refers to cutting or separating tissue. In most surgical procedures, you will either incise the scalp or the abdominal skin and body wall. The scalp of the rat is quite thin and is readily incised using a scalpel blade. Bleeding is rarely profuse from the incised scalp and can be readily controlled using gentle pressure from a dry cotton swab. The skin of the abdomen is thick and will require moderate pressure to incise using a scalpel. Bleeding may occur when incising the abdominal body wall. Such bleeding can often be cheeked by pressure from a cotton swab. Infrequently, you will have to use a hemostatic forcep to check abdominal wall bleeding. Locate and clamp the cut vessel using the tips of the forceps. Use considerable care in the amount of pressure that you exert on the tissue via the forceps because forceps can easily crush and destroy tissue. In some situations, gel foam can be be used to control bleeding. This material can be cut into small strips or chunks and placed near bleeding tissue. Bleeding from the skull may occur when scraping the periosteum from the surface of the skull as you prepare the skull for implantation of electrodes or cannulae (see Chapter 4). The hot tip of a small soldering pencil can be briefly applied to the skull to stop bleeding. An alternative measure to stop bleeding uses commercially available styptic powders (e.g. Kwik-Stop, Gimborn-Rich Health Company, Atlanta, GA).

Chapter 3: Surgery Techniques

<u>Wound Closure</u>

Surgical incisions must be properly closed in order for healing to occur. The following section details the techniques and materials that can be used to close surgical incisions in the rat.

Sutures.

Suture refers to a threadlike material that is used to literally sew tissue together and provide support during healing. Suture materials are a foreign substance within the body and as such are reacted to by tissue pierced by the suture. In fact, the bodily reaction to suture material serves as a reference to classify the suture. If the body reacts by absorbing (destroying) the suture, the material is termed as "absorbable" whereas if the suture material remains intact and is encapsulated by the tissue, the suture material is termed "non-absorbable".

Absorbable Suture Material. The typical material in this category is surgical gut or cat-gut. Depending on the extent to which the cat-gut is treated with chromic acid (a chemical that retards absorption), cat-gut can be expected to be absorbed within 7-40 days. Medium chromic cat gut absorbs within 20 days and is a typical suture material for rats. Cat-gut should not be sterilized or wetted as heat and dampness will reduce its strength. Use the cat-gut directly from the package and always discard the remainder. Never crush cat-gut with hemostatic forceps as it will lose its tensile strength.

Nonabsorbable Suture Material. Several varieties of nonabsorbable suture are available, each with advantages and specific uses. Surgical cotton should not be used as a suture material unless this is absolutely the only material available. Cotton is difficult to tie, cannot be sterilized and is not suitable for gut work in the rat. Surgical silk is a commonly used material for sutures in the rat. Vascular surgical silk, coated with silicon, is particularly useful in surgeries of the rat gut. Moreover, surgical silk offers the advantage that it can be autoclaved without significant loss of strength. Dry surgical silk is stronger than wet silk. The typical silk suture material used in rats is 5-0 surgical silk.

Stainless steel wire (iron-nickel-chromium alloy) is the least reactive of the suture materials and is the strongest. Steel wire can be used for both abdominal surgery and for closure of the scalp, although the latter may be overkill. Sutures made with wire remain in place indefinitely (until removed by the surgeon). Moreover, this suture material can be autoclaved frequently without loss of strength. Stainless steel wire should be discarded if bent or kinked.

<u>Suture Needles</u>

Suture needles are either traumatic (cutting edge) or atraumatic (no cutting edge). You will likely be using traumatic needles because these are designed for suturing skin and fascia whereas the atraumatic needle is used to suture soft tissue (stomach). Many

Chapter 3: Surgery Techniques

manufacturers and suppliers of suture provide needles already attached to the suture material (IDE Corporation, see Appendix B).

Suture Patterns

Figure 3.2 depicts several typical suture patterns. Interrupted sutures are independent; you pass the suture needle and material through the two opposing skin edges and tie the strands together (Figure 3.3). Push the suture needle through the skin using a forceps or needle holder while holding the skin using blunt tweezers; do not use your fingers. The suture ends are then tied together using a square knot (see knots below). The tissue is therefore held together at a number of separate sites along the incision. Such interrupted sutures are quite strong in that if one suture fails, the others will hold. Such a suture pattern would be appropriate for abdominal surgery in which the body wall must be tightly sutured or the scalp edges must be joined after stereotaxic surgery. The second pattern is that of the continuous suture in which you continue to use the same length of suture as you join the opposing skin edges (see Figure 3.2). Such a suture pattern, however, can easily fail if the tying knot fails. The final suture pattern is that of the "purse-string" pattern. Such a pattern is used when a cannula or length of plastic tubing is led out through the abdominal wall or neck. One passes one end of the suture in and out of the skin in a continuous circle and then pulls and knots the two ends thereby tightening the skin around the cannula. You should closely monitor the rat for infection of a purse suture (termed the "weeping" suture).

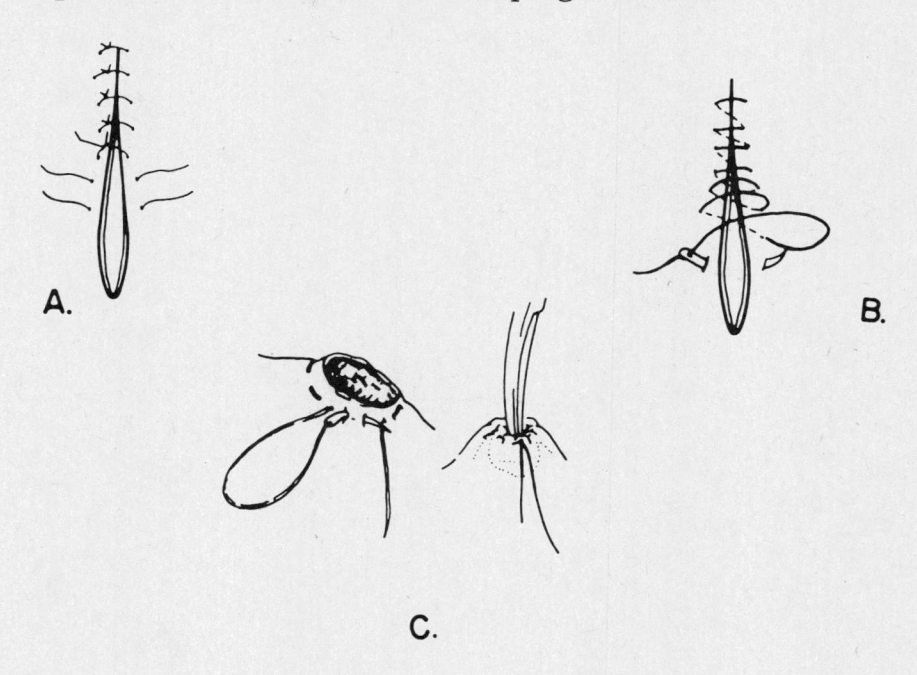

Figure 3.2. Examples of various suture stitch patterns including: a) interrupted stitches, b) continous stitch and c) "purse-string" stitch. (Figure reprinted with permission from D. Singh and D. Avery (Eds). (1975). Physiological Techniques in Behavioral Research, Belmont, CA: Wadsworth).

Chapter 3: Surgery Techniques

<u>Suture Knots</u>

A variety of esoteric knots are used to tie off suture material. The commonly used square knot is depicted in Figure 3.3. For additional information on suture knots refer to Nealson (1982) and Waynforth and Flecknell (1992).

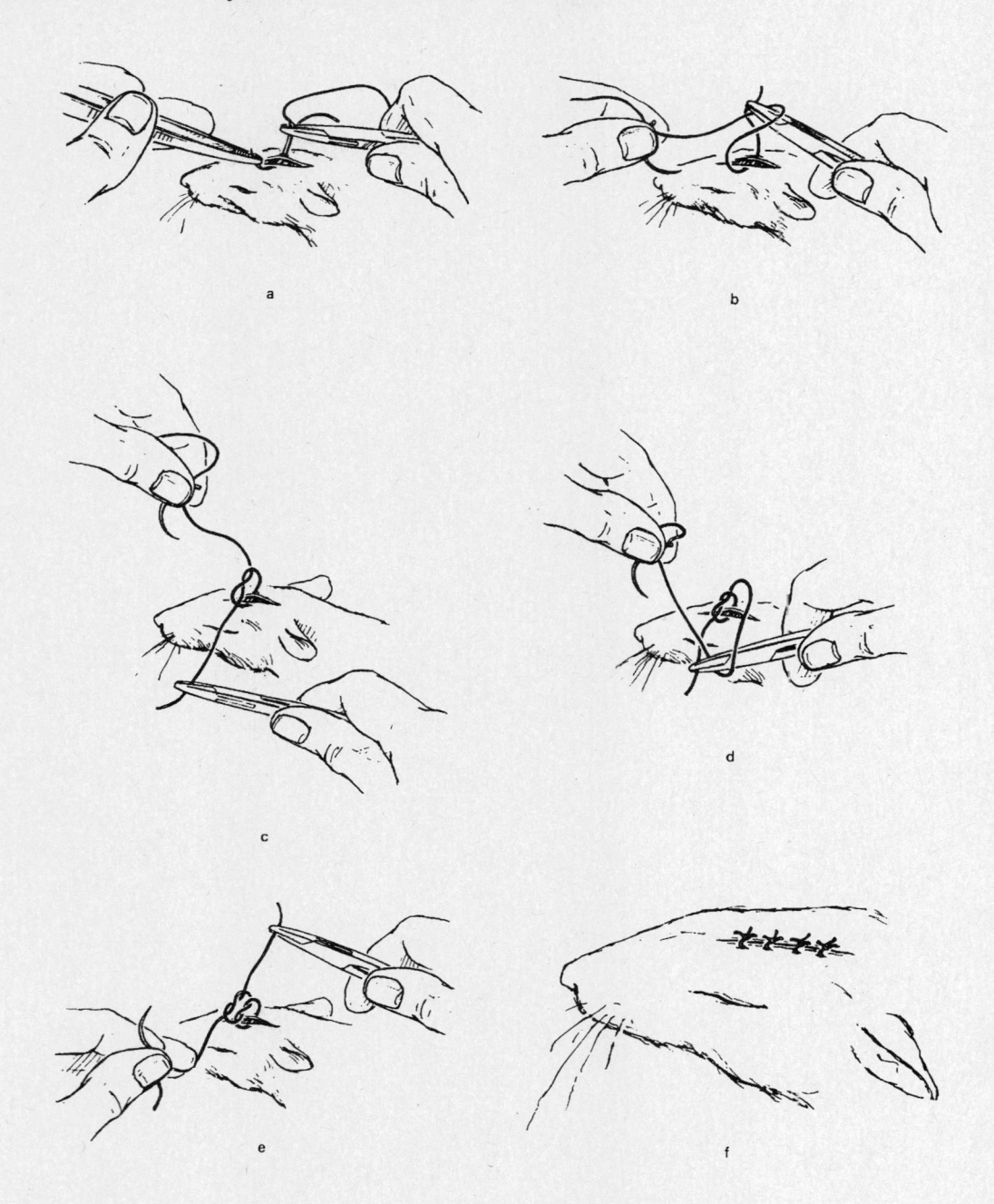

Figure 3.3. An example of how to tie a square knot using suture. (Figure reprinted with permission from B.L. Hart (Ed). (1976). Experimental Psychobiology, San Francisco: W.H. Freeman Co.).

Chapter 3: Surgery Techniques

Wound Clips

Stitches made using suture have largely been replaced by the metal wound clip as the typical wound closure technique. Incised tissue can be joined together using 9 mm metal wound clips (Clay-Adams). The skin is held together using blunt forceps while the wound clip applicator is used to mechanically force a curved metal clip over the skin (refer to Figure 3.4). Wound clips should be removed from the skin a week or so after surgery. This is accomplished using a special tool that forces the edge of the clip out from the skin. The clips offer the advantage of being reusable assuming, of course, that you clean and sterilize them (soak overnight in alcohol and then rinse with sterile water) prior to reuse.

A final note on sutures. It may be possible to join certain skin tissues together using cyanoacrylate glue. We have used a single drop of Superglue to hold intra-jugular cannulae in place and to join the skin around a scalp incision site after stereotaxic surgery. In some ways, this technique is preferable to using metal clips because this material does not require removal after healing has occurred.

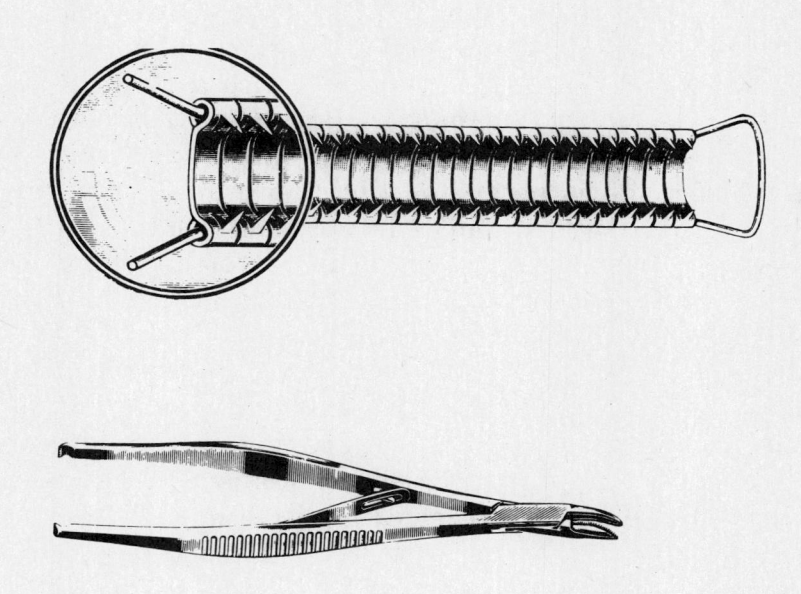

Figure 3.4. Metal (9 mm) wound clips and applicator used to close a wound in the rat. (Reprinted with permission from Roboz Surgical Instruments, Washington, D.C.)

Chapter 3: Surgery Techniques

COMMON SURGICAL PROCEDURES IN THE RAT

Physiological psychology has long been enamored of examining the effects of brain manipulations on behavior. Such an approach, however, fails to identify the significant control exerted by the autonomic nervous system and the peripheral glandular systems over behavior. Manipulations of the autonomic nervous system and of the various peripheral glands are described below. These include the use of gastric cannulae to deliver hormones and pharmacological agents into the digestive tract, the use of osmotic mini-pumps to chronically deliver hormones and drugs, the sectioning of a variety of peripheral motor and sensory nerves, the extirpation (removal) of the testes and the adrenal glands, and the chemical destruction of the sympathetic nervous system (sympathectomy) via guanethidine and the insulin-secreting cells of the pancreas by streptozotocin. Each technique is briefly described in the following section. Additional peripheral manipulations are described in Kraus (1980) and Waynforth and Flecknell (1992).

Gastric Gavage

Direct intragastric (intra-stomach) deposition of nutrients can be used to feed animals who for experimental reasons (i.e. lateral hypothalamic lesions) are not eating sufficient calories to maintain their body weight. Moreover, direct intragastric injections bypass the taste receptors of the tongue and oropharynx and is therefore an acceptable technique for delivering bitter or unpalatable drug compounds. The simplest technique for intragastric gavage is to outfit a 5 cc syringe with a 10 inch length of a number 8 French catheter (Davol Rubber Company). Grasp the rat with the thumb and left forefinger around the neck. Lubricate the tip of the catheter or feeding needle with a light mineral oil. Insert the catheter into the mouth and gently push the catheter tip some 6 cms down the esophagus and into the stomach (Kissileff, 1972). Verify that you have not inserted the catheter into the lungs (an outcome that produces squirming and respiratory distress in the rat). Another strategy is to use a 5.25 inch length of stainless steel tubing outfitted with a ball at the tip (refer to Figure 3.5). Again, restrain the rat and then insert the ball of the tubing down the esophagus into the stomach and then inject the solution (see Figure 3.5). If your intent is to limit the action of the injected solution to the stomach proper, you should be aware that solution volumes greater than 5 ml rapidly enter the duodenum from an empty stomach (Balagura and Fibiger, 1968). If your rat has just eaten prior to intragastric injection, the injected volume may move in a retrograde direction into the lungs thereby producing death.

Long-term implantation of catheters into the stomach and the duodenum have been extensively described by Kissileff (1972), Davis and Campbell (1975), and Snowdon (1975).

Chapter 3: Surgery Techniques

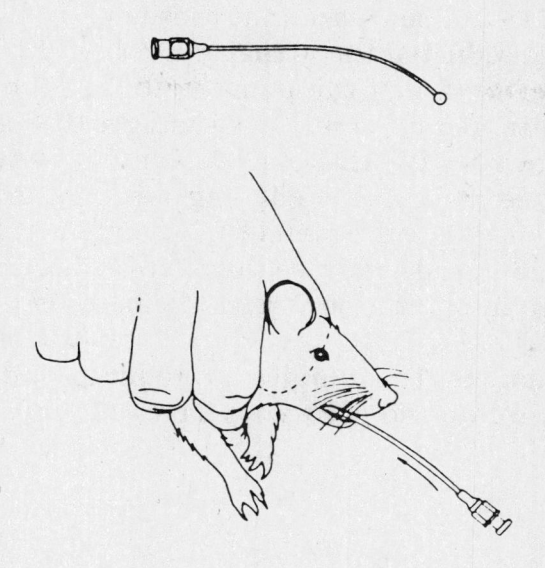

Figure 3.5. A metal-ball feeding tube used to make an intragastric injection into the rat (Reprinted with permission from Kraus, A. (1980). Research Methodology. In: H.J.Baker et al. The Laboratory Rat, Volume 2, New York: Academic Press).

Osmotic Delivery of Compounds

Drug injections produce drug effects that are variable in terms of time of onset and duration, depending on the route of injection, the vehicle used (oil vs saline), and the drug concentration. Even injections given several times a day do not provide for constant drug concentration in the blood but rather result in a series of drug "peaks".

An alternative to multiple daily injections for chronic drug/hormone exposure is that offered by the osmotic "mini-pump" (Alza Corporation). The mini-pump (refer to Figure 3.6) consists of a collapsible reservoir formed by a flexible material that is surrounded by a saturated osmotic solution. The fluid to be infused into the body is placed into the central reservoir and the pump is then implanted (see procedures below) into the body. Water from the bodily fluids enters the outer semipermeable membrane because of the attraction of the hyperosmotic fluid in the outer reservoir. This swelling of the outer layer serves to compress the volume of the inner reservoir, thereby forcing the drug\hormone solution out of the mouth of the pump, to be absorbed within the body. Depending on the physical characteristics of the outer membrane, the rate of delivery (between 0.5 and 1.0 ul/hour) is constant over a 7-14 day period.

The pump should be filled with the drug/hormone solution using a 10 cc syringe attached to a filler tube and then capped with the flow moderator. To determine that the pump is indeed full, weigh the pump before and after filling. If a pump weighs less than the value given for the pump, as would occur if air bubbles were trapped inside the

Chapter 3: Surgery Techniques

reservoir, you should repeat the filling process. If you are using a peptide such as angiotensin or insulin, you should be aware that these peptides can adhere to the inner surface of the pump thereby reducing the actual rate of peptide delivered. One simple solution is to coat the inner surface of the pump with a 1% solution of Siliclad (Clay-Adams) by injecting the solution into the reservoir using a 10 cc syringe and then storing each pump at room temperature for 72 hours. Use a 10 cc syringe to withdraw the Siliclad fluid and then oven dry (not above 40 degrees Centigrade) each pump for 1-2 hours. All glassware and syringe parts should be scrupulously cleaned and then rinsed in the silicon solution and then air-dried. Use this glassware to prepare the test solution and to fill the pump prior to implantation within the body as described below.

The following are descriptions of the surgical procedures used to implant a mini-pump into subcutaneous tissue and into the peritoneal cavity.

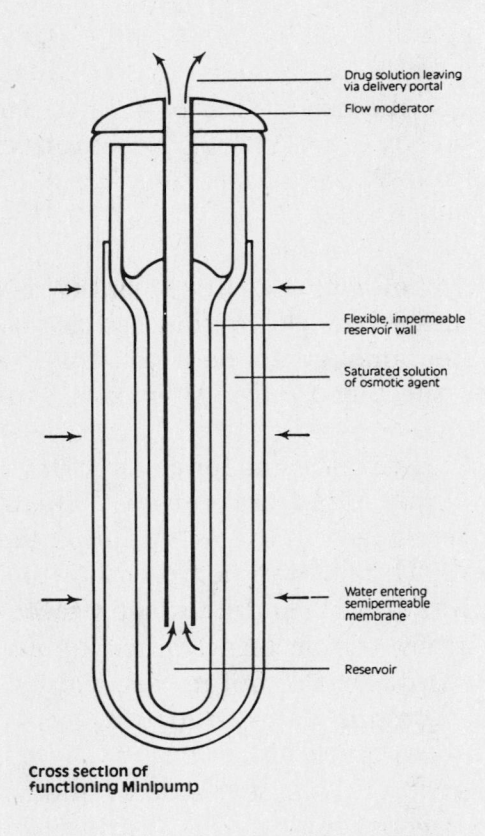

Figure 3.6. An osmotic mini-pump (courtesy of Alza Corporation, Palo Alto, CA).

Chapter 3: Surgery Techniques

Subcutaneous Implantation. This is a brief surgical procedure; therefore use an anesthetic such as ether or a combination of ketamine (60 mg/ml/kg, ip) and sodium pentobarbital (20 mg/ml/kg, ip) preceded by an injection (ip) of atropine sulfate (0.05-0.3 mg/ml/kg). Use electric clippers to shave the back of the rat and then clean the surgical site. Use sharp-sharp scissors to cut a 1 cm incision through the skin over the back and then use the tips of the scissors to divide the connective tissue of the back so as to create a subcutaneous pocket into which the mini-pump is inserted. Check that the flow moderator is pointing away from the incision as you insert the pump into the subcutaneous cavity. Clean the incision site and then suture the incision using 9 mm wound clips and an applicator. At the end of the 7-14 day infusion period, inject a fatal overdose of sodium pentobarbital and remove the pump to verify that the flow moderator is clear at the end of the study. Note that an osmotic mini-pump should be discarded after a single use.

Intraperitoneal implantation. This procedure is identical to that used for subcutaneous implantation. Anesthetize the rat, shave and clean the abdomen and then make a single 1 cm incision 2 cms below the rib cage and 1 cm off the midline. Use blunt scissors to divide the abdominal muscle layer so as to enter the peritoneal cavity. Insert the pump, moderator end first, into the peritoneal cavity. Clean the incision with sterile gauze, dust with Furacin powder and then close the peritoneal cavity using several 9 mm wound clips applied so as to join both the skin and underlying muscle layers.

Vagotomy

The vagus (Tenth cranial nerve) is the major neural pathway for the transmission of both sensory information from the gut and motor information to the viscera. As the vagus descends in front and back of the esophagus, several branches can be observed. The hepatic branch innervates the liver and is derived from the ventral (right) trunk of the vagus whereas the celiac vagal branch runs to the celiac ganglia and thence to other abdominal organs and is derived from the dorsal (left) vagal trunk (refer to Figure 3.7). The ventral vagal trunk descends to innervate the ventral aspects of the stomach whereas the dorsal vagal trunk innervates the dorsal aspects of the stomach. Given the recent emphasis of theories of feeding on receptors and controlling mechanisms within the gut (stomach, duodenum, intestines and liver), a promising research technique is to section the vagus so as to eliminate sensory information from the gut to the brain (see Snowdon, 1975; Tordofff and Novin, 1982). The following section details the surgical procedures used to section the dorsal and ventral branches of the vagus just below the diaphragm (sub-diaphragmatic vagotomy).

Weigh your rat to the nearest gram and treat it with atropine sulfate (0.05-0.3 mg/ml/kg, ip) followed by anesthesia induced by sodium pentobarbital (42 mg/ml/kg, ip). Use electric hair clippers to shave the abdomen from the rib cage to the genitals and then clean this area using Betadyne and 70% alcohol. A sharp scalpel blade should be used to make a 4 cm incision beginning just slightly off the midline of the abdomen at

Chapter 3: Surgery Techniques

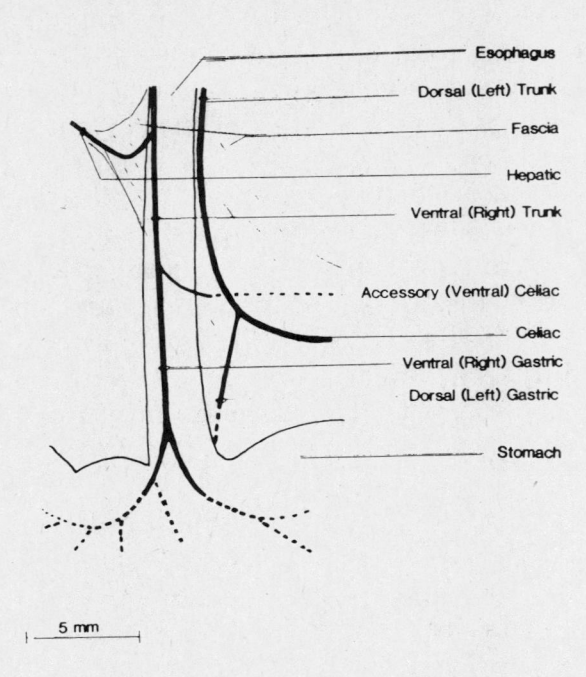

- Esophagus
- Dorsal (Left) Trunk
- Fascia
- Hepatic
- Ventral (Right) Trunk
- Accessory (Ventral) Celiac
- Celiac
- Ventral (Right) Gastric
- Dorsal (Left) Gastric
- Stomach

5 mm

Figure 3.7. The location and distribution of the various branches of the vagus nerve (Reprinted with permission from Tordoff, M.G. and D. Novin (1982). Celiac vagotomy attenuates the ingestive responses to epinephrine and hypertonic saline but not insulin, 2-deoxy-D-glucose, or polyethylene glycol. Physiology and Behavior, 29, 605-613).

the rib cage and extending toward the tail. Use blunt dissection via scissors to expose the peritoneal cavity. Locate the lobes of the liver and deflect these back so as to expose the stomach. Note the entrance of the esophagus into the stomach and then use blunt forceps placed under the esophagus to raise the esophagus from the peritoneal cavity. The vagus runs as two branches along the length of the esophagus: one is located just on top while the other is located beneath the esophagus. Use care not to crush or damage the esophagus (this will cause postoperative swallowing problems) and frequently moisten the tissue with 0.9% saline. Carefully use blunt forceps to separate the twin branches of the vagus from the esophagus and then use sharp iris scissors to cut a 0.25 inch length of nerve from each vagal trunk as the vagus enters the stomach. If you remove vagal tissue higher up the esophagus, the rat is likely to experience severe difficulty in swallowing because of esophageal denervation (Carpenter, King, Stamoutsos and Grossman, 1978). After checking that the vagus is completely interrupted, replace the esophagus into the cavity and reposition the liver. Sham vagotomies are carried out as above except that you handle the vagii rather than cutting each nerve. Clean the incision site using sterile gauze and then close the peritoneal cavity using 9 mm wound clips.

Vagotomized rats should be offered a liquid diet following surgery as these rats have problems with swallowing dry food. If a liquid diet is not available, then soak the chow

Chapter 3: Surgery Techniques

pellets with water to promote adequate hydration. A reliable sign of the completeness of vagotomy is that these rats will show normal food intake of liquid diet but will eat smaller, more frequent meals (Snowdon, 1975). Another simple but rough indicator of the completeness of the vagotomy is the "neutral red" test. Here, deprive the rat of food for 24 hours so as to clear the stomach. Anesthetize the rat(s), incise the abdominal wall and locate the stomach. Retract the stomach from the peritoneal cavity and then incise the stomach wall with a scalpel and wash the contents with 0.9% saline (37 degrees Centigrade). Now locate the heart and inject 1 ml of a 1% solution of neutral red (Sigma) via the left ventricle (see Chapter 5). Then apply white filter paper to the mucosal layer of the stomach for 15 minutes. If the vagus was completely transected, no red stains should appear on the filter paper, whereas remaining vagal secretory function would be indicated by red stains apparent on the filter paper.

Sympathectomy

The sympathetic nervous system is composed of neurons that are mixed in function, serving both afferent fibers (sensory) and efferent fibers (motor). As was the case with the surgical procedure of vagotomy, eliminating the sympathetic nervous system is a useful procedure for determining the contribution of this system to the regulation of behavior. Surgical transections of the sympathetic system, however, fail to eliminate all components of the sympathetic system. Because the sympathetic system uses the neurotransmitter norepinephrine (NE) at the post-ganglionic synapse, chemicals that destroy NE neurons can be used to disable the sympathetic nervous system. An effective neurotoxin for NE neurons within the sympathetic nervous system is the compound guanethidine sulfate. Subcutaneous injection of guanethidine sulfate (Ismelin: Ciba/Geigy) at a concentration of 40-60 mg/kg for 8-21 days will reduce heart NE levels by 80 to 97%. The sympathectomy induced by guanethidine is apparent in both neonate and adult rats and is permanent (Johnson et al, 1976). Two advantages accrue from using guanethidine rather than another neurotoxin such as 6-hydroxydopamine: guanethidine is less toxic and does not easily pass into the brain. Thus, any changes in behavior observed in guanethidine-sympathectomized rats are presumably a function of peripheral damage to catecholamine neurons.

Several procedural comments may facilitate the use of guanethidine sulfate. Prepare the guanethidine sulfate solutions fresh daily. Add hydrochloric acid in an amount sufficient to bring the pH to 7.2. The effect of guanethidine on the sympathetic post-ganglionic neuron can be verified by determining the level of NE in the heart (or other sympathetic post-ganglionic neuron can be verified by determining the level of NE in the heart (or other sympathetic tissue) using high-pressure-liquid-chromatography (HPLC). As the HPLC analytical procedure is somewhat beyond the scope of this course, an easily observed characteristic of guanethidine sympathectomy is polydipsia. Freeman, Wellman and Clark (1984, unpublished data) noted that adult rats treated with 40 mg/kg guanethidine sulfate per day over an 8 day period drank more water than controls not only during the treatment period but also for an additional 28 day period after the injections were discontinued. This polydipsia presumably reflects the denervation of the

Chapter 3: Surgery Techniques

salivary glands such that guanethidine-treated rats consume water to facilitate consumption of a dry chow diet.

Castration

Castration refers to the bilateral removal of the testes of the adult male rat. The surgical procedure for castration has been amply described in physiological surgery texts such as Wilsoncroft and Law (1967) and Hart (1976). Hormonal replacement procedures for castration include testosterone propionate (0.5 mg/rat, given in 0.1 ml of an oil vehicle, subcutaneously). The effect of castration on male sexual behavior has been elaborately described by Beach (1976), Leshner (1978) and by Feder (1984).

Ovariectomy

Removal of the ovaries of the adult female rat will induce a chronic state of diestrus or sexual non-receptivity. The procedures used to perform an ovariectomy are described in Exercise 8 of this manual as are the procedures for replacing the ovarian hormones. In addition to having an impact on sexual receptivity, removal of the ovaries also induces increased body weight, an effect termed ovarian obesity (refer to Gale and Sclafani (1977) for a comparison of ovarian and hypothalamic obesity syndromes).

Adrenalectomy

The adrenal glands of the rat greatly resemble two brown peas positioned just above the kidney on each side of the body. Each adrenal gland consists of the outer layer, termed the adrenal cortex and the inner adrenal medulla. The adrenal cortex secretes small amounts of the sex hormones (androgens) and secretes the glucocorticoids and the mineralocorticoids. The former hormones increase blood glucose concentration whereas the latter regulate water and electrolyte balance. The adrenal medulla is an important component of the sympathetic nervous system. Stimulation of the adrenal medulla results in the release of the hormones epinephrine (EPI) and norepinephrine (NE). These hormones circulate throughout the body and further stimulate and maintain stimulation of the sympathetic system by activating the sympathetic post-ganglionic receptors.

Weigh the rat to the nearest gram, atropinize (atropine sulfate, 0.05-0.3 mg/kg, ip) the rat and then use a short-acting anesthetic (ketamine plus pentobarbital, see Chapter 2). Use electric hair clippers to remove the fur from the abdomen on both sides of the body. Thoroughly clean the skin of the incision site using Betadyne and 70% alcohol. The incisions used for adrenalectomy are identical to those used for ovariectomy (refer to description in Exercise 8). Again, lay the rat on its side and use a scalpel to make a 3 cm incision through the skin. Then use sharp scissors to cut through the body wall for 1-2 cms. The adrenal gland will be found just above the kidney and will frequently be located in a mass of fatty tissue. A quick method to locate an adrenal gland that is obscured within fat is to roll the fat between your finger tips so as to palpate the adrenal. Retract the kidney and associated adrenal from the body. Cut the adrenal gland using the scalpel blade and replace the kidney and tissue into the abdominal

Chapter 3: Surgery Techniques

cavity. Repeat the procedure on the other side of the body. Carefully clean the incision sites using sterile gauze and then close each incision using several 9 mm wound clips.

The health of an adrenalectomized rat is fragile and special procedures must be performed to maintain these rats. Each rat should be kept in a clean and dry cage in a room maintained at 28 degrees Centigrade. Do not feed the rat for 3 days after surgery but do give access to 2 fluids: in one bottle provide 0.9% saline and in the other provide a 5% sucrose (w/v) solution. Because the adrenalectomized rat lacks the mineralocorticoids, offer a chow diet that is high in sodium and chloride but low in potassium (at the worst, sodium and potassium concentrations in the food should at least be equal).

Adrenal Demedulation

The procedures for adrenal demedullation are similar to those described above except that the outer cortex is left intact. Locate the adrenal gland and then use sharp iris scissors to nick one end of the gland. Use gentle pressure exerted by smooth-tipped forceps so as to force the medulla from the adrenal gland through the slit in the cortex. Sham-surgeries consist of cutting the cortex but not extruding the medulla. Replace the cortex into the peritoneal cavity and then close the wound. Rats that exhibit successful demedullation do not require maintenance on a high-salt fluid as the cortex supplies sufficient quantities of the mineralocorticoids to provide for adequate mineral and fluid balance.

Diabetes (chemically-induced)

The pancreas secretes two principle hormones, insulin and glucagon. Removal of the pancreas via surgical procedures results in diabetes, a condition characterized by high blood and urine glucose levels, enhanced breakdown (lipolysis) of fats, ketone bodies in urine, and high levels of water consumption and urine output. Diabetes is easily induced in the rat by a single injection of a drug such as alloxan monohydrate (200 mg/kg in a volume of 5 ml/kg, subcutaneously) or streptozotocin (100 mg/ml/kg, ip). Streptoxotocin is prepared in a citrate buffer to stabilize the solution. These compounds are somewhat selective in that each induces destruction of the insulin-secreting beta cells of the pancreas. The effects of diabetes on food intake, water intake, amphetamine anorexia and amphetamine hyperactivity have been described (Marshall, 1978; Thomas, Scharrer and Mayer, 1976). The presence of glucose in the urine of diabetic rats can be assessed using indicator strips (Lily Tes-Tape). The clinical signs of diabetes include polyuria (increased urine production; sometimes exceeding 100 ml/day), hyperphagia (increased eating of a low-fat diet), weight loss, and polydipsia (increased drinking; sometimes exceeding 100 ml/day), and, of course, the biochemical indices of urine (increased glucose levels ($\geq 2\%$) and ketones). The diabetic state can be reversed using daily injections of the long-lasting protamine-zinc insulin (PZI) at a concentration of 1-2 U/kg/day (subcutaneously).

Chapter 3: Surgery Techniques

REFERENCES AND SUGGESTED READINGS

Balagura, S. and H.C. Fibiger. (1968). Tube feeding: Intestinal factors in gastric feeding. Psychonomic Science, 20, 373-374.

Beach, F.A. (1976). Sexual attractivity, proceptivity and receptivity in female mammals. Hormones and Behavior, 7, 105-138.

Bradfield, J.F., T.R. Schachtman, R.M. McLaughlin and E.K. Steffen. (1992). Behavioral and physiologic effects of inapparent wound infection in rats. Laboratory Animal Science, 42, 572-578.

Carpenter, R.G., B.M. King, D.A. Stamoutsos and S.P. Grossman. (1978). VMH lesions in vagotomized rats: A note of caution. Physiology and Behavior, 21, 1031-1035.

Davis, J.D., and C.S. Campbell. (1975). Chronic intrajular, intraportal, gastric and duodenal cannulae for the rat. In: D. Singh and D. Avery (Eds). Physiological Techniques in Behavioral Research, Monterey, CA: Brooks/Cole.

Feder, H.H. (1984). Hormones and sexual behavior. The Annual Review of Psychology, 35, 165-200.

Johnson, E.M., F. O'Brien and R. Werbitt (1976). Modification and characterization of the permanent sympathectomy produced by the administration of guanethidine to newborn rats. European Journal of Pharmacology, 37, 45-54.

Hart, B.L. (1976). Experimental Psychobiology, San Francisco: W.H. Freeman.

Kissileff, H. (1972). Manipulation of the oral and gastric environments. In R.D. Myers (Ed). Methods in Psychobiology, Volume 2, New York: Academic Press.

Leshner, A.I. (1978). An Introduction to Behavioral Endocrinology, New York: Oxford University Press.

Marshall, J.F. (1978). Resistance of alloxan-diabetic rats to the behavioral activation induced by d-amphetamine: Partial restoration with a high fat/protein diet. Physiology and Behavior, 20, 319-322.

Nealson, T.E. (1982). Fundamental Skills in Surgery. Philadelphia: W.B. Saunders Co.

Olds, R.J. and J.R. Olds (1979). A Color Atlas of the Rat-A Dissection Guide. New York: John Wiley and Sons.

Snowdon, C.T. (1975). Gastrointestinal manipulation in the rat. In: D.Singh and D. Avery (Eds). <u>Physiological Techniques in Behavioral Research</u>, Monterey CA: Brooks/Cole.

Thomas, D.W., E. Scharrer and J. Mayer (1976). Effects of alloxan-induced diabetes on the feeding patterns of rats. <u>Physiology and Behavior</u>, <u>17</u>, 345-349.

Tordoff, M.G. and D. Novin. (1982). Celiac vagotomy attenuates the ingestive responses to epinephrine and hypertonic saline but not insulin, 2-deoxy-D-glucose, or polyethylene glycol. <u>Physiology and Behavior</u>, <u>29</u>, 605-613.

Waynforth, H.B. and P.A. Flecknell. (1992). <u>Experimental and Surgical Techniques in the Rat</u>, (2nd Edition). London: Academic Press.

Wells, T.A.G. (1964). <u>The Rat</u>. New York: Dover Publications

Wilsoncroft, W.E. and O.T. Law. (1967). <u>Laboratory Manual for Physiological Psychology.</u> Austin, TX: Psychonomic Press.

Waynforth, H.B. and P.A. Flecknell. (1992). <u>Experimental and Surgical Techniques in the Rat</u>, (2nd Edition). London: Academic Press.

Chapter 3: Surgery Techniques

Chapter 4
Stereotaxic Surgery

Stereotaxic surgery refers to the precise positioning of a surgical device, such as an electrode, a cannula or a wire knife, within a discrete area of the rat brain. Each of these surgical devices is designed to permit a different type of manipulation of brain tissue. An electrode, insulated except at the tip, can be used to create a lesion within the rat brain or to electrically stimulate the neurons that surround the electrode tip depending on whether high or low levels, respectively, of electrical current are used. A cannula is a thin metal tube that is implanted within the brain so that drug solutions can be infused into the brain tissue surrounding the tip of the cannula. A wire knife is a surgical device designed to cut neuron fiber bundles within the rat brain. The use of these devices will be described in this chapter.

The Stereotaxic Instrument

In order to accurately position a surgical device within the rat brain, the skull must be rigidly fixed in space using a stereotaxic instrument. This instrument, devised by Horsely and Clark in the early part of this century (Horsely and Clark, 1908), is illustrated in Figure 4.1. A stereotaxic instrument consists of a metal frame to which are affixed ear bars. These bars are designed to fit within each auditory meatus of the skull so as to hold the rat skull fixed in space. Additional support for the skull is provided by an upper incisor bar and tooth plate into which the jaw is clamped. Surgical devices such as electrodes or cannulae are attached to an electrode carrier arm that can be moved in 3 dimensions: anterior/posterior (A/P), dorsal/ventral (Height or H), and medial/lateral (L).

The movement of the carrier arm through the 3 planes (A/P, H and L) is calibrated in millimeters using vernier scales. Figure 4.2 illustrates such a vernier scale. Note that there are two juxtaposed sliding surfaces onto which are etched a series of lines. Note that there are 10 divisions, each representing 1 millimeter (mm), between each centimeter mark. An 80 mm scale is etched onto one surface, whereas a 10 mm scale is etched onto the opposite surface. To read the vernier scale, first note the position of the 0 line of the 10 mm scale. The position of this line relative to the marks on the opposing vernier scale denotes the digits before the decimal point. In Figure 4.2, the 0 line is located between the 38 and 39 mm marks. The trailing decimal is determined by noting which of the 10 mm scale marks lines up with any of the 80 mm scale marks. Note that in the figure the third mark of the 10 mm scale lines up with one of the lines of the 80 mm scale. Thus, this coordinate would be read as 38.3 mm. You should become very familiar with reading vernier coordinates. Also become familiar with the proper direction to turn the screw mechanism to move the carrier arm through each of 3 dimensions. Novice stereotaxic surgeons have bent more than one electrode because they turned the height mechanism clockwise rather than counterclockwise in order to raise the electrode.

Chapter 4: Stereotaxic Surgery

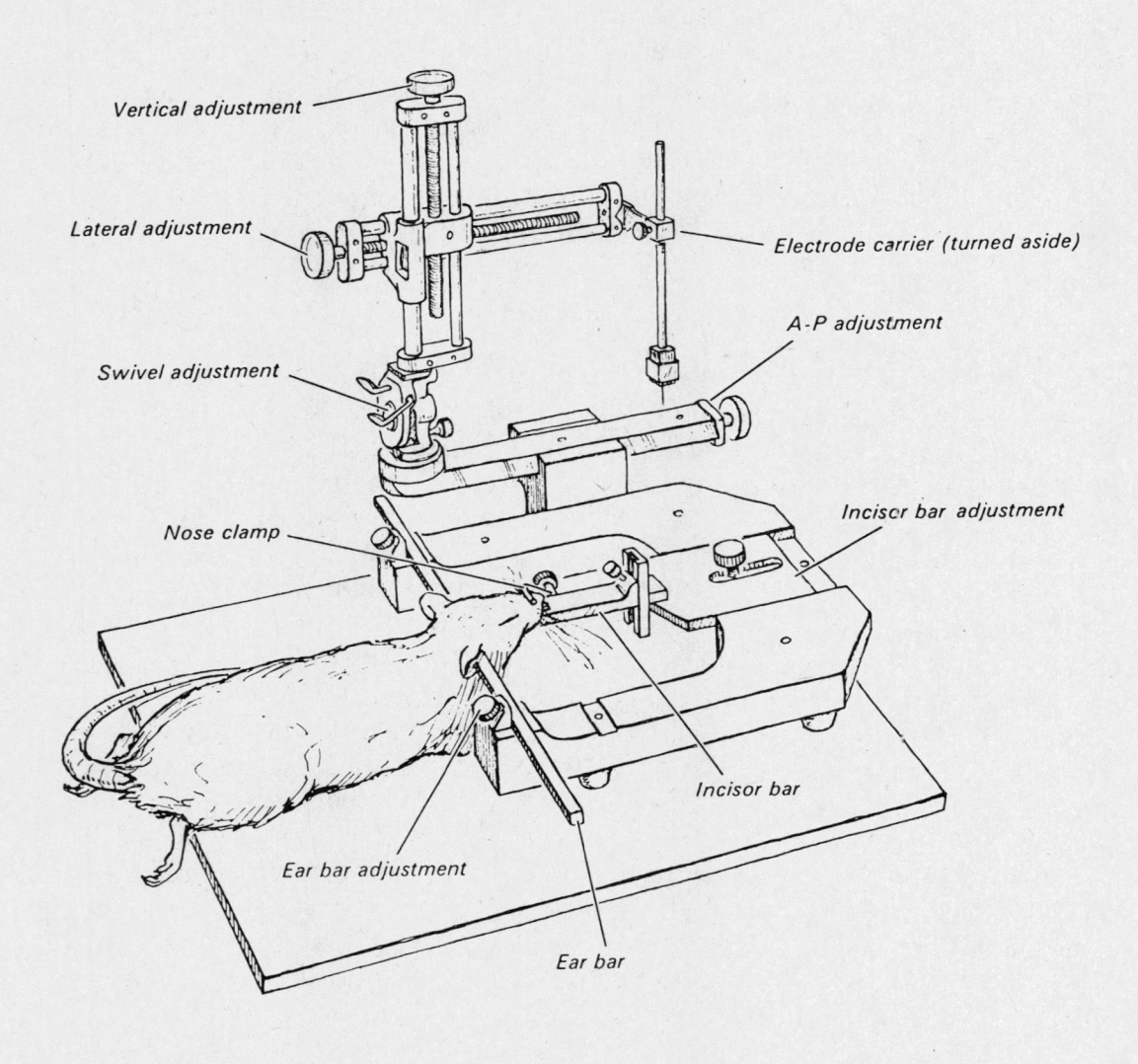

Figure 4.1. A rodent stereotaxic instrument. (Reprinted with permission from: Hart, B.L. (1976) <u>Experimental Psychobiology</u>, San Francisco: W.H.Freeman Co.).

Chapter 4: Stereotaxic Surgery

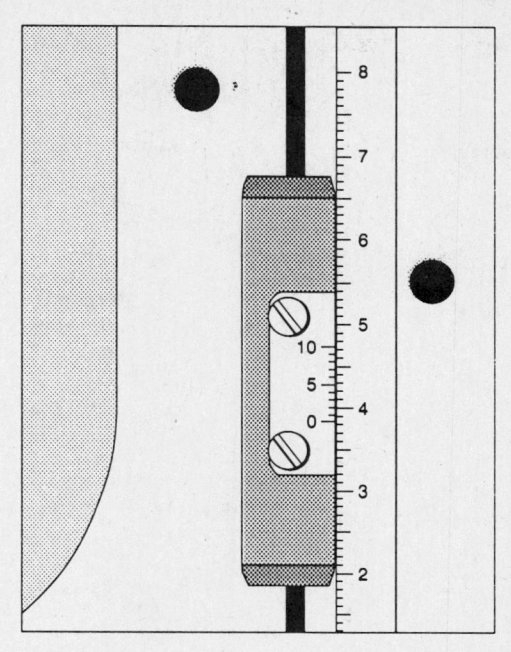

Figure 4.2. An illustration of stereotaxic vernier scales. The coordinate would be read as 38.3 mm. (Adapted with permission from Cooley, R.K. and C.H. Vanderwolf (1978). Stereotaxic Surgery in the Rat: A Photographic Series London, Canada: A.J. Kirby, Co.).

Atlases and Coordinate Systems

A stereotaxic atlas is a collection of coronal or transverse slices through the brain that were made at known intervals (say, every millimeter). Typically, the starting point for an atlas is the definition of the zero or reference point of the brain. Some atlases choose to use a line running through the center of each external auditory meatus (termed the interaural line or IAL) as the zero coordinate. The rat brain is then sliced in coronal sections anterior and posterior to the interaural line. The sections are then photographically enlarged and the major structures of each section are identified. A 3 dimensional system can then be constructed for identifying where a particular brain structure is located relative to the interaural line. Figure 4.3a depicts a plate from the atlas of König and Klippel (1963). In this line drawing, depicting the various brain structures, note the A/P, height and lateral dimensions. In the lower right corner is the A-P dimension (here given as 7.9 mm anterior to the interaural line). The vertical dimension gives height through the brain (dorsal/ventral) whereas the horizontal axis gives the lateral coordinates from the midline. The intersection of the lateral and height dimensions is the zero point of the brain for the König and Klippel (1963) atlas. This atlas also requires that the skull be placed in a level position by setting the upper incisor bar to -2.3 mm below the interaural line. Figure 4.4 depicts the relation between the horizontal and vertical zero planes of the König and Klippel (1963) atlas: you should note that the interaural line is exactly 4.9 mm below the height zero point. Thus, when you use coordinates derived from the König and Klippel (1963) atlas, you will add 4.9 mm to the interaural height vernier coordinate to approximate the true zero height coordinate.

55

Chapter 4: Stereotaxic Surgery

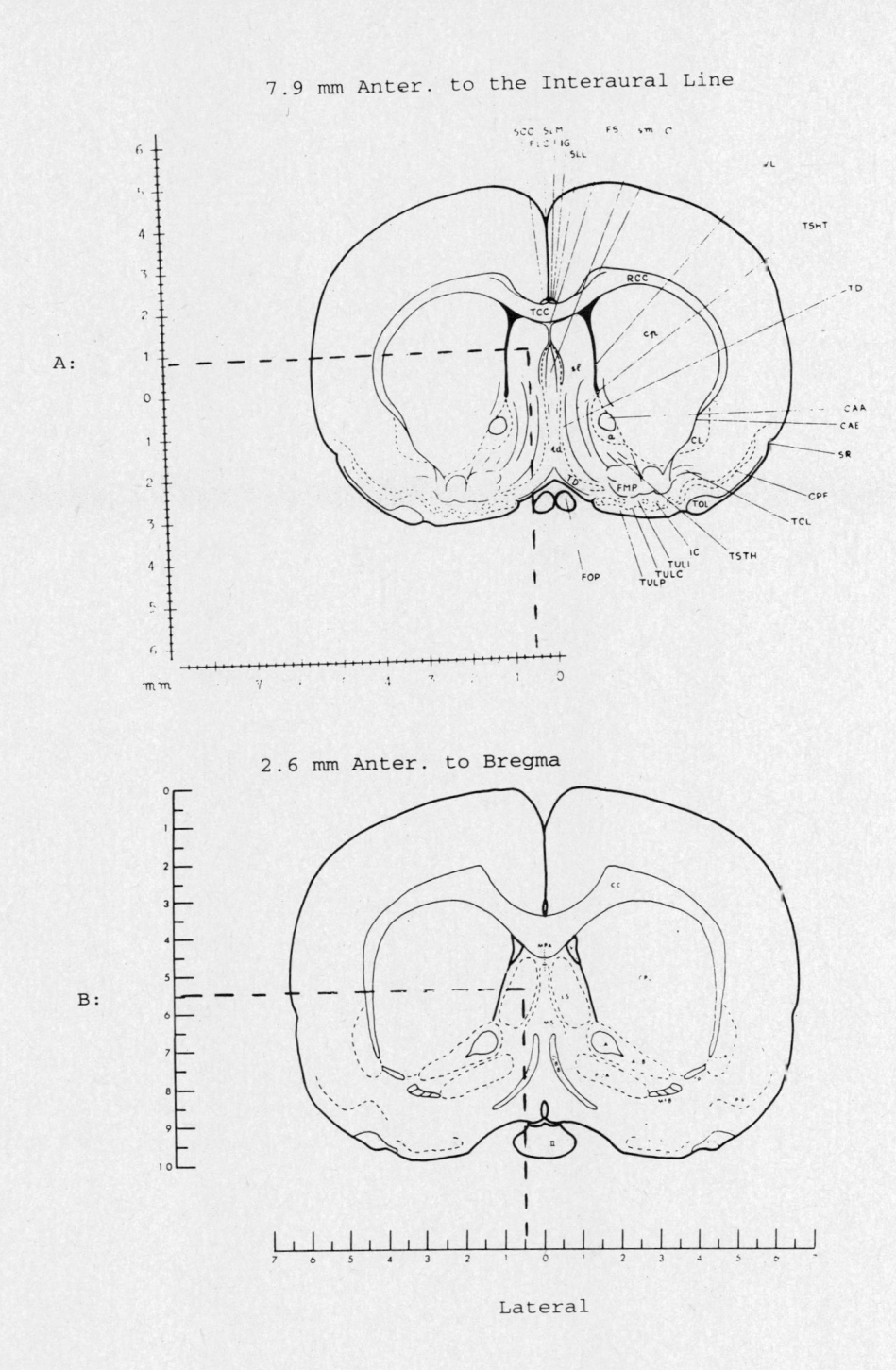

Figure 4.3. Representative coronal sections through the lateral septal nucleus illustrating the determination of A/P, height and lateral coordinates using different coordinate systems. a: König and Klippel (1963) atlas; b: Pellegrino, Pellegrino and Cushman (1979) atlas.

Chapter 4: Stereotaxic Surgery

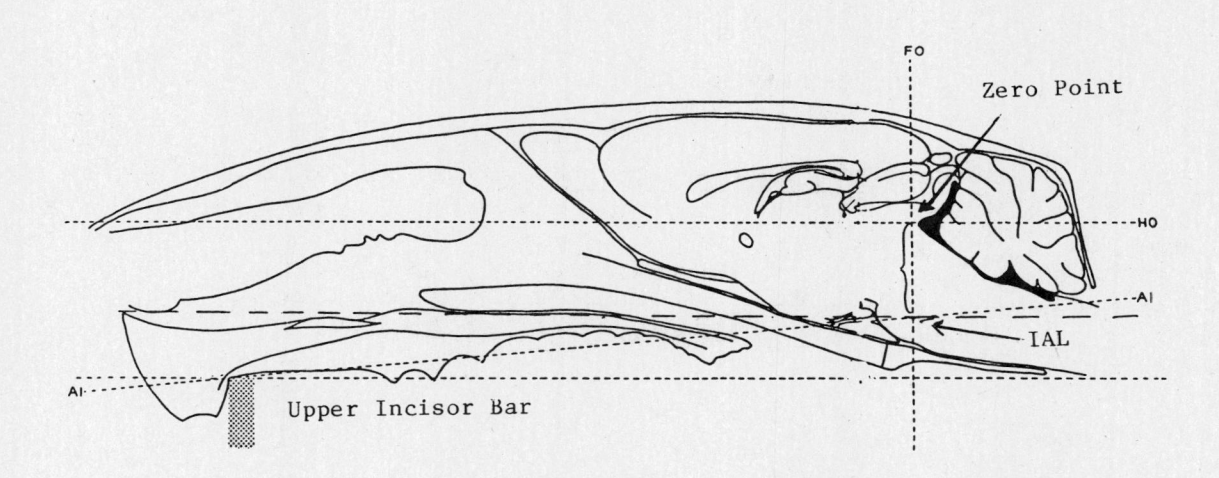

Figure 4.4. A sagittal section through the skull and brain illustrating the relationship between the interaural line and the zero point of the König and Klippel (1963) atlas (Reprinted with permission from König, J.F.R. and R.A. Klippel. (1963). <u>The Rat Brain.</u> Baltimore: Williams and Wilkins).

Stereotaxic atlases differ in terms of the size and sex of the animals used to construct the atlas, the definition of the zero point of the atlas and the angle of the skull. Table 1 depicts several of the various atlases currently in use and the specifics you should know in order to use each of them. The König and Klippel (1963) atlas assumes that the skull is level (thus, if you were to lower an electrode to the skull at bregma and at lambda, you would obtain the same height vernier reading). To accomplish this skull angle, the upper incisor bar must be set 2.3 mm below the interaural line (IAL). In contrast, the Pellegrino, Pellegrino and Cushman (1979) atlas assumes that the skull is tilted upward. To achieve this skull tilt, the upper incisor bar must be set at 5.0 mm above the IAL. The zero reference point also differs for each of the atlases. One can determine the zero point using either the interaural line or a skull landmark such as bregma (Pellegrino, Pellegrino and Cushman, 1979). Pellegrino, Pellegrino and Cushman (1979) and Paxinos and Watson (1986) provide coordinate systems that use either a skull landmark (bregma) or the interaural line. Finally, you should note that rats of different sexes and weights were used for the various atlases. You should try to use the atlas that most closely approximates the sex and weight of the animals you will be using in your studies. You would not, for example, use the König and Klippel (1963) atlas for male rats weighing 400-500 grams. Paxinos and Watson (1986) provide a discussion of some

Chapter 4: Stereotaxic Surgery

of the issues involved in adapting various rat atlases for use in different sexes and ages of rats.

Finally, Appendix C presents a number of stereotaxic plates derived from the Paxinos and Watson (1986) for use in this manual.

Table 4.1. Comparisons between the characteristics of several commonly used stereotaxic atlases.

Characteristic:	König and Klippel (1963)	Paxinos and Watson (1986)	Pellegrino et al (1979)
Subjects:	Female	Male/Female	Male
Weight Range:	150 g	250-350 g	280-320 g
Upper Incisor Bar Setting:	-2.4 mm	-3.3	5.0 mm
Zero Reference Points:			
A/P:	IAL	IAL or Bregma	IAL
Height:	IAL*	Skull	IAL # or Bregma
Lateral:	IAL	Midsaggital Suture	IAL or Midsaggital Suture

* Add 4.9 mm to the interaural line height coordinate.

\# Add 5.0 mm to the interaural line height coordinate.

Skull Preparation and Mounting

To minimize respiratory problems, your rat should be pretreated with atropine sulfate (0.3 mg/ml/kg, ip) 10 minutes prior to surgery and should be anesthetized as described in Chapter 2. After your rat has reached stage 3 anesthesia (see Chapter 2), use electric hair clippers to shave the rat's scalp from the middle of the eyes to the muscles of the neck and then around the ears. Now use sharp scissors to cut the flap of tissue immediately below the meatus of the ear. You should now be able to peer directly into the auditory meatus. This cut will heal quickly after surgery; its purpose is to facilitate placement of the skull into the ear bars of the stereotaxic instrument. The eyes of your rat may remain open even during anesthesia. In order to minimize eye irritation, place a small amount of Vaseline or mineral oil onto the eyes of your rat. Identify your rat using labelled tape wrapped around the base of the tail or use a marker pen to label the rat number on it's tail.

Chapter 4: Stereotaxic Surgery

If you are using an atlas that defines the middle of the interaural line between the ear bars as the reference point, determine the coordinates of this point prior to mounting the rat in the ear bars. Attach the electrode or cannula to the carrier arm and determine that the electrode is straight and parallel to the carrier arm. This is conveniently done using a 3x5 lined index card placed vertically to the instrument base and parallel to the electrode or cannula. Compare the electrode profile to that of the lines of the index card. If the electrode is bent or off-center, use the tips of your index fingers to straighten the electrode. Now bring the tips of the ear bars of the instrument within 1 mm of each other and determine that the ear bars are centered (i.e. the vernier settings on the ear bars are identical). Using the carrier arm manipulators, bring the tip of the electrode into the center of the space between the ear bars. Center the electrode tip between the ear bars in all three dimensions (see Figure 4.5). This point is the center of the interaural line and is the reference point for atlases such as König and Klippel (1963) and Pellegrino, Pellegrino and Cushman (1979). Next read the vernier settings of each manipulator of the carrier arm (i.e. A/P, height and lateral): these values are the instrument or implant zero coordinates. These values should be recorded on a surgery sheet such as that shown in Table 4.2.

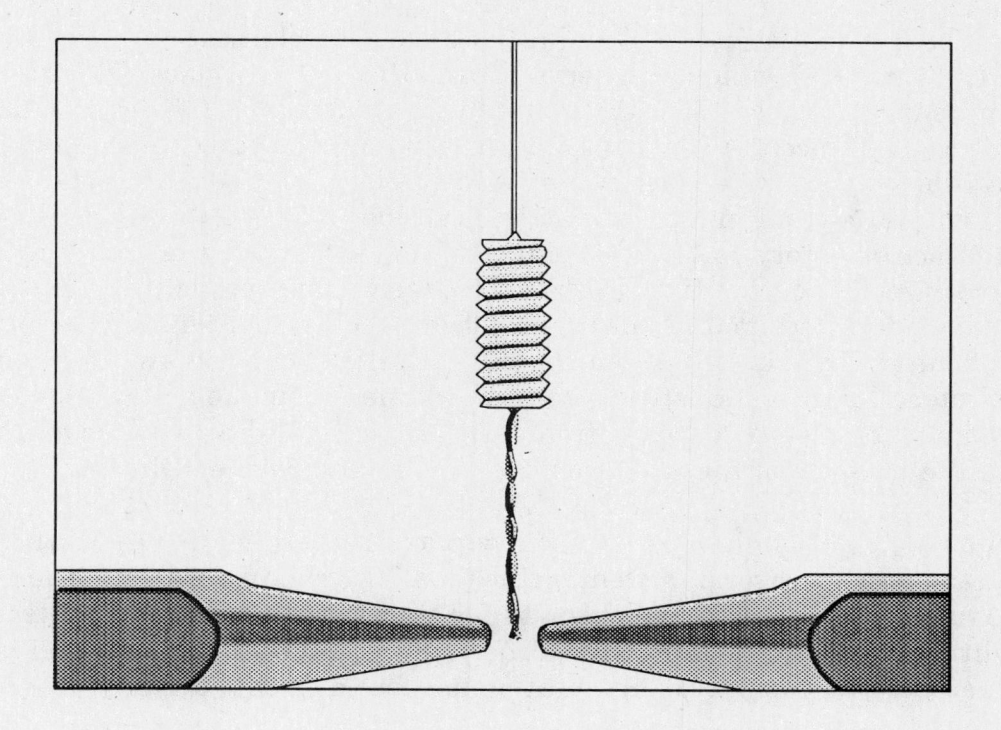

Figure 4.5. Positioning the tip of the bipolar electrode at the instrument zero point between the tips of the ear bars. (Adapted with permission from: Cooley, R.K. and C.H. Vanderwolf (1978) <u>Stereotaxic Surgery in the Rat: A Photographic Series</u>, London, Canada: A.J. Kirby Company).

Chapter 4: Stereotaxic Surgery

The most difficult procedure for novice students learning stereotaxic surgery technique is the proper mounting of the skull in the earbars of the instrument. If the earbars are not properly placed within the auditory meatus, the skull will certainly be in the wrong spatial position and if your coordinates are relative to this zero point, your electrode or cannula will be positioned within the wrong brain structure. Even if you use atlas coordinates that are relative to a skull landmark such as bregma, problems can arise if the ear bars are placed into the muscles of the neck. Such a placement will not be solid and the skull is liable to move downward during surgery (as, for example, when you attempt to drill holes into the skull).

You should practice handling your anesthetized rat with your left hand. To prevent the sharp tips of the ear bars from damaging the tympanic membrane of the rats, ear plugs (David Kopf, Appendix B) can be inserted into the auditory meatus prior to inserting each ear bar. You will use your right hand to insert the ear plugs into the meatus. First, turn the rat's head slightly to one side and insert one plug into the meatus of the rat's right ear. When the plug is in the auditory meatus, you should be able to locate a ridge just below it (felt by moving the plug down and then back up). Use the forefinger of your left hand to hold the ear plug in place while turning the head so as to expose the left auditory meatus. Insert the plug into the meatus and then use your left thumb to hold it in place. You should now have control of the rat's head with your left forefinger and thumb which also serve to hold the plugs in place. The right earbar of the instrument should be locked into place by tightening the set screw while the left earbar is left loose. Place the rat and the right ear plug onto the right earbar and hold it in place while you direct the left earbar into the left ear plug. If ear plugs are not available, then you should grasp the rat as described above and insert the ear bars directly into each auditory meatus. Center the earbars such that the same vernier reading is observed on each. If the skull is properly mounted at this point, the rat's head can be easily moved up and down but not laterally. Another indication of proper placement of the earbars is that when the rat's nose is tilted downward, the posterior skull ridge (refer to Figure 4.6) should be in the same A/P plane as the earbars. If the posterior ridge is observed to be in front of the earbars, then you have placed the earbars into the muscles of the neck: remove the rat and reinsert the ear bars.

Now, open the rat's mouth slightly and insert and center the rat's upper incisors over and through the upper incisor bar. Gently cinch the nose clamp down onto the rat's nose. Tighten the upper incisor plate and check to see that the upper incisor bar is set at the proper height position as dictated by the atlas you will use (refer to Table 4.1 or consult with your instructor if you are using an atlas not found in this table).

ELECTROLYTIC LESIONS

Lesions of discrete brain areas can be produced in the rat by inserting wire electrodes into the brain and passing high levels of electrical current through the electrodes. Electrodes to be used in making brain lesions can be made from metal insect pins (size 00). These pins should be insulated with an electrical insulating material such as

Chapter 4: Stereotaxic Surgery

Formvar (requires oven drying) or Insulx (air dried). If you choose to make your own electrode, first use sandpaper to remove all paint and other material from the electrode. Dip each pin into the insulating material and allow to dry. Only two points on the electrode should lack electrical insulation. The first is at the tip of the electrode: this is positioned within the brain structure to be destroyed. The other point is at the opposite end: here you will connect the electrode via an alligator clip and wire to the lesion maker.

Be sure to verify the completeness of the insulation process by connecting the electrode using the saline bubble test. For this test, connect the electrode to the cathode of a 9 volt battery. Now suspend the tip of the electrode into a small beaker of saline. Connect a wire to the anode of the battery and position the tip of this wire within the saline beaker. This connection should allow current to flow through the electrode and should produce some bubbles on the electrode. Bubbles should appear at the tip of the electrode (which is bare of insulation); bubbles appearing along the length of the electrode indicate a break in the insulation. If so, redo the insulation process.

Electrode wire can be purchased from several commercial sources. Insulated 30 gauge (0.010 inch) nichrome stainless steel wire can be obtained from Plastics One Corporation or California Fine Wire (see Appendix A). This wire makes an ideal electrode material. The wire can be easily cut into lengths using a scalpel blade (which is used only for this purpose). The wire can be straightened by repeatedly pulling the wire through your clenched thumb and forefinger. After straightening, a bare metal conical tip (0.5 mm) can be produced by holding the wire at an angle and gently turning the wire tip against a small separating disk (Moyco: 0.75 inch) mounted on a mandrel positioned in the stereotaxic drill. Examine the tip of the electrode under a microscope to ensure uniformity of the tip. A lighted match can be used to burn off the insulation after you mount the electrode in the stereotaxic arm. The burnt end is where you will connect the electrode to the lesion maker via a wire and alligator clip.

Lesion size is determined by the characteristics of the brain area in which the lesion is to be produced (i.e. more current is required for areas rich in myelinated axons), the size of the wire (greater diameter wire results in greater destruction), the amount of wire that is not insulated (e.g. the size of the electrode tip), and the current parameters chosen. You must take into account not only the amount of current used (amperage or amount of charge delivered) but also the amount of time during which the current is delivered. For example, 1.0 milliampere of current passed into the brain for 20 seconds will produce a lesion of approximately 1.0 mm in diameter (using a 0.5 mm tip electrode). As the amperage is increased while time is held constant, lesion size can be increased reliably (i.e. 5 milliamps at 20 sec will produce a 2 mm lesion). You should check the size of your lesion by performing one or more practice surgeries in advance and determine lesion size and placement using the histological procedures as described in Chapter 5.

Chapter 4: Stereotaxic Surgery

To produce an electrolytic lesion, the electrode should be connected to the anode of a DC lesion maker while the cathode of the lesion maker is attached to a metal banana plug inserted into the rat's rectum. It is important that your electrode connections be correct as anodal and cathodal current passed through an electrode will yield different lesion results. To verify that anodal current will be passed through your electrode, dip the electrode and the rectal cathode into a beaker of saline and pass a low level of current (1.0 milliamp for approximately 15 seconds). If bubbles are observed at the rectal plug, your connections are correct whereas if bubbles appear at the electrode, the electrode connections must be reversed. Use extreme caution when performing this check so as to avoid accidental electrocution.

Now that your rat is mounted firmly and properly in the earbars, make an incision of the scalp beginning at the eyes and ending a few millimeters short of the caudal neck muscles. Remember that the scalp wound will heal quickly if the incision is smooth (i.e. do not saw your way though the skin). To avoid profuse bleeding attendant on cutting the neck muscles, stop the incision just short of the posterior skull ridge and pull the scalp in an anterior direction past the blade. Mosquito clip forceps can be attached to the edge of the scalp to retract the scalp from your surgical field (see Figure 4.6). Use

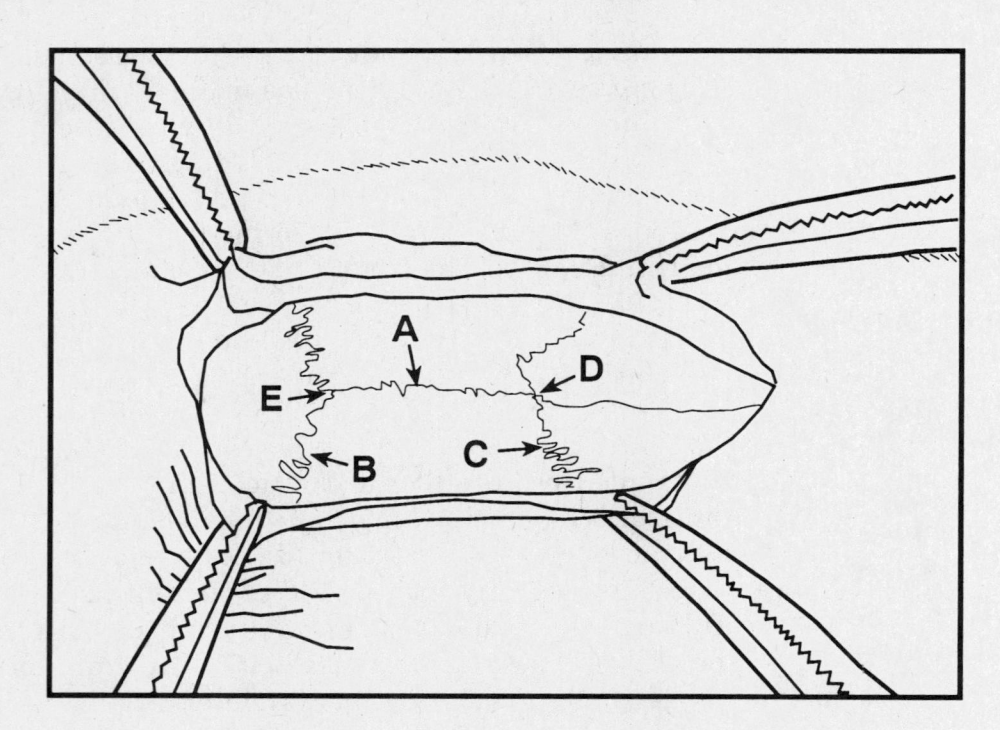

Figure 4. 6. Dorsal view of the skull illustrating the location of the skull landmarks. A: saggital suture; B: lambdoidal suture; C: Coronal suture; D: bregma; and E: lambda. The posterior skull ridge lies behind lambda. (Adapted with permission from Cooley, R.K. and C.H. Vanderwolf (1978). Stereotaxic Surgery in the Rat: A Photographic Series, London, Canada: A.J. Kirby Company).

Chapter 4: Stereotaxic Surgery

your scalpel blade to scrape the thin transparent membrane that overlies the skull, termed the periosteum, from the skull. The small amount of scalp and skull bleeding can be easily controlled by putting pressure on any bleeding area with a cotton swab. Sterile saline-soaked cotton should be used to clean the skull and scalp.

If your stereotaxic coordinates come from an atlas that uses skull landmarks (either lambda or bregma) as reference points, then determine the position of those landmarks in vernier coordinates after the rat has been mounted in the stereotaxic frame. For example, if you are using the Pellegrino, Pellegrino and Cushman (1979) atlas, then determine the coordinates for the midline sutures and the landmark bregma (refer to Figure 4.6). Bring your electrode to the midline at the level of bregma and position the electrode tip just above the skull. Record the vernier readings for bregma, height and the midline saggital suture (lateral). Now refer to the atlas and determine the stereotaxic atlas coordinates. For example, if your intended target is the lateral septal nucleus, a limbic system region involved in emotionality, then you would refer to the atlas plate at which this nucleus is most prominent (refer back to Figure 4.3b). This plate lies 2.6 mm in front of bregma, so the A/P coordinate would be +2.6 mm. The lateral coordinate would be 0.5 mm on each side of the midsaggital suture. The Pellegrino et al. (1979) atlas allows you to determine the height relative to the skull: on the left side of Figure 4.3b, the height coordinate would be -5.5 mm below the surface of the dura (the thick membrane that covers the cortex). Record these atlas values on the surgery sheet and then add the instrument values to obtain the coordinates at which you will position the electrode (see example given in Table 4.2b).

If you are using coordinates from an atlas such as König and Klippel (1963) that uses the interaural line as a reference point, then refer to that atlas to determine the atlas coordinates (see Figure 4.3a). Here the lateral septal nucleus is found some 7.9 mm anterior to the interaural line (A/P = +7.9 mm) and 0.6 mm lateral (L) from the midline (L= 0.6 mm). Because the zero point is 4.9 mm above the interaural line, add 4.9 mm to the atlas coordinate of +0.8 mm to obtain the correct height coordinate of 5.77 mm. These atlas values are recorded on the surgery sheet and added to the instrument interaural coordinates to obtain the final placement coordinates (see example given in Table 4.2a).

Chapter 4: Stereotaxic Surgery

Student Name   Paul Wellman

Animal Number: Psy 409-1

Strain: Long-Evans Hooded

Age: 90 days

Sex: Female

Weight:
  Preoperative: 233 g
  Operative: 218 g
  Post-operative   231 g

Operation Date: 2/6/1993

Anesthesia:

  Type: Sodium Pentobarbital/Ketamine

Atlas Coordinates:	**AP:**	7.9	**H:**	0.8	**L:**	± 0.6
Instrument Zero:	**AP:**	32.0	**H:**	2.4 (+4.9)	**L:**	31.0
Final Coordinates:	**AP:**	39.9	**H:**	8.1	**L:**	31.6/30.4

Surgery Comments:
  Type: Electrolytic lesions (1.0 mA for 20 sec)
  Upper Incisor Bar at: -2.4 mm
  Intended Structure-   Lateral Septal Nuclei
  Stereotaxic Atlas: König and Klippel (1963)

Sacrifice date :

Histology Results:

Table 4.2a. A sample stereotaxic surgery sheet that illustrates the calculation of stereotaxic coordinates for the lateral septal nuclei using the König and Klippel (1963) atlas.

Chapter 4: Stereotaxic Surgery

Student Name   Paul Wellman

Animal Number: Psy 409-2

Strain: Long-Evans Hooded

Age: 90 days

Sex: Female

Weight:
  Preoperative: 233 g
  Operative: 218 g
  Post-operative   231 g

Operation Date: 2/6/1993

Anesthesia:
  Type: Sodium Pentobarbital/Ketamine

Atlas Coordinates:	**AP:**	2.6	**H:**	-5.5	**L:**	± 0.5
Instrument Zero:	**AP:**	37.8	**H:**	12.0	**L:**	31.0
Final Coordinates:	**AP:**	40.4	**H:**	6.5	**L:**	31.5/30.5

Surgery Comments:
  Type: Electrolytic lesions (1.0 mA for 20 sec)
  Upper Incisor Bar at: +5.0 mm
  Intended Structure-   Lateral Septal Nuclei
  Stereotaxic Atlas: Pellegrino et al. (1979)

Sacrifice date :

Histology Results:

Table 4.2b. A sample stereotaxic surgery sheet that illustrates the calculation of stereotaxic coordinates for the lateral septal nuclei using the Pellegrino et al. (1979) atlas.

Chapter 4: Stereotaxic Surgery

Given the bilateral aspects of brain neuroanatomy, lesions are typically placed within both sides of the brain. The electrode should be placed at the proper A/P coordinate and positioned at one of the lateral coordinates (either will do). Lower the electrode to within 1 mm of the skull. Use a sharp pencil to mark the skull under the electrode and then repeat the marking process on the other side of the skull. Place the carrier arm out of the way and drill through the skull at the positions marked in pencil. As you drill, exert downward pressure with one hand and a slight upward pressure with the other hand. This will give you better control over the drill bit and will prevent your rat from receiving the ultimate lobotomy were your drill bit to pass through the skull and the brain. As you drill, stop frequently to allow heat to dissipate and to check the progress of the bit through the skull (see Figure 4.7a). As your bit finishes the hole (Figure 4.7b), avoid drilling through the dura.

Check that the electrode will in fact easily pass through each skull hole: if not, then redrill the hole(s) until the electrode will easily clear each hole. Then use an alligator clip to connect the anode of the lesion maker to the uninsulated end of the electrode and insert the cathode banana plug into the rectum. You must cut the dura with a sterile needle prior to lowering the electrode to its final height. This thick membrane will easily bend an electrode if not cut prior to lowering the electrode into the brain. You should be aware that there is a large blood vessel, the midsaggital sinus, that runs along under the skull below the midsaggital suture. If you are working close to the midline of the skull, you may puncture this sinus and will observe considerable bleeding. Use cotton swabs to control this bleeding before continuing the lesion procedure.

If possible, check the current level to be delivered prior to creating the lesion. Be sure that you are not touching the stereotaxic instrument, electrode or the wires connecting the electrode to the lesion maker. Deliver the current for the specified interval. After current offset, remove the electrode and repeat the lesion process on the other side of the brain.

Remove the forceps that serve to retract the scalp. Clean the skull and scalp with damp sterile cotton. Use a flat metal spatula covered with bone wax (Ethicon) to smear bone wax into the skull holes. The sterile bone wax will seal the skull holes and will serve to minimize intracranial infections. To suture the scalp using 9 mm wound clips, grasp and bring together the tissue with curved forceps. Apply 2 or 3 wound clips (9 mm) over the tissue and use a moderate amount of force exerted through a clip applicator or forceps to bend the clips into place. For a description of suture techniques see Chapter 3 (Figures 3.2 and 3.3).

Chapter 4: Stereotaxic Surgery

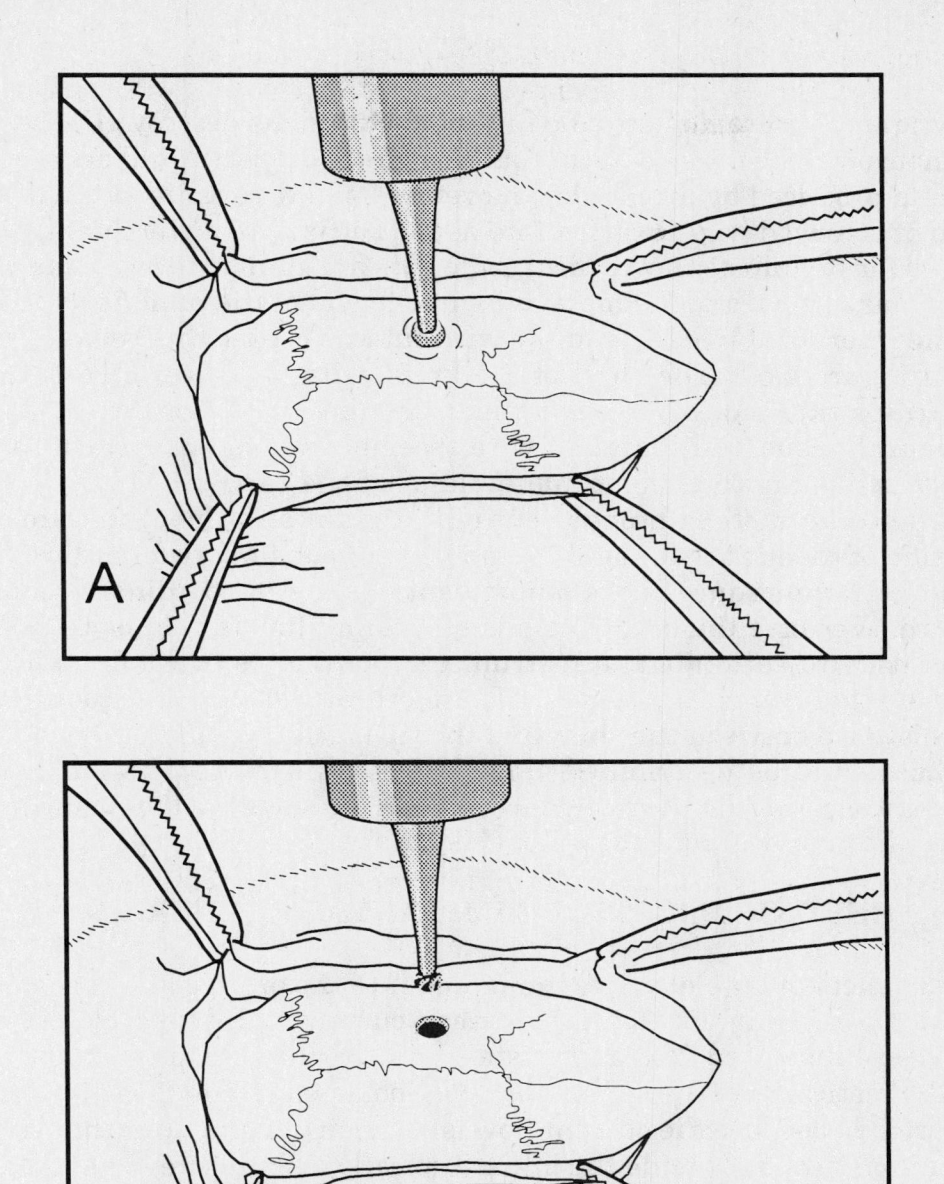

Figure 4.7. Drilling through the rat skull. A: The skull hole is partially complete. B: The hole is through the skull but not the underlying dura. (Adapted with permission from Cooley, R.K. and C.H. Vanderwolf. (1978). Stereotaxic Surgery in the Rat: A Photographic Series, London, Canada: A.J. Kirby Company).

KNIFE CUTS

Electrolytic lesions are non-specific in that such lesions destroy glial cells, fibers of passage and neuron cell bodies. A technique designed to interrupt fibers of passage (i.e. axons) uses cuts produced by mechanical movement of a wire knife in the brain. A wire knife consists of a curved wire inserted into a shaft affixed to a stereotaxic carrier arm. The procedures for producing mechanical knife cuts are similar to those used to produce electrolytic lesions. The tip of the metal wire at the end of the knife is used to calibrate the knife to the interaural line (extend the wire out and center this between the earbars as depicted in Figure 4.5). The shaft of the knife, with the wire retracted, is lowered through the drilled skull holes into the brain, the knife wire is then extended down and out. To cut neural tissue, the shaft and wire assembly are repeatedly (usually 3 times) raised and lowered using the height manipulator of the carrier. The wire is retracted into the shaft and the knife is brought out of the brain and the procedure is repeated on the other side of the brain. It should be noted that one important difference between the lesion and knife procedure is the adjustment of the A/P coordinate required in the knife procedure. Because the knife extends several millimeters in back of the shaft, if the shaft was used to calibrate the instrument coordinates, the knife will cut tissue several mm's to the rear of the shaft. Therefore adjust the A/P coordinate by the difference in distance between the shaft and the tip of the wire knife (this will vary with each knife and should be determined empirically). Knives can be purchased (David Kopf; Stoelting Corporation: Appendix B) or can be constructed using inexpensive materials (Hamilton and Timmons, 1976; Gold, Kapatos and Carey, 1973).

CHRONIC ELECTRODE IMPLANTS IN RAT BRAIN

Bipolar and monopolar electrodes implanted into the brain can be used to stimulate discrete brain sites using low-level electrical current. Bipolar electrodes can be constructed from insulated nichrome stainless steel wire or can be purchased commercially (Plastics One: Appendix A). A bipolar electrode is more useful than a monopolar electrode because the current flow is restricted to the tip rather than between an electrode and a cathode outside the brain (typically a skull screw) as is the case with a monopolar electrode.

To implant a bipolar electrode within the rat brain, you must first determine the coordinates to be used. Select an appropriate atlas. If the atlas uses the interaural line as the reference point, determine the vernier coordinates for A/P, height and lateral prior to mounting the rat in the ear bars. As before, position the ear bar tips within 1 mm of each other and center the bars. Place the tip of the electrode within the center of the interaural point (see illustration in Figure 4.5) and record the vernier coordinates.

Mount your rat in the ear bars after preparing it for aseptic surgery. Incise and retract the scalp. Clear the skull of periosteum and blood. Because you will be gluing the electrode base to the skull, the skull surface must be very clean and dry. Control all

Chapter 4: Stereotaxic Surgery

bleeding with pressure from dry cotton balls. Styptic powder can also be used to stop skull bleeding. Calculate the coordinates for the final placement of the cannula. If the coordinates come from an atlas that uses bregma, then position the tip of the cannula at the bregma and determine instrument coordinates.

Position the tip of the electrode at the final A/P coordinate and one of the lateral coordinates (this is usually a unilateral procedure). Set the carrier arm and electrode to one side, mark the entry hole with a pencil and then drill a half-hole using a medium dental burr. Now drill a series of half-holes around the entry site so as to roughen the skull surface and increase the bond between the final electrode pedestal and the skull. Now drill through the skull at four sites positioned around the entry site. Leave sufficient room between the screws and the skull hole so that the electrode can be lowered into the hole without touching the screws. Use curved forceps and a small screwdriver to position four jewelers screws into the skull to a depth of 1 mm (refer to Figure 4.8). Superglue placed at the base of the screw will strengthen the grip of these screws to the skull. Control any bleeding that might occur around the screws and clean and dry the skull again.

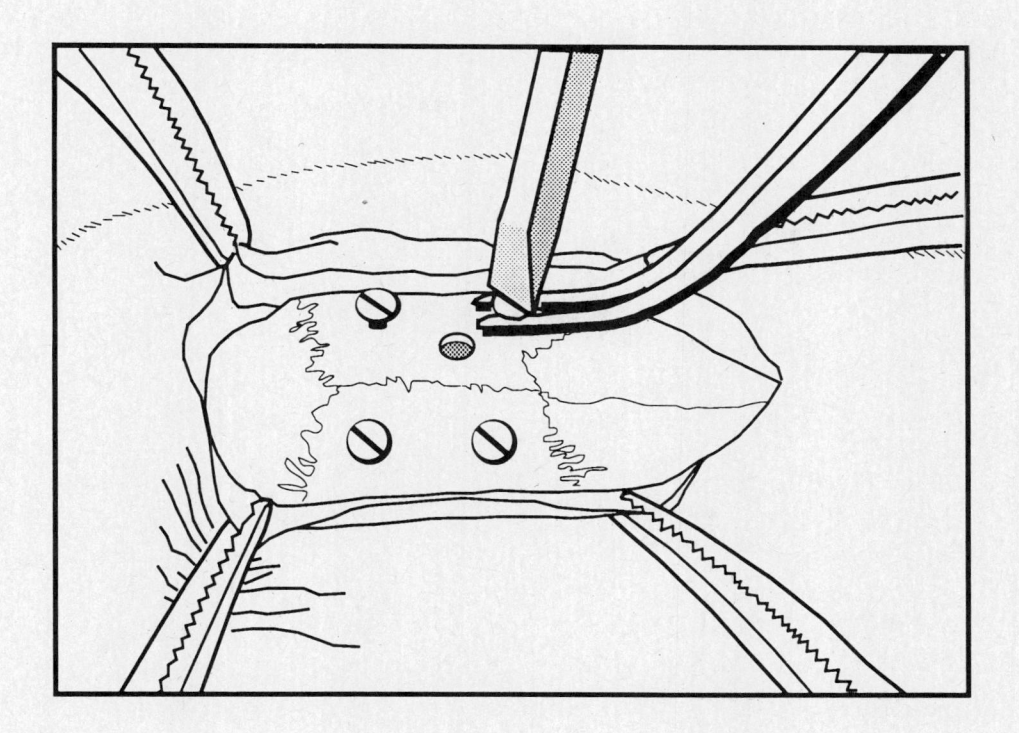

Figure 4.8. Metal screws are twisted into the skull to a depth of 1 mm to provide support for the electrode pedestal. (Adapted with permission from: Cooley, R.K. and C.H. Vanderwolf (1978). Stereotaxic Surgery in the Rat: A Photographic Series, London, Canada: A.J. Kirby Co).

Chapter 4: Stereotaxic Surgery

Finish drilling through the skull and then pierce the dura with a sharp needle. Control any bleeding from the entry site with sterile cotton swabs and then position the electrode tip at the proper A/P and lateral coordinates. You should verify that the electrode will easily enter the skull hole prior to lowering the electrode to the proper height (see Figure 4.9). Again clean the skull using sterile saline and cotton swabs and allow it to dry. Apply a thin layer of cyanocrylate cement (e.g. Superglue) over the screws and the surface of the skull and allow to dry. Now mix a thin paste of dental acrylic in the watchglass (approximately equal amounts of powder and liquid). Use a thin metal spatula to apply a thin layer of dental acrylic over the screws and the skull. After this layer is dry, apply successive layers of dental acrylic on the skull and the screws. Use the thin spatula to apply successive layers of dental acrylic around the electrode base and over the pedestal base. Build the pedestal so as to enclose the electrode base (see Figure 4.10). Smooth the edges of the acrylic cement so as to avoid sharp edges which will irritate the healing edges of the skin.

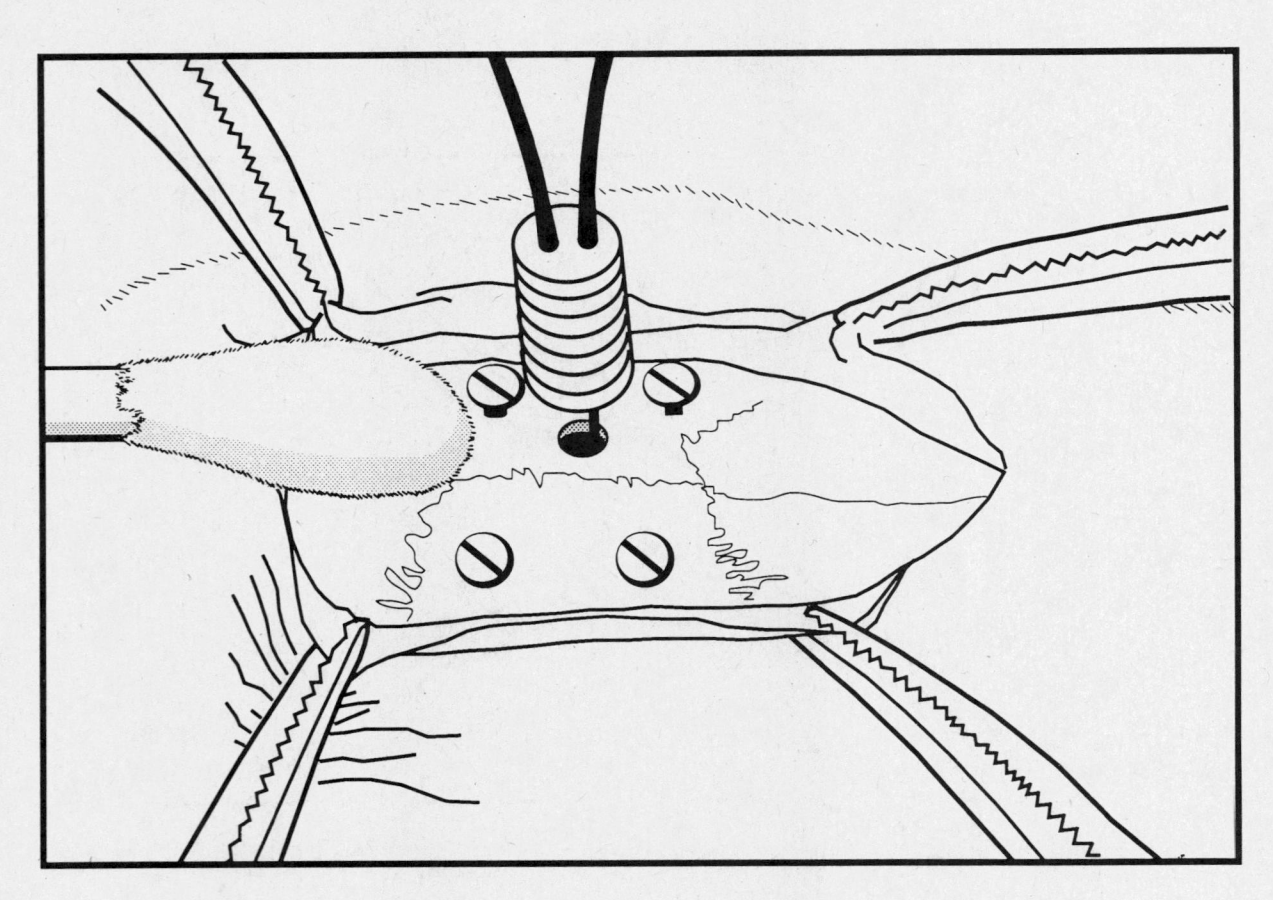

Figure 4.9. The electrode is lowered to the proper height within the rat brain while a sterile cotton swab is used to absorb any blood from the entry hole. (Adapted with permission from Cooley, R.K. and C.H. Vanderwolf. (1978). <u>Stereotaxic Surgery in the Rat: A Photographic Series</u>, London, Canada: A.J. Kirby Company).

Chapter 4: Stereotaxic Surgery

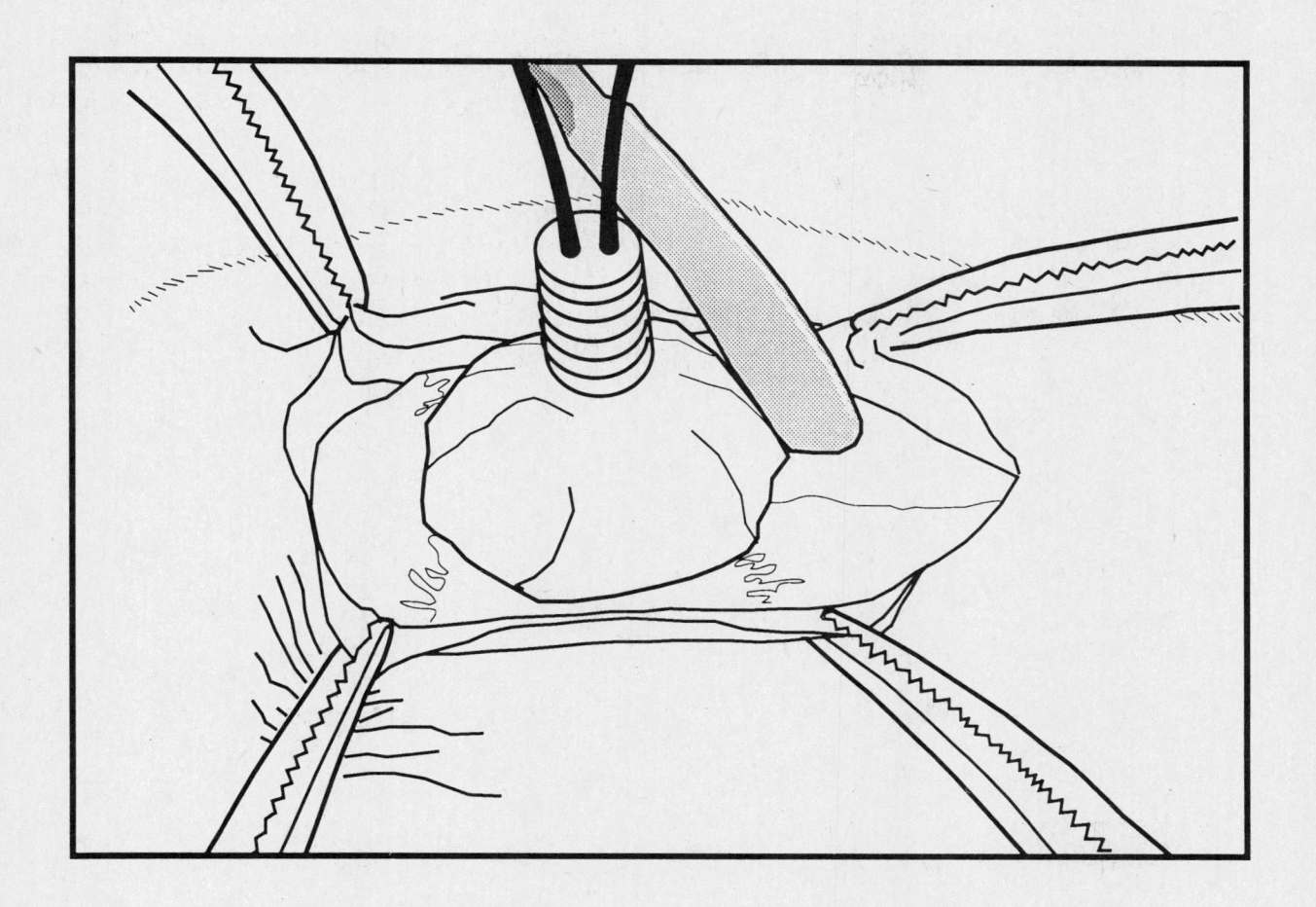

Figure 4.10. A metal spatula is used to apply the cranioplastic cement around the electrode to build the smooth pedestal that will hold the electrode in place. (Adapted with permission from Cooley, R.K. and C.H. Vanderwolf. (1978) <u>Stereotaxic Surgery in the Rat: A Photographic Series</u>, London, Canada: A.J. Kirby Company.)

When the electrode pedestal is solid, carefully remove the carrier arm from the electrode. Remove the mosquito clips from the incision edge and clean the scalp with sterile saline-soaked cotton swabs. Apply a topical disinfectant (i.e. Furacin) to the scalp and close using 9 mm wound clips applied anterior and posterior to the cannula. An alternative means of closure is to glue the skin edges together using a few drops of Superglue. Remove the rat from the stereotaxic instrument and give post-operative care as described in Chapter 2.

CHRONIC CANNULATION OF THE RAT BRAIN

Discrete regions of the brain can be stimulated by infusion of chemical solutions through a cannula or metal tube. A cannula consists of a metal or plastic base that is

Chapter 4: Stereotaxic Surgery

mounted to the skull and a thin metal tube that extends through the base into the brain (see Figure 4.11). The outside tube or guide cannula is stereotaxically positioned just above the site to be stimulated chemically. A stylet or injection cannula (see Figure 4.11) is constructed of metal tubing of a diameter that can be positioned within the outer barrel and of a length such that the tip of the stylet extends beyond the outer barrel by about .5-1.0 mm. Crystalline chemicals can be tapped into the tip of the stylet. When placed into the brain, these crystals will diffuse out of the stylet into brain tissue. In other situations, the stylet can be connected to a 10 microliter syringe (Hamilton Syringe Company) for infusion of a chemical in solution. An obdurator (dummy cannula) can be constructed from a 30 gauge needle cut to the same length as the stylet but crimped at one end so as to wedge within the outer cannula barrel. The purpose of the dummy cannula is to prevent the outer barrel from becoming blocked by dirt or CSF between injection tests.

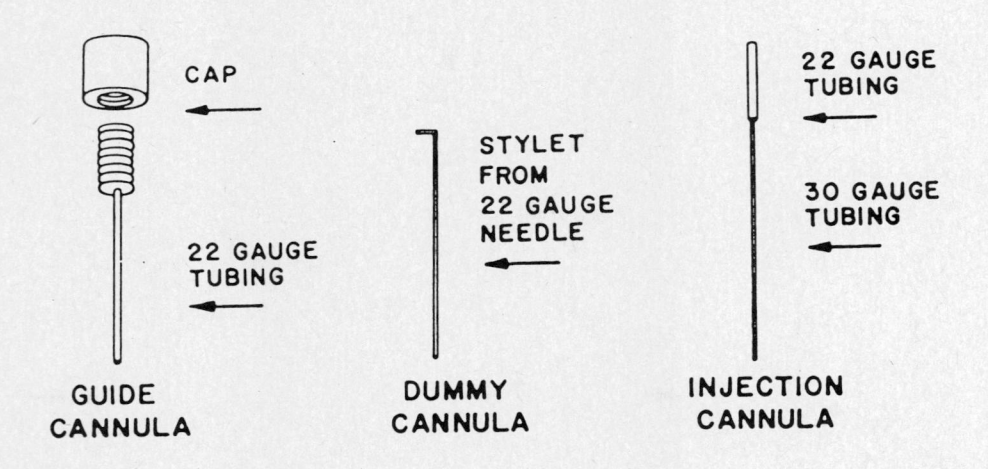

Figure 4.11. A cannula assembly consisting of the guide cannula, the injection cannula and the dummy cannula (obdurator). (Adapted with permission from Singh, D. and D. Avery (1975). <u>Physiological Techniques in Behavioral Research</u>, Belmont, CA: Brooks/Cole).

The surgical procedures used to implant an injection cannula are identical to those described above for the bipolar electrode. Adjust the height coordinate by adding 0.5 mm so as to place the tip of the cannula slightly above the intended target. If the tip invades the intended target, your data may be compromised by mechanical damage of neural tissue.

Chapter 4: Stereotaxic Surgery

REFERENCES AND SUGGESTED READINGS

Carpenter, M.B. and J.B. Whittier. (1952). A study of the methods for producing experimental brain lesions of the central nervous system with special reference to stereotaxic techniques. Journal of Comparative Neurology, 97, 73-131.

Hart, B.J. (1976). Experimental Psychobiology, San Francisco: W.H. Freeman, 110-113.

deGroot, J. (1959). A brain atlas. Journal of Comparative Neurology, 113, 389-300.

Gold, R.M., G. Kapatos and R.J. Carey. (1973). A retracting wire knife for stereotaxic brain surgery made from a microliter syringe. Physiology and Behavior, 10, 813-815.

Hamilton, L.W. and C.R. Timmons. (1976). Knife cuts while you wait: A simple and inexpensive procedure for producing knife cuts in freely moving animals. Physiology and Behavior, 16, 101-103.

Horsely, V. and R.H. Clark. (1908). The structure and function of the cerebellum examined by a new method. Brain, 31 31-123.

König, J.F.R. and R.A. Klippel. (1963). The Rat Brain Baltimore: Williams and Wilkins.

Krieg, W.,J.S. (1936). Accurate placement of minute lesions in the brain of the albino rat. Quarterly Bulletin of the Northwestern University Medical School,. Chicago, 20: No. 2.

Massopust, L.C. Jr. (1961). Stereotaxic Atlases. A. Diencephalon of the rat. In: D.E. Sheer (Ed). Electrical Stimulation of the Rat Brain, Austin, TX: University of Texas Press.

Nealson, T. E. (1982). Fundamental Skills in Surgery. Philadelphia: W.B. Saunders Co.

Olds, R.J. and J.R. Olds. (1979). A Color Atlas of the Rat- A Dissection Guide. New York: John Wiley & Sons.

Paxinos, G. and C. Watson. (1986). The Rat Brain in Stereotaxic Coordinates, 2nd edition. New York: Academic Press.

Pellegrino, L.J. and A.J. Cushman. (1967). A Stereotaxic Atlas of the Rat Brain, New York: Appleton-Century-Crofts.

Pellegrino, L.J., A.J. Pellegrino and A.J. Cushman. (1979). A Stereotaxic Atlas of the Rat Brain. 2nd Edition. New York: Plenum.

Chapter 4: Stereotaxic Surgery

Sheer, D.E. (1961). <u>Electrical Stimulation of the Brain,</u> Austin: University of Texas Press.

Sherwood, N.M and P.S. Timiras. (1970). A <u>Stereotaxic Atlas of the Developing Rat Brain</u> . Berkeley: University of California Press.

Skinner, J.E. (1971). <u>Neuroscience: A Laboratory Manual</u> , Philadelphia: W.B. Saunders.

Thompson, R. (1971). Introducing subcortical lesions by electrolytic methods. In: R.D. Myers (Ed) <u>Methods in Psychobiology</u> , Vol 1, New York: Academic Press.

Thompson, R. (1978). A <u>Behavioral Atlas of the Rat Brain.</u> New York: Oxford University Press.

Chapter 5
Histology

Histological procedures are used to examine and describe the brain, especially those structures that have been experimentally altered or manipulated (via lesions, chemical or electrical stimulation). Histology of the rat brain requires that the brain be removed from the calvarium or skull, hardened or fixed in a solution of formalin and then sectioned using a microtome. This chapter will describe these techniques and the procedures used to photographically enlarge brain sections or to stain sections. Finally, this chapter will describe how to describe the location of a brain manipulation such as an electrolytic lesion.

Perfusion of the Rat Brain

The purpose of perfusion is to remove blood from the brain (exsanguination) and to start the fixation of the brain. Perfusion involves pumping saline into the left ventricle of the heart, through the body and then out through a cut placed in the right auricle of the heart. Following exsanguination with 0.9% saline, a solution of 10% buffered neutral formalin can be passed through the vascular system to harden the brain.

The following materials will be required to perfuse and fix (harden) the rat brain:

Rongeurs (bone cutters)
0.9% saline (9 gms NaCl in 1000 mls water)
10% buffered neutral formalin solution:
    -9 gms NaCl
    -100 ml formalin (stock solution is 37%)
    -900 ml water
    -4.0 gm sodium dihydrogen phosphate-1-hydrate
    -8.25 gm disodium hydrogen phosphate-2-hydrate
Scalpel handle (#3) with blade (#10)
50 cc plastic syringes (2)
20 gauge (1.5 inch) needles
Sharp-tipped 5 inch scissors
Iris scissors
Film canisters (35 mm, plastic)
1 cc syringe with 27 gauge needle
60 mg/ml sodium pentobarbital
20% alcohol solution
Flat metal spatula
Dissection pan
Forceps
Latex examination gloves

Chapter 5: Histology

The rat should be deeply anesthetised (see chapter 2) with sodium pentobarbital (60 mg/ml/kg, IP) prior to perfusion. Because formalin is toxic, wear gloves when you perfuse the rat and work in a well-ventilated area. Lay the rat on its back in a dissection pan. Use sharp scissors to open the abdominal cavity by cutting through the skin and body wall at the midline between the genitals and the thoracic cage. Continue this midline incision in an anterior direction until your scissors encounter the ribs. Angle the points of the scissors up (so as to avoid cutting the heart) and continue cutting through the ribs until the heart is visible. Cut the diaphragm (which appears as brownish horizontal sheets of tissue just below the heart and lungs) on each side. If the heart is still covered with a transparent tissue, remove this using blunt forceps and gently grasp the heart between the thumb and forefinger of your left hand.

Lift the heart up and identify the left ventricle and the right auricle (see Figure 5.1). Use the scissors to gently cut the right auricle and then place the tip of the saline syringe (50 ml) needle into the left ventricle. Use constant pressure on the plunger to push saline out of the syringe; blood should exit from the auricle. The perfusion will proceed more rapidly if the heart beats during exsanguination but this is not an absolute requirement. As the exsanguination process continues, the fluid exiting from the right auricle should become increasingly clear. If the saline solution is very cold, you will observe some twitching of the limbs; if so, these do not indicate that the rat is regaining consciousness. Now remove the saline needle and note the position of the entry site into the heart. While still holding the heart in an upright position, position the formalin syringe needle into the same entry site and begin to push formalin into the heart. Formalin will produce marked contraction and rigidity of the body musculature. As you continue to inject formalin into the left ventricle, you should observe contraction of the muscles of the head and neck. A proper perfusion of the brain is often accompanied by spastic contraction of the neck muscles. As the formalin hardens the body tissues, a leak may develop where the needle enters the heart. Seal the leak using your thumb and forefinger or by clamping a forcep onto the heart at the point of entry.

Now use sharp scissors to separate the head from the torso. To remove the lower jaw from the skull, you will first have to cut the skin and muscles along an imaginary line running horizontally in a posterior direction from the mouth on each side of the skull. This cut can be made by inserting the lower edge of your iris scissors into the mouth and then cutting the skin on each side along the bone of the skull (see Figure 5.2a). Grasp the tip of the skull with one hand and remove the jaw from the skull using the rongeurs. To remove the skin over the skull, grasp the base of the skull with your left hand. Then grasp the distal end of the scalp with the rongeurs and roll the rongeurs sideways to remove the skin from the skull. All muscle and tissue should be removed from the skull prior to removing the brain.

Chapter 5: Histology

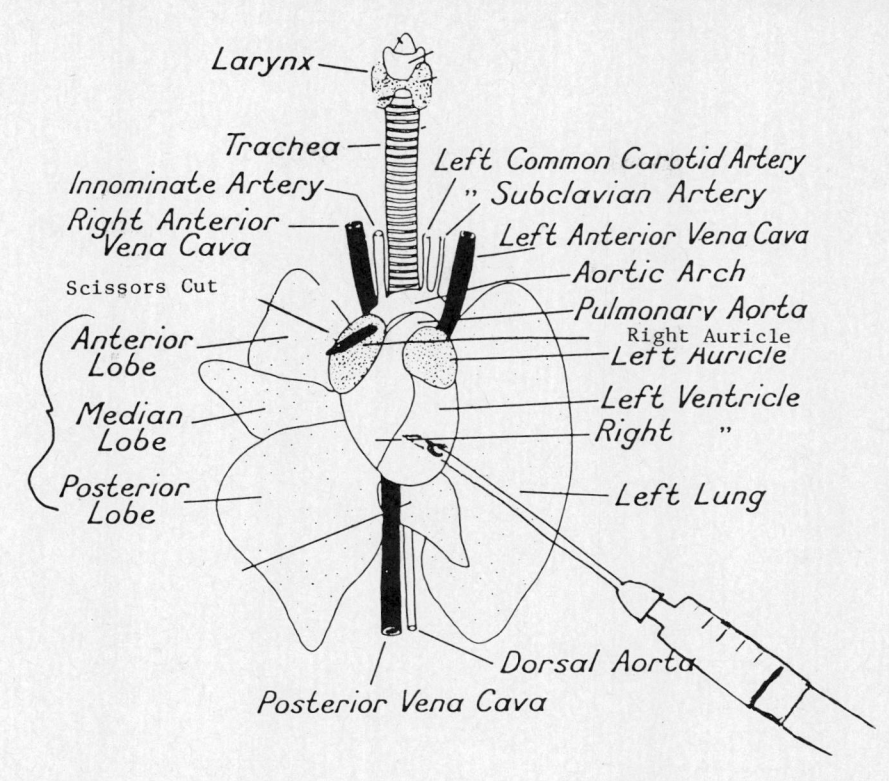

Figure 5.1. Ventral view of the heart and lungs of the rat illustrating the location of the right auricle and the left ventricle. (Figure adapted with permission from The Rat: A Practical Guide by T.A.G. Wells (1963). NY: Dover Publications).

Extraction and Fixation of the Brain

A simple technique for removing the brain from the skull is the "hinge" technique in which two cuts are made through the skull in an anterior direction along the lateral ridges. To do this, use scissors to cut the spinal cord from the skull: you should now see a 1-2 mm diameter opening in the skull, termed the foramen magnum, through which the spinal cord enters the skull (see Figure 5.2b). Insert one of the iris scissors tips through the foramen and cut along each lateral ridge. When you have reached the orbits of the eye on each side, you should be able to grasp the skull and remove the skull plate between each lateral ridge. Now you must remove the bone from each side of the brain using gentle outward chipping movements of the rongeur tips. When the brain is exposed on 3 sides, turn the skull over and lift the brain down and away from the skull using a flat metal spatula. Use the iris scissors to cut any nerve fibers that connect the brain to the skull. To complete the debraining process, make a coronal cut through the brain at the orbits and allow the brain to fall into a 35 mm plastic film container containing 30-40 ml of 10% buffered neutral formalin. The brain should be immersed in the formalin for at least 48 hours to allow the fixation process to proceed. Fixation times less than 48 hours may result in poor sectioning of the brain.

Chapter 5: Histology

The hinge technique is useful for the rapid removal of lesioned brains but not for brains into which electrodes or cannulae have been implanted. To remove the implanted device from a brain, clean the skull of tissue and muscle. Use the rongeur tips to gently break the bone of the skull out and off beginning at the foramen magnum. Chip the bone away in an anterior direction until you have reached the cranioplastic pedestal that holds the electrode or cannula affixed to the brain. Gently chip the skull around the pedestal base until you can lift the pedestal in a vertical direction off the brain. Use great caution at this step that you not twist the implant around as it exits the brain. Then continue removing bone until the brain is exposed on the top and sides. Now turn the skull over and allow the brain to drop down and away from the base of the skull. As before, cut any nerve fibers to the brain and then make a coronal cut at the orbits of the skull and allow the brain to drop into a container of 10% buffered formalin.

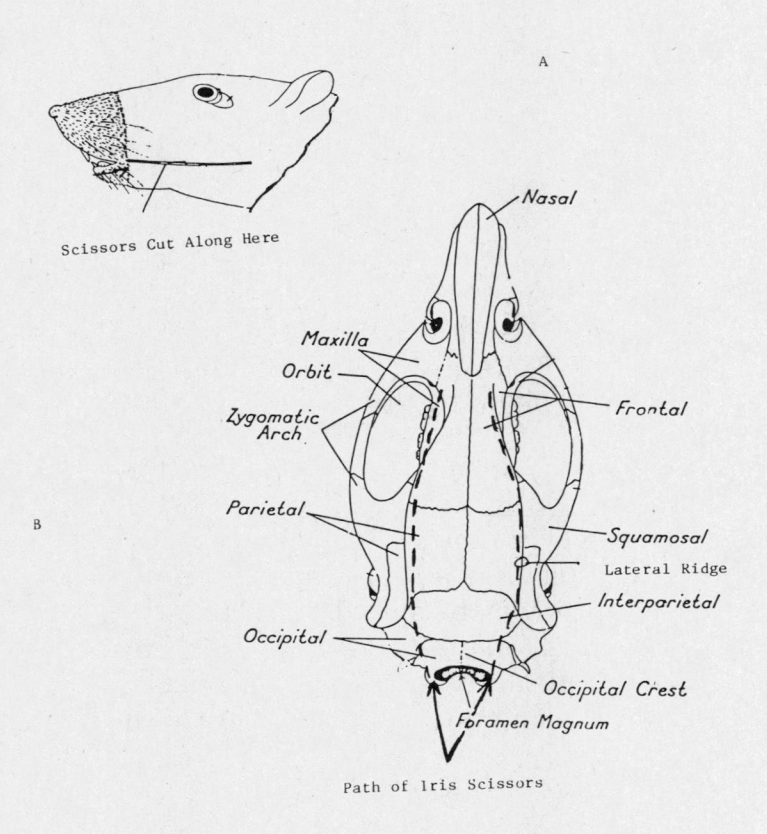

Figure 5.2. Removing the brain from the skull. A: Cutting the skin along the lateral aspect of the skull. B: Making the "hinge" cuts beginning at the foramen magnum and continuing to the anterior end of the zygomatic arch. (Figure adapted with permission from: The Rat: A Practical Guide by T.A.G. Wells (1963). New York: Dover Publications.)

Chapter 5: Histology

Microtomes and Brain Sections

As explained in Chapter 4, the skull angle used during stereotaxic surgery is a critical factor for precisely locating a brain structure. Similarly, when the brain is sectioned, you should attempt to duplicate the angle dictated by the various atlases. If you used an atlas that dictates that the skull be level, then simply place the brain on a flat surface and block the brain by making two coronal cuts; one cut should be several millimeters posterior to the entry site (visible on the cortex) while the other cut should be made several millimeters anterior to the entry site. Blocking the brain refers to removing excess brain tissue in front of and behind the coronal area of interest. This will save time in both freezing and sectioning the brain. The angle of the posterior cut is critical because this is the surface that is placed on the microtome platform. If the atlas dictates an angle of 5 degrees (i.e. König and Klippel, 1963) then place the brain on a block of wood that has been cut at an angle of 5 degrees and make the two perpendicular (here from the counter top) blocking cuts. To facilitate sectioning the brain, place the brain into a solution containing 10-20 % alcohol for several hours after blocking and prior to sectioning.

The microtome is a device used to freeze and to section the brain. Microtomes consist of a stage or platform on which the brain is placed (posterior blocking cut down) into a drop of mounting medium (Figure 5.3 depicts one type of microtome). The stage is often connected via metal tubing to a carbon dioxide canister so that carbon dioxide passed through pores in the stage will freeze the brain. The microtome also consists of a blade that can be moved in a direction parallel to the brain stage; thus, coronal slices of the brain can be obtained by moving the blade toward and then away from you. The scale below the stage allows the thickness of a single cut to be set: if the scale is set at 50, each pass of the blade will cut a section of brain tissue that is approximately 50 microns thick. Most sections you will make will be in the range of 50-100 microns (note: 1 micron = .001 mm). Prior to mounting the brain, verify that the knife is at the highest possible vertical height and that the scale is positioned at the proper thickness setting.

To mount the brain onto the microtome stage, place several drops of mounting medium (Biomeda: Fisher Scientific) onto the freezing stage. To keep track of which side of the brain is which, use a scalpel to notch the right hemisphere through its A/P length. Immerse the posterior surface of the brain within the medium and position the brain on the stage in such a way that the knife blade will cut the brain squarely. If the probe track is to be located within the ventral portion of the brain, then position the dorsal surface of the brain toward the knife and vice versa for probe tracks that are in the dorsal portion of the brain. Open the CO_2 valve for several seconds several times in succession to freeze the brain. The stage will freeze first as will the brain tissue closest to the stage. Check the progress of the freezing process frequently. You may wish to make several cuts through the brain at this point to gain familiarity with tissue that is not quite frozen. Use a wet camel-hair brush to moisten the microtome blade prior to each cut and to remove sections from the microtome blade. Place each section into distilled water and note the thickness of each. Practice picking these sections up with the brush and placing them onto slides.

Chapter 5: Histology

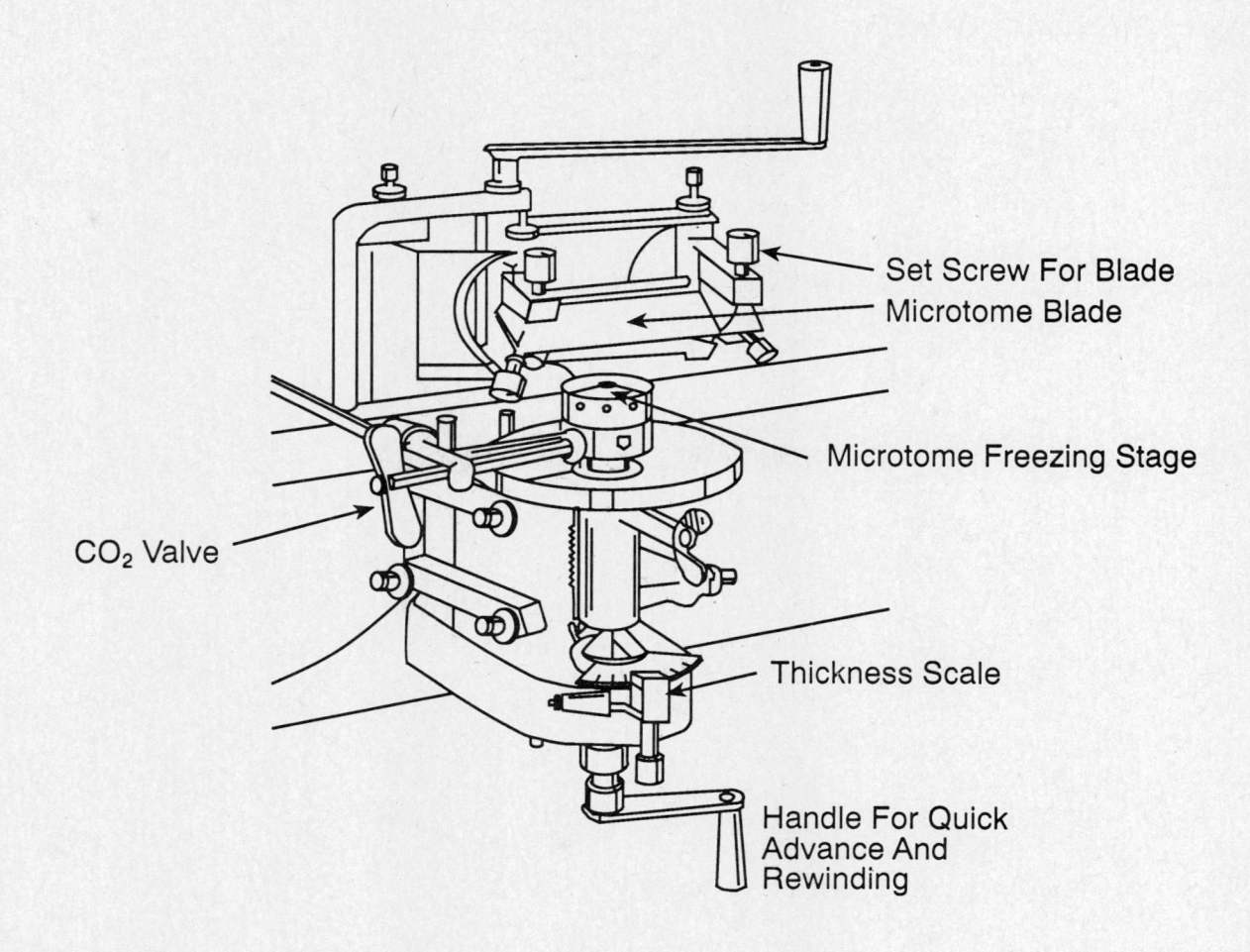

Figure 5.3. A freezing microtome.

As you slice toward the site of interest, compare the brain sections you see with the sections depicted in your stereotaxic atlas. As you begin to approach the brain site of interest, watch for signs of brain manipulation: lesions will appear as spots of discoloration whereas a cannula or electrode track will appear as a dark vertical line. If the brain is properly frozen, each 80-100 micron section should come easily off the blade with no scratch marks (a sign of overfreezing or a dull blade) and will not shatter when placed in water. Each serial section should be floated in water to remove any material and to facilitate the mounting process. If you place the sections in a clear glass cell that is positioned on a black paper background, each section can be easily viewed and you can then decide whether a section should be photographically enlarged or stained. Typically, you would keep one section every 200 microns through the area of interest.

Chapter 5: Histology

<u>Photographic Enlargement of Brain Sections.</u>
If a darkroom and black/white photographic equipment are available, photographic enlargement of unstained brain sections is a rapid and permanent method for recording brain histology (see Figure 5.4) In the photographic technique, the brain section is mounted in a photographic enlarger. Passing light through the section onto photographic paper results in a positive print of the brain similar in appearance to those that are presented in the König and Klippel (1963) and the Thompson (1978) stereotaxic atlases.

<u>Materials for Photographic Enlargement</u>
   Photographic enlarger (35 mm)
   Easel for photographic paper
   Safelight
   Photographic paper (5 x 7 inch; Polycontrast F is suitable)
   Plastic developing trays (3)
   Paper tongs (3)
   Developing solutions (Kodak):
       Dektol-1500 ml (mix 1 part Dektol stock solution with 2 parts
          water)
       Indicator stop-1000 ml (mix 16 ml stop solution with 983 ml water)
       Fix-1600 ml (200 ml fix stock solution with 1400 ml water)
   Paper dryer
   Microscope slides (75 x 25 mm)
   Indelible marker pen
   Camel hair brush
   Glass cell filled with distilled water
   Paper safe (to store photographic paper)

<u>Procedure</u>
Set up the developing trays in order (developer, stop, fix and water wash). Clean a microscope slide in acetone and wipe dry with tissue. Most photographic enlargers are equipped with a removable 23 x 35 mm aperture into which 35 mm negatives can be mounted. Tape the microscope slide over the inside portion of the aperture. You can now float the section onto the glass slide (see Figure 5.4). After you have flattened the brain section and have removed all air bubbles (by gently teasing the section with a camel hair brush), drain excess water off the slide by holding the section in place with the brush while slightly tilting the slide. Position the sections onto the slide in a predetermined order. For example, if you place 6 sections onto the slide, you might always put the most anterior section at the upper left corner. As you move in a posterior direction, position the sections in a row from left to right. The last section in the right hand position of the second row would be your most posterior section.

Insert the mounting aperture (with your slide and brain sections mounted within) into the enlarger and turn on the enlarger light so as to view the enlarged projection of the section onto the easel placed beneath the enlarger. Douse the darkroom lights, turn

Chapter 5: Histology

on the darkroom safelight and then focus the projected image. If the section image is not large enough, you will have to raise the height of the enlarger aperture and then refocus the image. Center the image onto the photographic easel. Turn off the enlarger light and remove a piece of photographic paper from a paper safe. Label the back of the paper (i.e. dull surface) with the rat number, section number and date (i.e. #12-1, 3/21/1992) using the marker pen. Position the photographic paper onto the easel so that the image will center on the paper and then turn on the enlarger light for 2-8 seconds to expose the paper. The exact exposure time should be determined beforehand. Exposure time depends on the thickness of the section; thicker sections require longer exposure times.

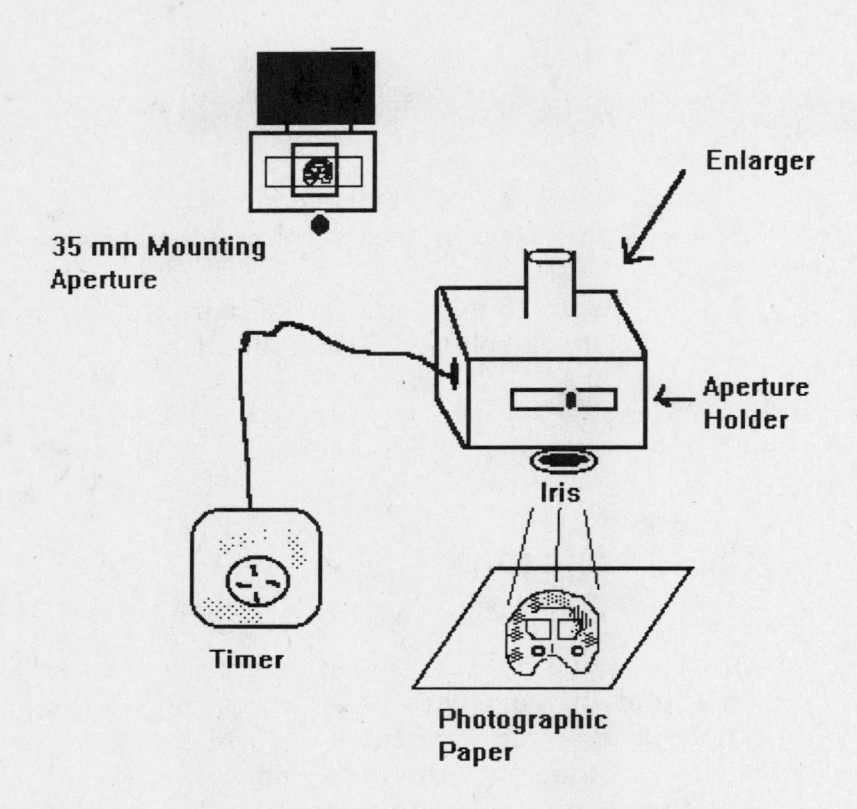

Figure 5.4 Photographic enlargement of brain tissue sections.

Place the exposed paper into the developer tray for 5-25 seconds; watch for contrasting black and white shades within the brain section and a dark border around the brain section. Remove the developed paper using the tongs and place into the stop tray for 10-20 seconds. Use extreme caution when handling the stop solution as it contains a potent acid that can damage skin and clothing. Remove the acid-stopped paper from the stop tray and place into the fix tray for 5 minutes. After you have verified that the paper safe is closed, you can now turn on the darkroom lights and examine the quality of your photographic enlargement. If the brain section is too light

Chapter 5: Histology

(no contrast between areas of the brain), then lengthen the exposure time. If the section is indistinct, it may be too thick; a thinner section will be required. You may also have to further adjust the focus of the enlarger. After fixation, wash each paper in running water in a tray for 5-10 minutes and then dry. The latter can be done by hanging the prints from a line, by blotting each print dry using paper towels, or by using a commercial print dryer.

To estimate the amount of magnification in each photographic enlargement, use a diamond tipped pencil to etch a 5 mm line onto the microscope slide in the enlarger just below the section area. Measure the length of the enlarged line on the photographic paper to calculate the extent of magnification. If the enlarged line is 50 mm, then the magnification is x10. Ordinarily, magnification is between x7 and x15.

Staining of Brain Sections

Stains are dyes that are taken up by different elements of neural tissue. Different stains have different affinities for different cellular components of the brain. Stains such as cresyl violet are taken up primarily by cell bodies so that nuclei within the brain sections are highlighted. Other stains, such as hematoxylin, color the myelin material and thus distinguish axons from cell bodies. The key to staining brain tissue sections is to achieve a state of differentiation in which great contrast is achieved between those cell groups that concentrate the stain and those that do not.

Stain procedures for cresyl violet and for hematoxylin are presented in the following sections (modified from those described by Wolf, 1971). More advanced staining procedures can be found in Bures, Buresova and Huston (1983) and Kiernan (1981).

Cresyl Violet Staining Procedure

Materials
  Alcohol (50, 75, and 100 %)
  Xylene
  Cresyl violet (0.25 g in 100 mls water: filter before use;
      store in dark bottle at room temperature)
  Acid/alcohol solution:
      -1 part 10 % acetic acid
      -9 parts 100% alcohol
  Microscope slides (25 x 75 mm)
  Preservaslide mounting medium
  Cover slips (22 x 30 mm)
  Slide warmer
  Stain cells (or Tissue-Tek stain tray)
  Muffin pan
  Gelatin solution (0.5%: 0.5 g gelatin, 0.05 g potassium chrome III sulfate,
      100 ml distilled water; stirred at 60-70 degrees C)
  Camel hair brush
  Diamond-tipped pencil (to label glass slides)

Chapter 5: Histology

<u>Procedure</u>

Clean several microscope slides in acetone, dip each in the gelatin solution and then air-dry each for 35-60 minutes. The gelatin solution will serve to bind each brain section to the glass slide during the staining procedures. Etch the section information (i.e. rat number and date) onto one end of the slide using the diamond tipped pencil. Float the sections onto the slide in a sequential order (i.e. place the most anterior sections near the etched end of the slide) and orient each section in the same direction. Remove any air bubbles from each section and drain excess water off the slide while holding each section in place with the camel hair brush. Dry each slide on a slide warmer (low heat, 2-5 minutes) or air-dry for 60 minutes. Prepare a series of stain compartments, each containing one of the fluids described in Table 1. If you have no glass stain cells, use a muffin pan to hold the stain solutions. If you do this, however, reduce the number of brain sections on each slide so that the sections can be completely immersed in each muffin compartment. After each slide is dry, mount the slides in a slide holder and then place the slides into each compartment sequentially for the time periods listed in Table 5.1.

Table 5.1. Sequential steps for the cresyl violet stain procedure.

Stain Compartment:	Duration:
Distilled water	5 dips
Alcohol series: (dehydration)	
50% alcohol	10 min
70% alcohol	10 min
100% alcohol	5 minutes
Xylene	10-20 minutes
Alcohol series (hydration)	
70% alcohol	5 minutes
50% alcohol	5 minutes
Distilled water	5 minutes
Cresyl violet	1-2 minutes
Distilled water	5 dips
Acid/alcohol	2-5 minutes (until differentiation)
Xylene	2 dips

Hematoxylin Staining Procedure

<u>Materials</u>
  Acetone
  Iron-Hematoxylin solution:
      -1 part 10% alcoholic hematoxylin (1 g hematoxylin in 10 ml alcohol)
      -9 parts distilled water
      -10 parts 4% aqueous ferric ammonium sulfate

Chapter 5: Histology

Decolorizing solution:
- -25 gram potassium ferricyanide
- -25 grams sodium borate in 1000 ml water

Procedure

Prepare a different series of staining fluids using the order given in Table 5.2. After you have dried the sections on the slide, stain the slide using the order and times given in Table 5.2.

Table 5.2. Sequential steps for the hematoxylin stain procedure.

Stain Compartment:	Duration:
Distilled water	5 dips
Acetone	5 minutes
Distilled water	5 dips
Hematoxylin	60 minutes
Distilled water	5 dips
Decolorizer solution	2-10 minutes (until differentiation)
Distilled water	5 dips
Alcohol	5 minutes
Distilled water	5 dips

After the slide has been run through the series of staining fluids for either the cresyl violet or hematoxylin stain procedures, use tissue paper to gently blot the slide dry. A drop or two of preservaslide mounting medium is placed onto the slide and a cover slip is then placed over the sections. Tap any air bubbles from under the sections and air-dry the slide overnight. The preservaslide solution will prevent loss of stain and dehydration of sections. After the slide has dried, the slide can then be examined under a light microscope to evaluate the locus and extent of lesion damage.

The two staining procedures outlined above allow one to examine the relative composition of different cellular components (cell bodies versus axons) in a specific area of the brain. Other procedures exist to determine the degeneration of axons from their source to the area of final termination. Axons depend on nutrients from the cell body which are transported out to the axon terminals. If the axon is disrupted, the portion of the axon distal to the point of disruption begins to degenerate. As the axon segments degrade, these segments can be impregated with silver which make them appear a dark brown. The following method for identifying degenerating axons is based on that described by Eager (1970) and Bures, Buresova and Huston (1983). This stain procedure is used after some interval has elapsed since an insult to a specific brain region. For example, if a small lesion were to the medial hypothalamus, after 7 days, the brain

Chapter 5: Histology

would be removed and processed. Presumably, this interval would capture the maximal extent of axonal degeneration.

Axonal Silver Stain Procedure

Materials
  Distilled water
  100% alcohol
  Microscope slides (25 x 75 mm)
  Preservaslide mounting medium
  Cover slips (22 x 30 mm)
  Slide warmer
  Stain cells (or Tissue-Tek stain tray)
  Muffin pan
  Camel hair brush
  Diamond-tipped pencil
  Uranyl nitrate (2.5% solution in water)
  Ammoniacal silver solution:
    -160 ml 1.5% silver nitrate
    -96 ml 95% ethanol
    -16 ml ammonium hydroxide
    -14.4 ml 2.5% sodium hydroxide
  Reducer solution:
    -400 ml distilled water
    -45 ml 100% ethanol
    -13.5 ml 1% citric acid solution
    -13.5 ml 10% formalin
  Sodium Thiosulfate solution (0.5% in water)

Procedure

After perfusion and debraining, the brain is stored in a 30% sucrose-10% formalin solution for about 14 days. Very thin sections (about 30 microns) are used for this procedure. The stain solutions and times are given in Table 5.3. In this procedure, use the muffin pan to process sections prior to mounting them onto microscope slides. After the final rinse, mount the sections and let them airdry. Before applying preservaslide and coverslipping the sections, place the slides into 100% alcohol (1 min) and then xylene (1 min).

Chapter 5: Histology

Table 5.3. Sequential steps for the silver impregnation stain procedure.

Stain Compartment:	Duration:
Distilled water	5 dips
Uranyl nitrate	5 minutes
Ammoniacal silver	5-15 minutes
Reducer	2-5 minutes
Distilled water	5 dips
Thiosulfate solution	2 minutes
Distilled water	5 dips

A number of exciting staining procedures have been developed over the last 30 years which are beyond the scope of this manual for description. These include retrograde tracing procedures in which a chemical such as horseradish peroxidase is injected into a brain region and is then transported from the axons back to the cell bodies. These procedures allow one to determine which brain areas project to and innervate other brain regions. This procedure and others are described in some detail in Bures, Buresova and Huston (1983).

Evaluation of Brain Material

The data you collect in the exercises that involve manipulating the brain (using lesions, electrical stimulation or chemical stimulation techniques) become meaningful only when you are able to verify the neural structures that were actually manipulated. Histological description of the brain sections will allow you to state what brain areas were involved in some behavioral effect and to eliminate data from animals in which the wrong brain site was manipulated.

Histological reconstruction involves determining the anterior/posterior, the dorsal/ventral and the medial/lateral position of your manipulation. To evaluate the locus of a lesion, you should select, from either the photographs or the slides you have made, three different coronal sections. The first section will be the anterior region at which the lesion was first apparent, the second will be the section at which the lesion is the largest, while the third section will be the most posterior extent of the lesion. For electrode and cannula placements, you should select for decription the section at which the tip of the electrode or cannula is apparent.

Figure 5.5 depicts a line drawing of the rat brain from the atlas of König and Klippel (1963). For purposes of illustration, assume that I wish to demonstrate the effects of a bilateral electrolytic lesion of the red nucleus on feeding behavior. I measured feeding behavior before and after the lesion and then performed perfusion and histology of this rat brain. I have sketched in Figure 5.5, the approximate location and size of this lesion at its greatest extent. Moreover, I have sketched in vertical and horizontal lines that

Chapter 5: Histology

bound the lesion. This hypothetical lesion has destroyed the red nucleus (r) on both sides of the brain and has not invaded structures on the border of this nucleus.

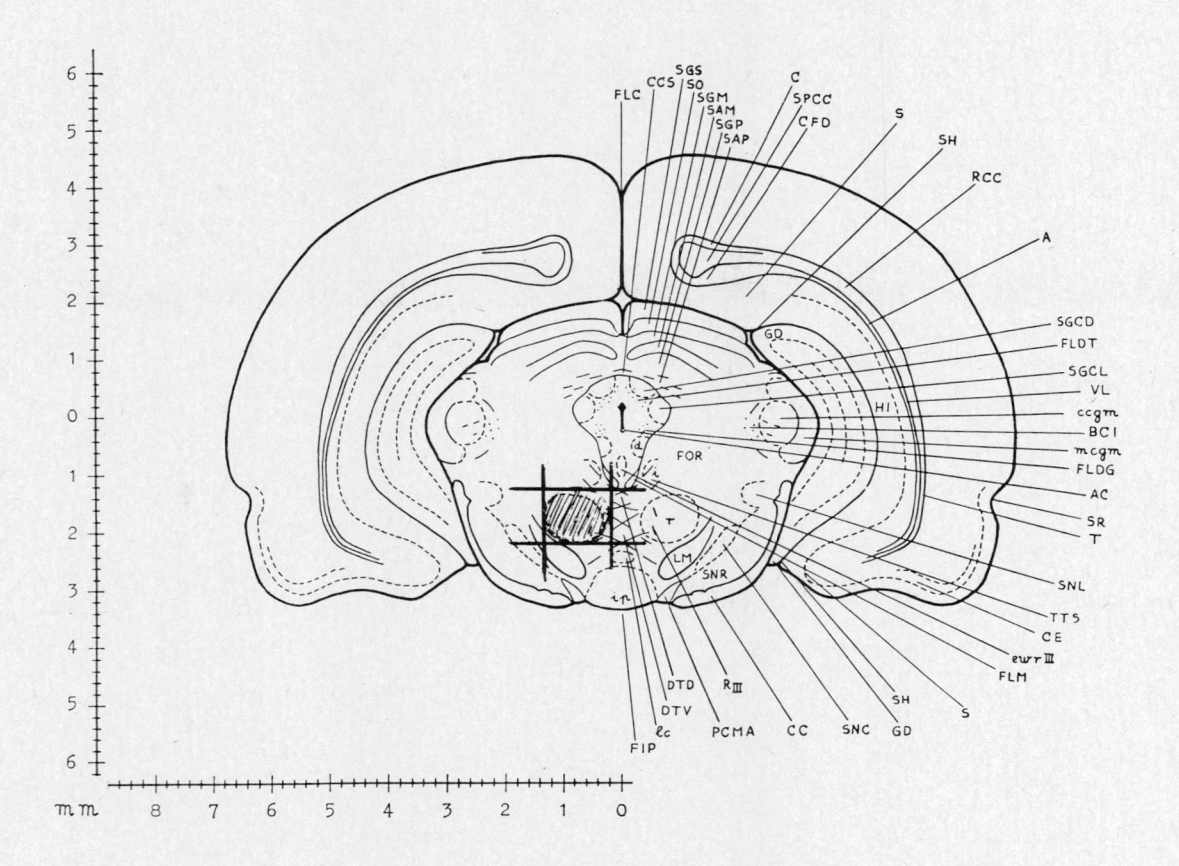

Figure 5.5. Line drawing of a hypothetical bilateral lesion of the red nucleus. (Atlas plate reprinted with permission from König, J.F.R. and J.Klippel (1963). <u>The Rat Brain</u> Baltimore: Williams and Wilkins Co.).

To describe the lesion in your report, you need to know the starting and ending anterior/posterior extent of the lesion, the dorsal/ventral extent of the lesion and the medial/lateral extent of the lesion. In this figure, the hypothetical lesion has destroyed neural tissue in a lateral direction to the dorsomedial border of the medial lemniscus (LM) and in a medial direction to the lateral edge of the midline tegmental decussation (DTV). The dorsal extent of the lesion is to the ventral border of the medial longitudinal fasciculus (MLF) while the ventral extent is to a horizontal plane that bisects the medial lemniscus. The text above described the D/V and M/L extent of the lesion leaving only the anterior/posterior extend to be described. To do this, determine a neural structure whose A/P extent coincides with the A/P extent of your lesion. In this hypothetical red nucleus lesion, the lesion correponds in A/P extent with that of the interpeduncular nucleus (IP), a structure found on the midline at the base of the brain.

When you describe the sections, state whether the lesion was bilaterally symmetrical (did it destroy the same site on both sides of the brain?). If the lesion was asymmetrical, you will have to give slightly different descriptions for each side. This is another reason for notching one side of the cortex so as to allow you to keep track of which side of this which. State the shape of the lesion and its approximate size at it greatest extent. Size can be estimated by measuring the diameter of the lesion on the photograph and then comparing this value with the length of your etched line. If the observed lesion value was 30 mm on the photograph and your 5 mm etched line is 50 mm, then the magnification would be X 10. The lesion size would be 30 mm/ 10 for an actual lesion size of 3 mm. For a further discussion of the methods of localization, see Akert and Welker (1961) and Wolf (1971).

REFERENCES AND SUGGESTED READINGS

Akert, K. and W.I. Welker. (1961). Problems and methods of anatomical localization. In: D.E. Sheer (Ed). Electrical Stimulation of the Brain. Austin: University of Texas Press.

Bures, J., O. Buresova and J. Huston. (1983). Techniques and basic experiments for the study of brain and behavior. New York: Elsevier.

Davenport, H.A. (1960). Histological and Histochemical Technics. Philadelphia: W.B. Saunders.

Eager, R.P. (1970). Silver stain. Brain Research, 22, 137-141.

Humason, G.L. (1971). Animal Tissue Techniques . San Francisco: W.H. Freeman.

Kiernan, J.A. (1981). Histological and histochemical methods: Theory and practice. Pergamon Press: Oxford.

König, J.F.R. and J. Klippel. (1963). The Rat Brain, Baltimore: William and Wilkins Company.

Paxinos, G. and C. Watson. (1986). The Rat Brain in Stereotaxic Coordinates, 2nd edition. New York: Academic Press.

Chapter 5: Histology

Pellegrino, L.,J., A.S. Pellegrino and A.J. Cushman (1979), <u>A Stereotaxic Atlas of theRat Brain</u>, New York: Plenum Press.

Skinner, J. E. (1971). <u>Neuroscience: A Laboratory Manual,</u> Philadelphia: Saunders.

Thompson, R. (1978) . <u>A Behavioral Atlas of the Rat Brain</u> New York: Oxford University Press.

Wells, T.A.G. (1963). <u>The Rat: A Practical Guide</u>. New York: Dover Publications.

Wolf, George. (1971). Elementary histology for neurophysiologists. In: R.D. Myers (Ed). <u>Methods in Psychobiology</u> , Volume 1, New York: Academic Press.

Exercise 1
Human Psychophysiology

Background and Problem

Bioelectric potentials are generated by activity in skin, muscle and nerve (Cacioppo and Tassinary, 1990; Stern, Ray and Adams, 1980). Our skin, for example, exhibits electrical activity, due in part to the activity of sweat glands. A common measure of skin electrical activity involves measuring the resistance of the skin to a small electrical current passed between two electrodes attached to the skin. These changes in skin resistance have been referred to as galvanic skin response (or GSR). As sympathetic nervous system activity increases, the amount of sweat secreted increases and the resistance of skin decreases (that is, it is easier to pass current through the skin). Psychophysiologists have shown that variations in arousal which alter activity of the sympathetic nervous system produce reliable changes in skin resistance. The purpose of this lab exercise is to introduce general issues in psychophysiology and specifically to introduce the measurement of skin resistance in humans.

Materials

This exercise is written without precise knowledge of the specific electrophysiological equipment available to your department and your instructor. Rather, I have chosen to present general principles of psychophysiology which can be adapted to meet the specific equipment available.

Skin resistance is recorded by passing a small amount of electrical current between two electrodes. As skin resistance changes, the magnitude of the potential difference between the two electrodes will change. Many different instruments have been devised to record skin electrical activity. The basic components of a GSR system include:

✿ Electrodes: These are normally fashioned from small lead plates (2 cm x 3 cm) and are each connected to a separate wire. These plate GSR electrodes can be lightly taped to the skin or can be held in place on skin using a Velcro strip. If GSR style electrodes are not available, you can substitute EMG electrodes which consist of a silver-silver chloride plate which is encapsulated in a plastic ring. The GSR electrodes are filled with an isotonic conducting jelly and then applied to the skin using double-sided adhesive disks. The electrodes are connected to wires which lead to a preamplifier.

✿ Physiograph (recording unit): This common instrument is actually composed of a number of units. Figure E1.1 presents a schematic of the components of a GSR system. The following discussion is related to general functions that are found on many GSR systems.

Exercise 1: Psychophysiology

The purpose of the recording unit is to detect electrical potentials, amplify them, and then display the output on a paper record. As summarized in the figure, the GSR electrodes are connected to a GSR preamplifier. The preamplifier has an output connection to one of the amplifier channels of the Physiograph. A GSR preamplifier may have several controls. An amplitude control will allow you to adjust the gain or amplification of the GSR signal. This control can be used to make the system more sensitive to small changes in GSR that occur in some subjects. A second control is a calibration button which allows you to produce a known resistance change in the circuit which is then amplified and displayed. This allows you to calibrate the magnitude of the pen deflection. We will come back to the use of this control later in the exercise.

The output of the GSR preamplifier is fed to an amplifier via a connecting cable. This amplifier has several controls. One control alters the sensitivity of the recording channel and can be used to alter the magnitude of the output of the channel. In Figure E1.1, this control is labelled "amplitude." The other control on the amplifier is used to center the output record. Separate controls on the amplifier are provided to power the amplifier and to send the output to the pen mechanism (record switch).

The typical output of a physiological recorder is via ink pens whose horizontal motion describes the amplitude of the input signal. A paper drive moves the paper past the pens at a constant speed (1 cm/sec is standard). Time on the paper record is indicated by another pen, which regularly (i.e. 1 per second) provides a short movement of the timing pen. The resulting record is a display of time and amplitude of the signal.

Procedure

You or one of your lab partners will be the subject in a series of tests designed to detect changes in skin resistance in response to changes in arousal. The exercise assumes that a GSR-style Physiograph is available. The following description provides general information as to the setup of the exercise; your instructor will provide specifics as to the setup of your GSR recorder.

The subject should be sitting for this exercise in a comfortable chair which supports the hand from which skin resistance measures will be recorded. Clean the skin over two of the fingers on one hand. If plate-style electrodes are available, lightly attach these to separate fingers (e.g. forefinger and ring finger) on one hand. If concentric electrodes are available, fill each with a small amount of a conducting solution (i.e. EKG gel) and then attach to the fingers. Attach these wire leads to the GSR preamplifier. Have the subject face away from the GSR recording device.

Exercise 1: Psychophysiology

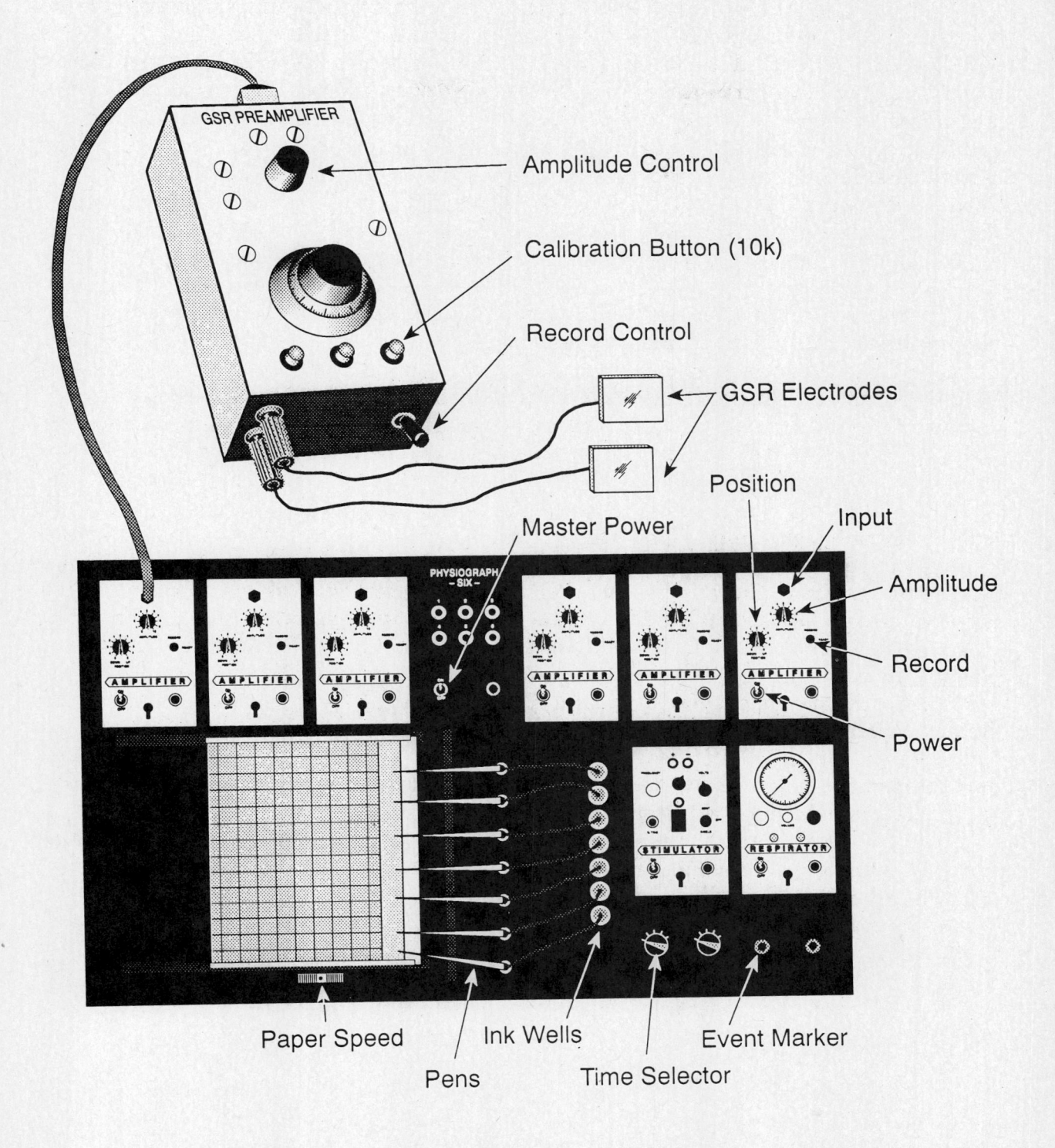

Figure E1.1. A representation of a GSR recording system. Depicted in the figure are a GSR preamplifier, its connections and controls, a physiograph control panel and its components.

Exercise 1: Psychophysiology

The following general actions should be accomplished:

You should turn on all power switches that power the main recording system, the amplifiers and the GSR preamplifier.

If the output of the GSR device is a pen-and-paper mechanism, the you should check that the ink wells are filled and are placed in a raised position. Remove the ink pad from the storage position under the ink pens. These are gravity fed and will cause ink to flow to the tips of the pens. Check the setting of the paper speed switch (0.1 mm/sec) and engage the paper feed mechanism. Verify that the time interval control (1 per second) is providing a record of time on the paper chart.

The next step in setting up the GSR device is to center the pen on the paper record so that you can observe both increases and decreases in skin resistance. Different systems have different means to center the pen: some may do so via a dial provided on the GSR preamplifier.

After centering the pen, you must determine the sensitivity of the recording unit to changes in resistance. This requires that you calibrate the output record in terms of changes in resistance. Recall that the GSR preamplifier may have a calibration button which imposes a 10,000 ohm (or 5,000 ohm) resistance into the recording circuit. If you now press that button and observe a 4 cm pen deflection on your chart recording, then you know the calibration of the system: 2500 ohm/cm vertical deflection. If only a small movement of the pen is observed, you should alter the gain on the preamplifier so that a known resistance change produces an observable response on the pen record.

After calibrating the system in terms of time (chart paper speed and time marker) and voltage (how large an excursion of the pen per unit change in resistance), you are ready to record resistance changes from your subject. An additional check on subject sensitivity is to have the subject draw a deep breath which should induce a change in skin resistance.

Exercise manipulations:

Measures of skin resistance must distinguish between baseline levels (so-called tonic measures) and phasic responses which change rapidly to external stimuli. Thus, you will in this exercise record GSR over some period of time. You will want to know how much variability in skin resistance your subject shows over time (tonic measures) so that you can compare their sensitivity to external stimuli (phasic measures).

1. Response to a loud noise: Our nervous systems are tuned to detect novel stimuli including unexpected noises. Demonstrations of how noise induces changes in GSR can use a variety of noise sources. A starters pistol provides a strong noise stimulus. A book

Exercise 1: Psychophysiology

slammed on the table can also be an effective noise stimulus. In this portion of the exercise, you should record GSR for 3-5 minutes. Determine the amplitude of GSR changes during this baseline period. What is the largest tonic excursion of the GSR record for this subject? Then introduce the noise stimulus. As you do so, hit the channel event marker so that a record can be made of when the noise stimulus was introduced.

You should be aware that subject variables can often influence the effect of a noise stimulus on GSR. One semester, I conducted this GSR exercise and found that a starter's pistol produced a small GSR response. The male subject who volunteered for this exercise turned out to be a member of the University Corps of Cadets (a military training organization) and a sharpshooter. Although he exhibited a minimal GSR response to this loud noise, he exhibited a very marked locomotor response (ducking to the floor) and a loud verbal response ("Incoming...").

2. Response to a memorization passage. Another means by which to produce a change in arousal and a subsequent change in GSR is to have the subject memorize a difficult passage. The subject is given a card containing a difficult passage (usually taken from an introductory physiological psychology text) dealing with staining of neural tissue. To increase the difficulty level, one can substitute fictitious words in the text passage. The following is an example:

"Cell body stains invade the Nissl substance within the myenteric plexus of the cell membrane. Membrane stains provide partial and lasting contrast between the cell body, the dendrites and the neural axon. Oligodendrites are rarely stained by membrane stains unless the pH of the stain solution is adjusted downward. Cresyl violet, magenta blue and true yellow are some examples of cell membrane stains."

Start a baseline recording for 3-5 minutes (use the event marker to indicate the start of the recording period). This period will serve to record baseline fluctuations in GSR. The subject is given the card to begin memorization with an instruction that s/he has 30 seconds to memorize the passage. At the end of that period, they are expected to recite the passage. Provide a an event mark on the GSR channel to indicate the start of the memorization period.

<u>Summary and Interpretation</u>
Indicate time marks on the horizontal axis and voltage scale on the vertical axis. For each class of stimuli, calculate the amplitude of the GSR response and the latency of the response. Indicate the magnitude of the baseline fluctuations in GSR.

Exercise 1: Psychophysiology

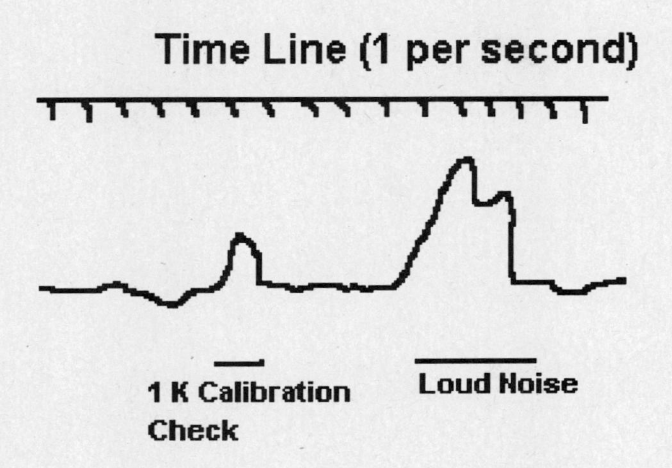

Figure E1.2. An example of a GSR record. The upper channel represents the time channel while the lower trace represents changes in skin resistance.

REFERENCES AND SUGGESTED READINGS

Cacioppo, J.T. and L.G. Tassinary. (1990). <u>Principles of Psychophysiology: Physical, Social and Inferential Elements</u>. New York: Cambridge University Press

Stern, R.M., W.J. Ray and C.M. Davis. (1980). <u>Psychophysiological Recording</u>, New York: Oxford University Press.

Exercise 2
Adrenergic Control of Brown Adipose Thermogenesis in Rats

Background and Problem

The peripheral nervous system consists of the somatic nervous system that controls striated muscles and the autonomic nervous system that controls activity of the glands and smooth muscles. The latter system consists of sympathetic and parasympathetic divisions. Neurons in the sympathetic division originate from the thoracic and lumbar sections of the spinal cord and use the neurotransmitter norepinephrine (NE) at the junction between a postganglionic neuron and a target organ. In contrast, parasympathetic neurons originate from the cranial and sacral sections of the spinal cord and use acetylcholine (ACh) as a transmitter at both pre-ganglionic and post-ganglionic synapses.

The purpose of this exercise is to demonstrate the pharmacology of the postganglionic sympathetic noradrenergic neuron. You will examine the effects of a noradrenergic receptor agonist and a noradrenergic receptor antagonist on the heat-producing (thermogenic) tissue, brown adipose (BAT). This tissue is found in large amounts (30-40 mg per 100 grams of body weight) between the scapulae (shoulder blades) of the rat (see Figure E2.1) and is innervated by sympathetic neurons that course through the intercostal nerves (Foster, Depocas and Zuker, 1982). BAT thermogenesis is normally activated by release of norepinephrine from the sympathetic fibers onto brown adipose tissue. Brown adipose tissue can be activated experimentally by using drugs that induce the release of norepinephrine (i.e. indirect agonists) or by drugs that directly activate the receptors that control thermogenesis within this tissue. Moreover, its easy access on the dorsal surface of the rat make this tissue a good bioassay to illustrate the pharmacology of a sympathetic synapse.

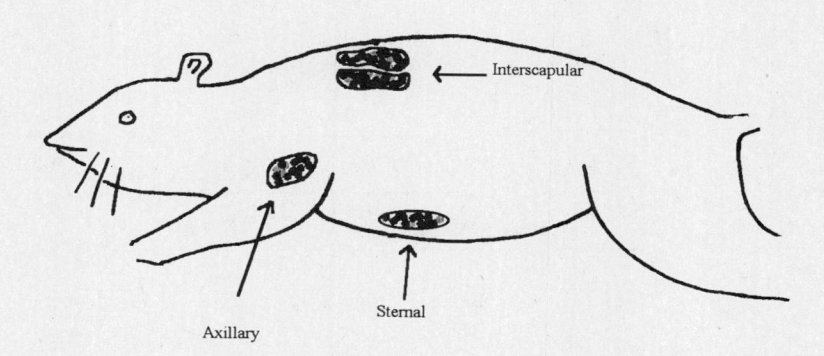

Figure E2.1. A diagram illustrating the location of the lobes of brown fat situated between the shoulder blades of the rat.

Exercise 2: Brown Fat Thermogenesis

Thermogenesis in brown adipose tissue is controlled by beta-adrenergic receptors located on the postsynaptic membrane (Rothwell and Stock, 1982; Rothwell, Seville and Stock, 1981). In this exercise, you will use one of several drugs that serve as BAT agonists (activate the heat-producing system within BAT) and one of several drugs that serve as BAT antagonists (that block this system). For example, isoproterenol, a drug that stimulates primarily beta receptors, will produce thermogenesis in BAT but fails to do so in a rat that is pretreated with the beta antagonist propranolol. Injection of an alpha agonist has minimal effect on BAT thermogenesis and the thermogenesis produced by isoproterenol is not prevented by pretreating the rat with phentolamine, an alpha receptor antagonist.

Table E2.1 lists a variety of drug treatments, their mode of action, dose level, route of injection (see Chapter 2) and the expected effect on brown adipose heat production. It should be noted that norepinephrine (NE) is listed here as a beta agonist for brown adipose tissue. Although this drug stimulates both alpha and beta receptors (primarily alpha receptors), brown adipose tissue contains primarily beta receptors and is therefore stimulated by the weak beta effects of NE. Paredrine (4-hydroxyamphetamine) is a useful form of amphetamine that does not easily cross the blood-brain-barrier and does not produce the changes in activity and arousal that are characteristic of amphetamine yet paredrine activates brown adipose tissue thermogenesis (Wellman and Watkins-Freeman, 1984). Phenylpropanolamine (PPA) is the active ingredient in many over-the-counter diet aids. PPA also induces marked BAT thermogenesis; the activation is due to release of NE from the sympathetic terminals within BAT (Wellman, 1985). Thus, PPA is an indirect agonist in this system. Moreover, these drugs are not controlled substances and are therefore easily obtained for use in this laboratory exercise.

TABLE E2.1: Drugs That Alter Brown Adipose Tissue Thermogenesis

Drug:	Mode:	Dose (IP):	BAT Effect:
Isoproterenol	Beta-agonist	1.0 mg/kg	Increase
Norepinephrine	Beta-agonist	40 ug/kg	Increase
Propranolol	Beta-antagonist	0.5 mg/kg	Decrease
Paredrine	Sympathomimetic	2.0 mg/kg	Increase
Phenylpropanolamine	Sympathomimetic	5.0 mg/kg	Increase

Exercise 2: Brown Fat Thermogenesis

Materials

Electric hair clippers
2 mercury thermometers (each accurate to 0.2 degrees C)
1 foam urethane pad (15 cm x 25 cm x 1 cm)
1 pair 5 inch surgical scissors (sharp tip)
1 pair iris dissecting scissors (blunt tip)
1 cc syringe with 27-gauge (0.5 inch) needle
5 cc syringe with 27-gauge (0.5 inch) needle
9 mm wound clips and applicator or hemostatic forceps
Drug solutions (see Table E2.1)
60 mg/ml sodium pentobarbital
Anesthetic: urethane (Sigma Chemical: 1.2 g/10 ml/kg)
Adjustable ring stand with horizontal extension and clamp
Label tape

Procedure

This exercise will require rats that are of the same sex and age. The rats should be given free access to food prior to the thermogenesis test as food deprivation can reduce the thermogenic activity of BAT. Weigh each rat to the nearest 10 grams and anesthetize it with urethane (1.2 grams/10 ml/kg, ip) using a 5 cc syringe. Avoid using a barbiturate anesthetic as this drug class greatly reduces BAT thermogenesis. After your rat displays plane 3 anesthesia (no response to a toe pinch or corneal stimulation), use hair clippers to shave the skin overlying the scapulae, which are easily felt on the back just below the neck. Then place the rat on a foam pad (to prevent heat loss through its ventral surface) in a room maintained at least at 25 degrees C. Use sharp scissors to make a 4 cm longitudinal cut through the skin overlying the scapulae. The tips of the scissors should be used to cut through the skin and you should keep the scissors perpendicular to the skin as you make the incision. Use care as you cut the skin so that you avoid damaging the underlying tissue. You should now see a thin layer of connective tissue that overlie the lobes of the interscapular brown adipose deposit. Separate this tissue and the lobes by placing the closed tips of your blunt dissecting scissors on the midline between the lobes and then gently opening the scissors. Only use longitudinal motions of the scissor tips as transverse movements will tear the lobes and greatly reduce thermogenesis within this tissue.

Insert one of the thermometers 4 cm into the rectum to record core temperature (tape the thermometer to the tail to prevent movement). The second thermometer can be suspended over the rat by attaching it with tape to the adjustable ring stand. The tip of this thermometer should be positioned between the lobes of BAT. The thermometer tip should be in an oblique angle and should be completely covered by BAT. Use either metal wound clips or hemostatic forceps to close the skin around the thermometer shaft.

Exercise 2: Brown Fat Thermogenesis

Experimental Design:
Your instructor will dictate the precise design to be used for this exercise. One option is to merely demonstrate that a beta agonist such as NE or paredrine or PPA will induce brown adipose tissue thermogenesis. If so, you will record baseline temperatures every minute for 10 minutes and then administer a dose of the drug as dictated by your instructor. Record temperature changes every other minute for 30 minutes after injection. Use care when you make the injection that you do not disturb the placement of the thermometers.

One potential design which documents stimulation of BAT by an beta-agonist and blockade of BAT thermogenesis by a beta-antagonist requires 8 rats in a 2 x 2 factorial. In this design, rats are pretreated with either saline or propranolol and then treated with either saline or 5 mg/kg PPA (or another agonist chosen by your instructor). You will test one rat at a time and you should vary the order of running (that is, do not run the saline-PPA rats first followed by another group and so on). Record rectal and BAT temperature every other minute for 10 minutes (no-injection baseline) and then pretreat each rat with either saline (n=4) or propranolol (n=4) in a volume of 1.0 ml/kg, ip. You should use considerable care when making the intraperitoneal injection so as not to disturb the placement of the thermometers. Record temperature every other minute for an additional 10 minutes (pretreatment baseline). Then inject your rat with either saline (n=2 from each pretreatment group) or 5 mg/kg PPA (n=2 from each pretreatment group) and then measure temperature every other minute for 30 minutes. Then inject each rat with an overdose of sodium pentobarbital (60 mg/kg, ip). Following euthanasia, dispose of each carcass as directed by your lab instructor and then clean your work area.

Data Presentation and Interpretation
You should graph your data using the graphic axes provided in Figure E2.2. You may wish to average group temperature scores over a 10 minute block prior to and after saline or propranolol pretreatment and then over successive 10 minute blocks after either saline or drug treatment. Remember that this is a factorial experiment with the following Pretreatment/Treatment groups: Saline-Saline, Saline-Agonist, Propranolol-Saline and Propranolol-Agonist. Each group will have an n of 2; therefore, compute group averages for the temperature scores at each time period. Use open or closed symbols (triangles, squares or circles) to represent the IBAT temperature scores for the various groups. In writing this exercise for your instructor, you should briefly summarize the procedures you used and then describe and interpret the data. Some points you should consider are the following:

   a. Was BAT and rectal temperature stable in rats pretreated and then treated with saline? (if not, could the lack of stability affect your interpretation of your results?)

   b. How large of an increase in BAT temperature (if any) did rats in the saline-agonist group display? Compare the increment in BAT temperature

Exercise 2: Brown Fat Thermogenesis

produced by the various agonists with the increases in temperature reported in the literature (Perkins et al. 1981; Wellman, 1985; Wellman and Watkins-Freeman, 1985). Did rectal temperature remain stable throughout the experiment? If rectal temperature also increased, was this increase at some time interval after an increase in BAT temperature? How would you explain a rise in rectal temperature?

c. If you compare the BAT temperatures of rats pretreated with either saline or propranolol and treated with saline, did propranolol by itself produce a decline in BAT temperature? Did the beta-agonist produce enhanced BAT thermogenesis in propranolol pretreated rats? Are your data consistent with a beta noradrenergic receptor model of BAT heat production?

d. If there were any problems with the procedures be certain that you note these in your experiment summary.

REFERENCES AND SUGGESTED READINGS

Foster, D.O., F. Depocas, and M. Zuker. (1982). Heterogeneity of the sympathetic innervation of rat interscapular brown adipose tissue via intercostal nerves. Canadian Journal of Physiology and Pharmacology, 60, 747-754.

Perkins, M.N., N.J. Rothwell, M.J. Stock, and T.W. Stone. (1981). Activation of brown adipose tissue by the ventromedial hypothalamus. Nature, 289, 401-402.

Rothwell, N.J., M.E. Seville, and M.J. Stock. (1981). Acute effects of food, 2-deoxy-d-glucose and noradrenaline on metabolic rate and brown adipose tissue in normal and atropinized lean and obese (fa/fa) Zucker rats. Pflugers Archives, 392, 172-177.

Rothwell, N.J. and M.J. Stock. (1989). Neural regulation of thermogenesis. Trends in Neurosciences, April, 124-126.

Wellman, P.J. (1984). Brown adipose tissue thermogenesis: A simple and inexpensive laboratory exercise in physiological psychology. Teaching of Psychology, 11, 115-116.

Wellman, P.J. (1985). Influence of phenylpropanolamine on brown adipose tissue thermogenesis in the adult rat. Physiological Psychology, 12, 307-310.

Wellman, P.J. and P.A. Watkins-Freeman. (1984). Effects of 4-hydroxyamphetamine on in vivo brown adipose tissue thermogenesis and feeding behavior in the rat. Behavioral Neuroscience, 98, 1060-1064.

Exercise 2: Brown Fat Thermogenesis

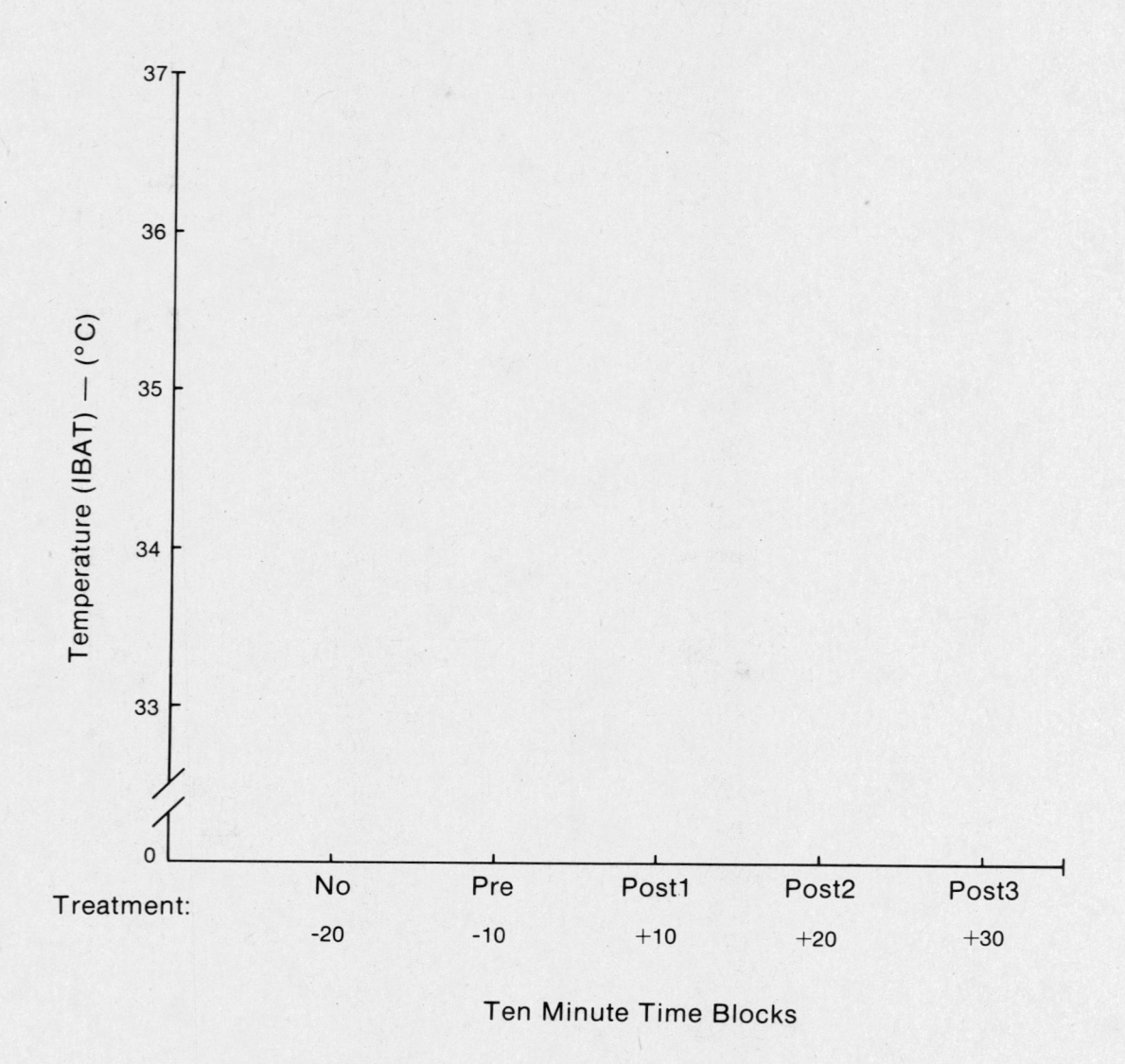

Figure E2.2. Graphic axes used to depict the IBAT temperature data of Exercise 2. Mean group temperature scores are plotted over 10 minute blocks prior to treatment (NO), prior to pretreatment with either vehicle or propranolol (PRE) and at 10, 20 and 30 minutes following the drug treatment (POST1, POST2 and POST3). Separate symbols should be used to represent the 4 groups of this exercise (VEH-VEH, VEH-PPA, PROPANOLOL-PPA and PROPRANOLOL-VEH).

Exercise 3
Gross Anatomy of the Sheep Brain

Background and Problem
   Neuroanatomy refers to the detailed description of the central and peripheral nervous systems. In this exercise, you will become familiar with the terminology of neuroanatomy and with the general external and internal features of the sheep brain.

Materials
   Sheep (or cow) brain (stored in 10% Formalin)
   Dissection tray (aluminum or plastic)
   Paper towels
   Dissection instruments:
      -Virchow brain knife
      -5 inch scissors
      -iris scissors
      -forceps
      -tweezers
      -scalpel handle (#3) with blade (#10)
   Vinyl examination gloves (to handle brain tissue)

Directional Terms
   By now you are somewhat familiar with the operation and general structures of a car. As you learned to drive a car, you learned several terms that refer to directions that can be taken by the car. You can move forward, backward, turn to either side and, in some instances up and down. You are aware that certain mechanical devices are found at the front of the car (i.e. the engine), at the back of the car (muffler), at the sides of the car (the doors), at the center of the car (the stickshift) and on the bottom of the car (the floorboard) as well as the top of the car (the headliner). When you examine the brain, you will learn to use similar terms to refer to directions and locations of the brain.

   Because the brain exists in 3 dimensions, we need 3 axes to describe locations within the brain. Figure E3.1 illustrates these dimensions in an animal brain. You can refer to structures found toward the front of the brain; these are in an "anterior" direction. Structures found toward the back of the brain are in a "posterior" direction. A similar set of terms are rostral ("toward the beak") and caudal, respectively. "Dorsal" refers to structures that are found toward the top of the brain whereas "ventral" refers to structures that are found at the base of the brain. The final axis is perpendicular to the anterior/posterior axis. "Medial" refers to whether a structure is located near the middle of the brain whereas "lateral" refers to structures that are located away from the midline.

   Just as we use terms to refer to the three axes of the brain, we also use special terms to refer to the various angles from which one can view the brain. If you position

Exercise 3: Sheep Brain Anatomy

a brain with its ventral surface on a table, and look down onto the dorsal surface, you are employing a dorsal view. Similarly, it you turn the brain over so that now the dorsal surface lies on the table, you are employing a ventral view. If you now examine the side of the brain, you are using a lateral view (refer to Figure E3.1). There are also specific terms that refer to views of the interior aspects of the brain. For example, if you slice the brain as you would a loaf of bread, you are dividing the brain into anterior and posterior sections (refer to Figure E3.2). This plane of section is referred to as coronal, transverse or frontal. If you were to slice the brain down the middle along an anterior/posterior axis, the section would be referred to as a sagittal cut. A sagittal cut made exactly down the center of the brain that divides the brain into left and right halves is a midsagittal cut. As you view the inside surface of a brain after a sagittal cut, you are examining the medial surface of the brain.

Overview of the Brain

The brain can be conveniently separated into 3 major divisions: the forebrain, the midbrain and the hindbrain (refer to Table E3.1). Each of these divisions represents an addition to the spinal cord during evolution (i.e. the forebrain is the latest addition to the brain). Each of these divisions is further divided into sub-sections resulting in 5 subdivisions. The forebrain is separated into the telencephalon and the diencephalon. Structures within the telencephalon are concerned with emotion (limbic system), motor movement (basal ganglia) and cognitive behavior (cortex). The diencephalic structures include the thalamus, a sensory relay region and the hypothalamus, a region that integrates autonomic nervous system activity and controls pituitary hormone release. The mesencephalon is divided into the dorsal tectum and the ventral tegmentum. The tectum consists of the superior and inferior colliculi; a collection of nuclei that are involved in the processing of auditory and visual information. You will observe these nuclei when you examine the dorsal surface of the brainstem. The tegmentum contains the reticular-activating system, a series of nerve fibers and nuclei that are involved in the regulation of arousal and sleep as well as the nuclei for the 3rd and 4th cranial nerves. The hindbrain is divided into the metencephalon and the myencephalon. The metencephalon consists of the cerebellum (a motor control region) and the pons, a swelling on the ventral surface of the brain that contains numerous cranial nerve nuclei as well as nerve fibers that ascend and descend from the spinal cord and cortex. Finally, the myencephalon consists of the medulla oblongata, an extension of the spinal cord that contains numerous nuclei that control vital functions (heart rate, breathing).

Sheep Brain Preparation

You will be provided with a sheep brain that has been stored in 10% formalin. Recall from Chapter 5 that formalin hardens brain tissue so that one can handle and section the tissue. Carefully wash the brain under a stream of water and blot the brain dry using paper towels (use gloves as you handle the brain tissue). The sheep brain may be covered by a thick layer of tissue termed the dura mater. This covering is a part of the meninges and serves to protect the brain. Remove the dura if it is still present on the brain using the large scissors. Because some blood may have pooled within the dura, you should wash the brain and blot it dry prior to examining its features.

Exercise 3: Sheep Brain Anatomy

LATERAL VIEW

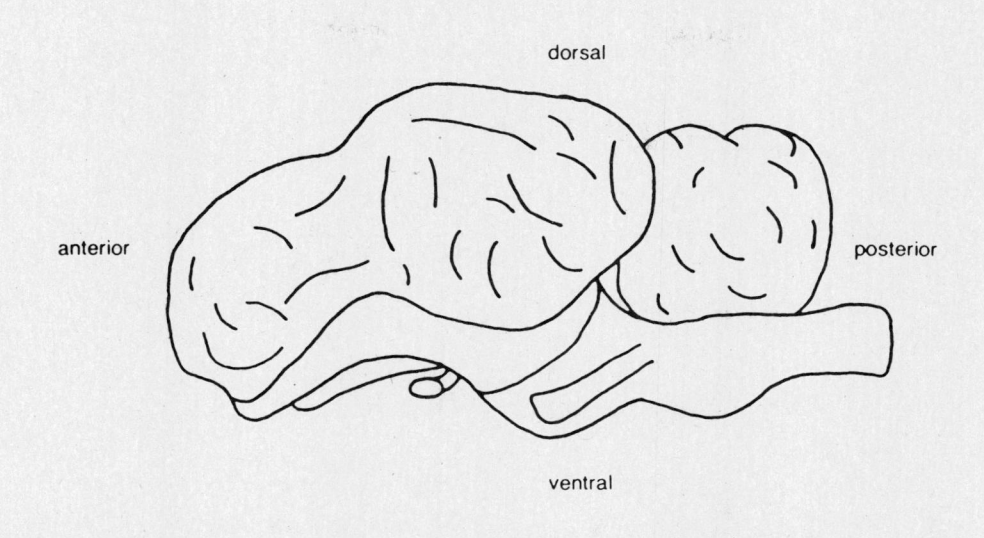

DORSAL VIEW

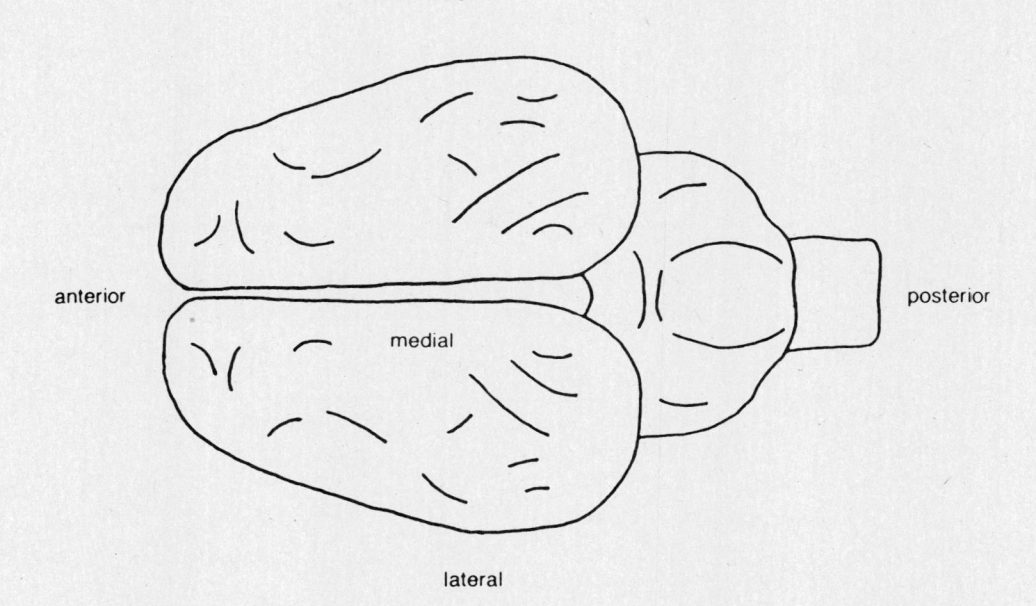

Figure E3.1. Illustration of the three axes of the brain (Anterior/Posterior, Dorsal/Ventral and Medial/Lateral) as well as the lateral and dorsal views of the brain. (Adapted with permission from: Ferguson, N.B.L. (1977) Neuropsychology Laboratory Manual, San Francisco: Freeman, Cooper & Company.)

Exercise 3: Sheep Brain Anatomy

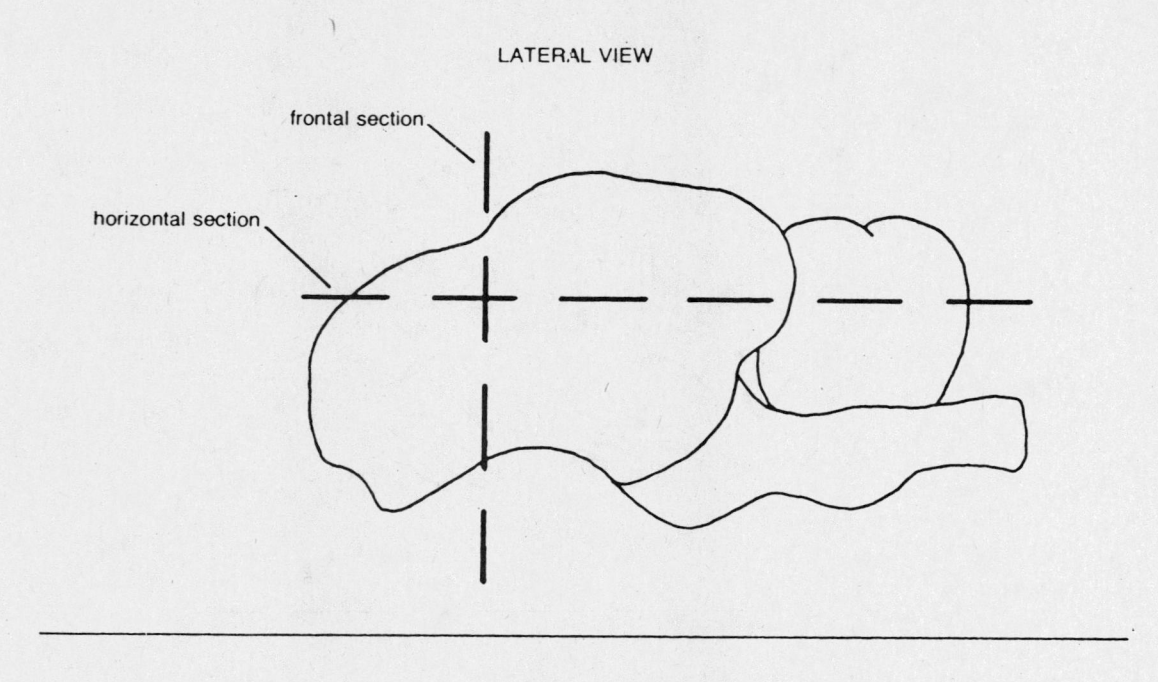

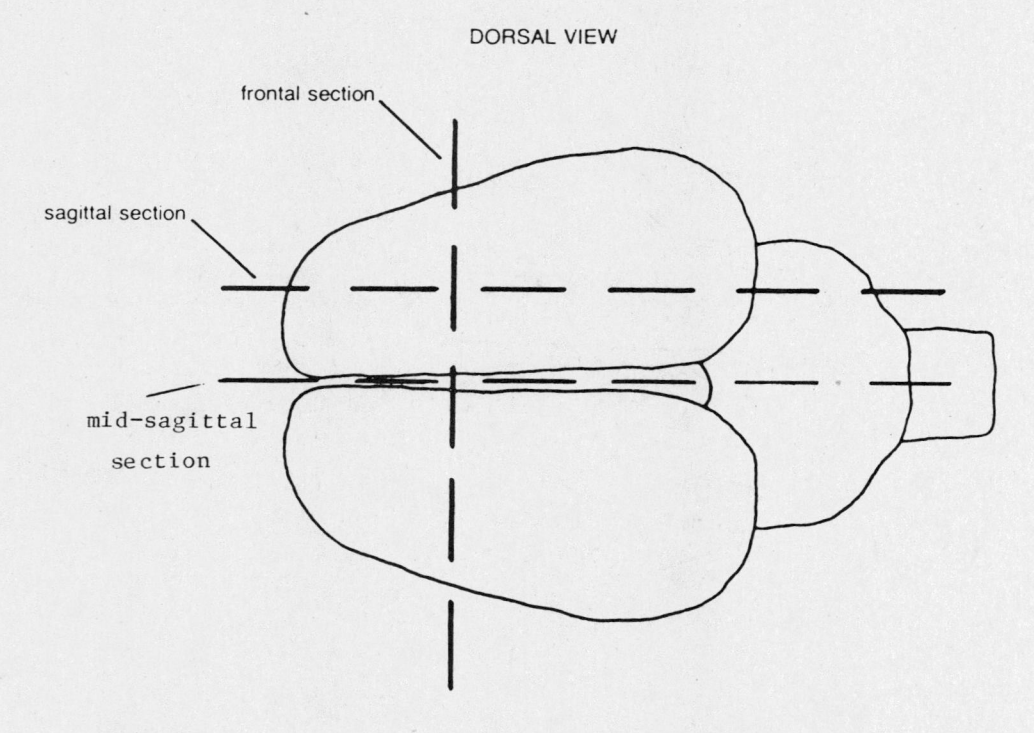

Figure E3.2. Illustration of the various planes of the brain including the frontal (or coronal or transverse), the horizontal and the sagittal sections. (Adapted with permission from: Ferguson, N.B.L. (1977). <u>Neuropsychology Laboratory Manual</u>, San Francisco: Freeman, Cooper & Company.)

Table E3.1 Major Divisions and Subdivisions of the Brain.

Forebrain Telencephalon Cerebral cortex
              Basal ganglia
                Caudate Nucleus
                Putamen
                Globus Pallidus
              Limbic system
                Hippocampus
                Amygdala
                Septum
                Mammillary Bodies
                Lateral ventricles

       Diencephalon Thalamus
              Hypothalamus
              Third ventricle

Midbrain Mesencephalon Tectum
                Sup., inf. colliculi
              Tegmentum
                Reticular Formation

Hindbrain Metencephalon Cerebellum
              Pons

       Myencephalon Medulla Oblongata

Exercise 3: Sheep Brain Anatomy

Dorsal Aspects of the Sheep Brain

Position the base of the sheep brain on the dissecting tray and compare the dorsal surface of the brain with the diagram given in Figure E3.3. You should note that three structures are apparent in a dorsal view of the sheep brain. Beginning at the most posterior extent of the brain, the spinal cord continues into the brain as the medulla oblongata. Just above the medulla you will observe the cerebellar hemispheres. The cerebellum is involved in motor coordination and perhaps learning. The cerebellum consists of an outer layer of cortex and an inner set of deep cerebellar nuclei. The cerebellar cortex is divided into many small ridges termed folia. The nuclei within the cerebellum communicate with the brain via three large fiber bundles (peduncles) that connect the cerebellum with the brainstem. Between the cerebellum and the overlying cerebral cortex you may observe the tentorium, a tough sheet of tissue (dura) that separates the cerebellum and the cerebral cortex. If the tentorium is still present, gently cut it free using the small iris scissors. Now gently pry the cerebellum away from the overlying cerebral cortex. Underneath these structures you will view four brainstem structures, the colliculi. These are arranged in pairs of bumps on the dorsal brainstem. The anterior pair are termed the superior colliculi and are slightly larger than the inferior colliculi.

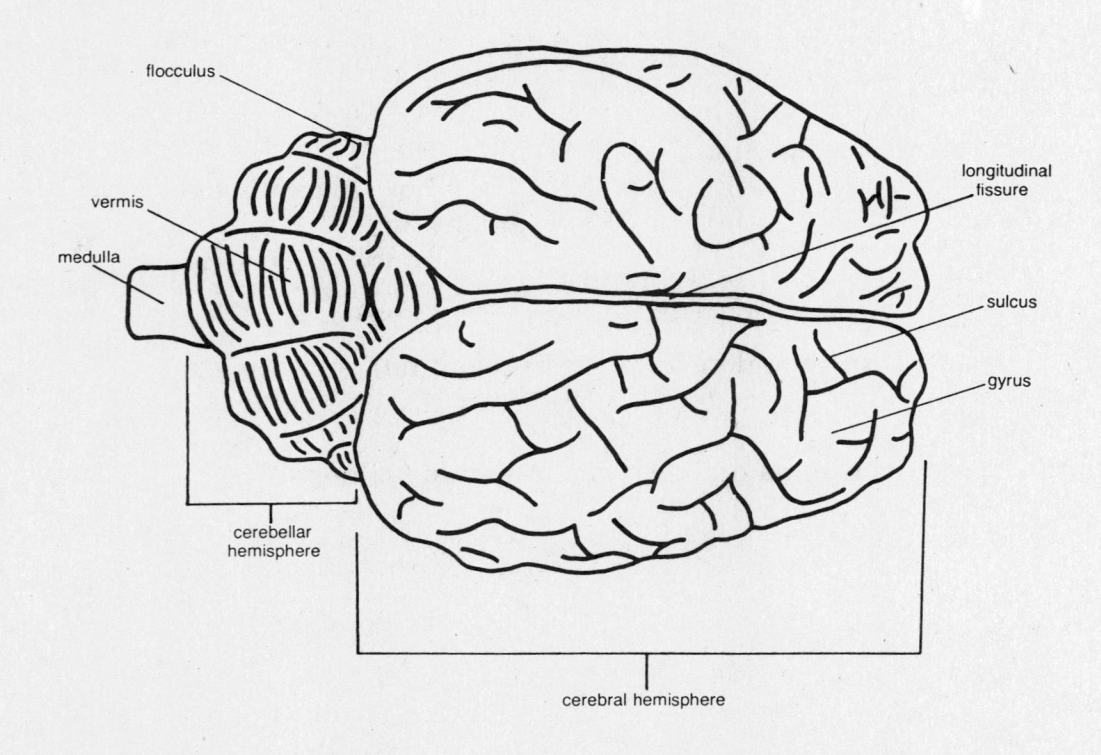

Figure E3.3. Dorsal view of the sheep brain illustrating the medulla, the cerebellar hemispheres and the cerebral cortex. (Adapted with permission from: Ferguson, N.B.L. (1977). Neuropsychology Laboratory Manual, San Francisco: Freeman, Cooper & Company.)

Exercise 3: Sheep Brain Anatomy

Anterior to the cerebellum lie the two hemispheres of the cerebral cortex which form the cerebrum. The cerebral cortex is convoluted by a series of ridges, termed gyri and a series of grooves or fissures, termed sulci. As you will observe when you attempt to identify the major lobes of the cerebral hemispheres, the major fissures serve as convenient landmarks to separate brain cortical areas. Along the midline of the cerebral cortex you will observe a deep groove, termed the medial longitudinal fissure. If you gently pry the cerebral hemispheres apart along this fissure, you will observe a series of white transverse fibers termed the corpus callosum. This structure is a commissure or body of fibers that interconnect similar areas within the two hemispheres.

Lateral Aspects of the Sheep Brain

As you view the sheep brain from the side, begin your observations at the anterior extent of the brain. The cerebral cortex can be divided into a number of lobes, including the occipital, temporal, parietal and frontal lobes (refer to the lateral view in Figure E3.4). You should attempt to identify these lobes in the sheep brain. Locate the transverse sulcus; this fissure separates the anterior motor cortex from the posterior sensory cortex. The lateral fissure serves to separate the frontal and temporal lobes. It is more difficult to identify the demarcation of the parietal and occipital lobes. At the base of the brain, ventral to the cortex, locate the rhinal sulcus which separates the pyriform lobe from the overlying cerebral cortex. As you move in a posterior direction, identify the cerebellum and the pons and medulla. In a lateral view, it possible to observe several of the cranial nerves that exit the brainstem. Although many of the smaller nerve bundles may have been torn from the brain during the removal of the dura, you should attempt to locate the larger bundles including the olfactory tract, the optic nerve and the trigeminal nerve (see Table E3.2 and Figure E3.4).

Table E3.2   Cranial Nerves and Their Function

Nerve:	Name:	Function:
1	Olfactory	Sensory (smell)
2	Optic	Sensory (vision)
3	Oculomotor	Motor (eye movement)
4	Trochlear	Motor (eye movement)
5	Trigeminal	Sensory (face and tongue)
		Motor (jaw movement)
6	Abducens	Motor (eye movement)
7	Facial	Motor (facial expression)
8	Auditory/Vestibular	Sensory (hearing, balance)
9	Glossopharyngeal	Sensory (mouth, tongue)
10	Vagus	Sensory (heart, viscera)
		Motor (heart, viscera)
11	Spinal Accessory	Motor (neck, viscera)
12	Hypoglossal	Motor (tongue movement)

Exercise 3: Sheep Brain Anatomy

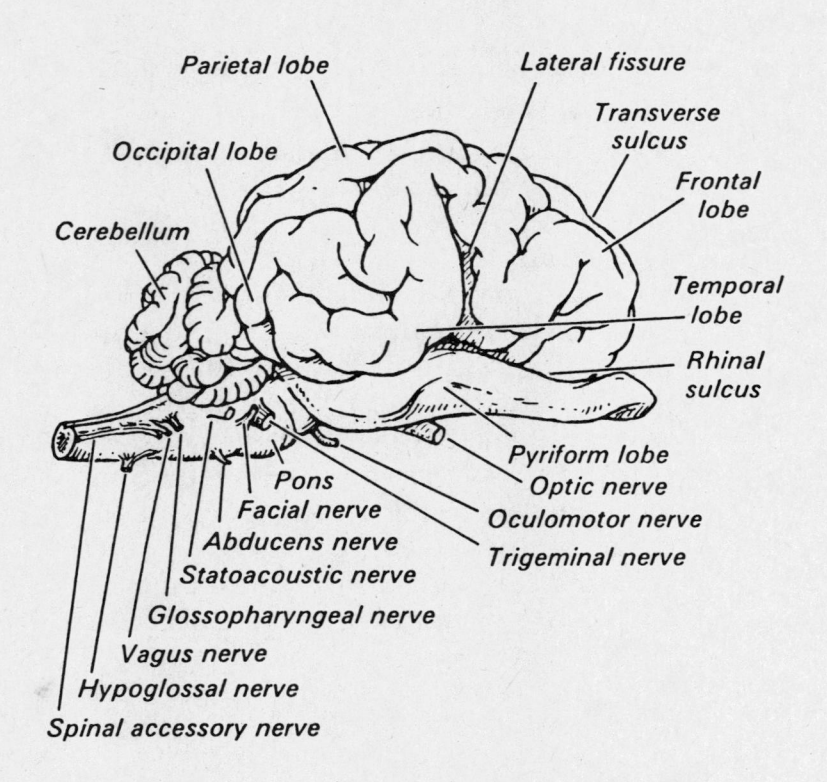

Figure E3.4. Lateral view of the sheep brain illustrating the locations of the cortical lobes and the cranial nerves. (Reprinted with permission from: Hart, B.L. (1976) <u>Experimental Psychobiology,</u> San Francisco: Freeman, Cooper & Company.)

<u>Ventral Aspects of the Sheep Brain</u>

Position the sheep brain so that the dorsal surface rests on the dissection tray and the ventral surface is clearly visible. The 12 cranial nerves (refer to Table E3.2 and Figure E3.5) should be identified beginning at the anterior extent of the ventral surface of the brain. You should observe the laterally positioned rhinal fissure that separates the pyriform and cerebral cortices. The optic chiasm is located between the olfactory tract and the infundibular recess and is where the optic fibers from the retina cross over prior to entering the brain. The infundibular recess lies below the hypothalamus. Immediately posterior to this recess you will observe two bumps on the base of the brain, the aptly named mammillary bodies. Two large fiber bundles, the cerebral peduncles, are located laterally from the mammillary bodies; these peduncles connect the pons with the anterior brain. As you move in a posterior direction, you will note the pons and the remaining cranial nerves.

Exercise 3: Sheep Brain Anatomy

Medial Aspects of the Sheep Brain

Place the brain onto the dissection tray so that the ventral surface lies on the tray. To obtain a medial view of the brain you must cut the brain in half along the medial longitudinal fissure. Use the Virchow brain knife to cut through the corpus callosum and the subcortical brain structures. Use an even cut; do not saw the brain into jagged halves.

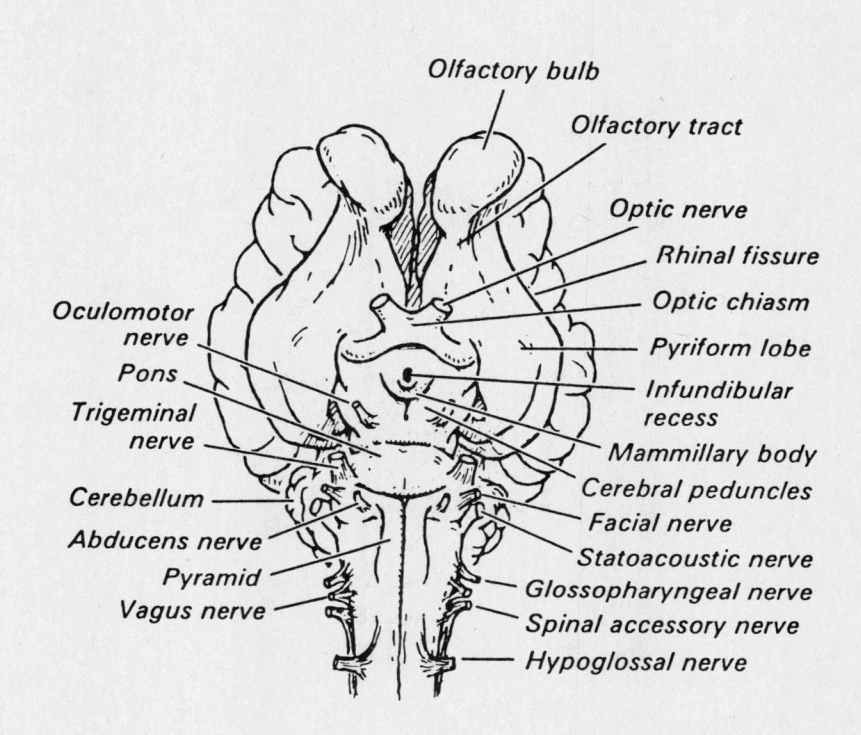

Figure E3.5. Ventral view of the sheep brain illustrating the cranial nerves, the cerebral peduncles and the pons. (Reprinted with permission from: Hart, B.L. (1976) *Experimental Psychobiology* San Francisco: W.H. Freeman Co.)

Refer to Figure E3.6 for a medial view of the sheep brain. You should begin your observations at the caudal end of the brain. Identify the following structures in the medial view:

medulla	pineal body
pons	thalamus
midbrain	hypothalamus
4th ventricle	3rd ventricle
cerebral aqueduct	optic nerve
cerebellum	corpus callosum
superior colliculus	fornix
septum pellucidum	

Exercise 3: Sheep Brain Anatomy

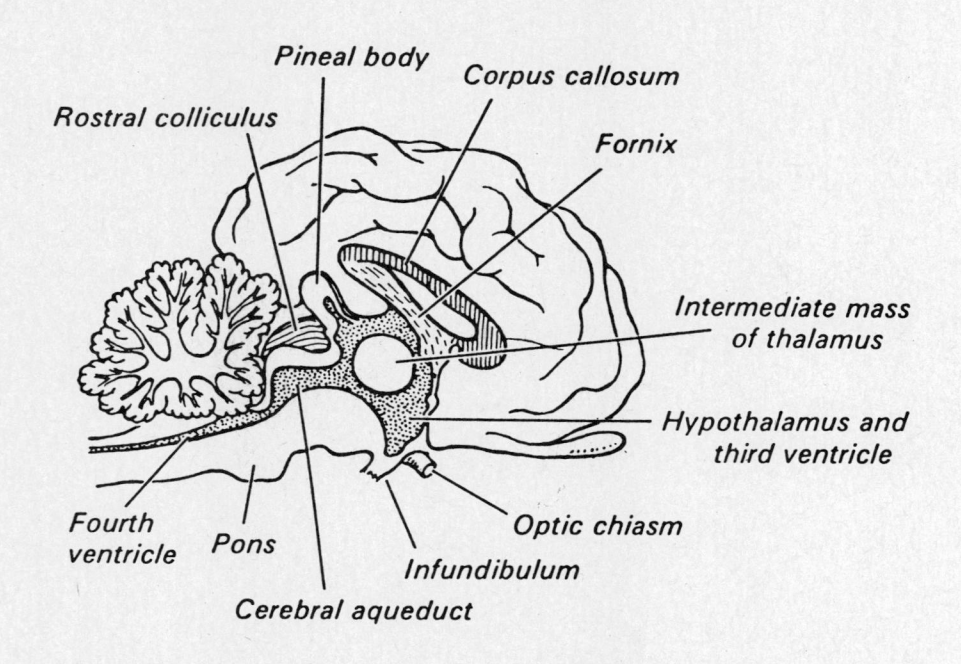

Figure E3.6. Medial view of the sheep brain subjected to a mid-sagittal cut illustrating the structures observed along the midline of the brain (Adapted from Hart, B.L. (1976). <u>Experimental Psychobiology,</u> San Francisco: W.H. Freeman Co.)

REFERENCES AND SUGGESTED READINGS

Carpenter, M.B. (1972). A <u>Core Text of Neuroanatomy.</u> Baltimore: Williams and Wilkins Co.

Cooley, R.K. and C.H. Vanderwolf. (1979). The Sheep Brain: <u>A Basic Guide</u> .London, Ontario Canada: A.J. Kirby Co.

Ferguson, N.B.L. (1977). <u>Neuropsychology Laboratory Manual</u>, San Francisco: Albion Publishing Company.

Moyer, K.F. (1980). <u>Neuroanatomy</u>. New York: Harper and Rowe.

Paxinos, G. (1989). <u>The Rat Nervous System: Forebrain and Midbrain</u>, New York: Academic Press.

Exercise 4: Motor Cortex

Exercise 4
Electrical Stimulation of Rat Motor Cortex

Background and Problem

The concept of motor cortex, that is, cortical tissue directly controlling discrete muscle groups, originated in the 1800's with the work of Fritsch and Hitzig (1870). These scientists demonstrated that low-level electrical stimulation of the anterior and medial regions of the cortex of the dog would produce reliable muscle contractions of the limbs. Of particular interest was their observation that stimulation of one side of anterior cortex produced contractions in the opposite or contralateral side of the body and that spatially distant sites in this cortex seemed to control similarly separated muscle groups. The motor region of the rat cortex, like that of the dog, is situated in the anterior regions (refer to Figure E4.1).

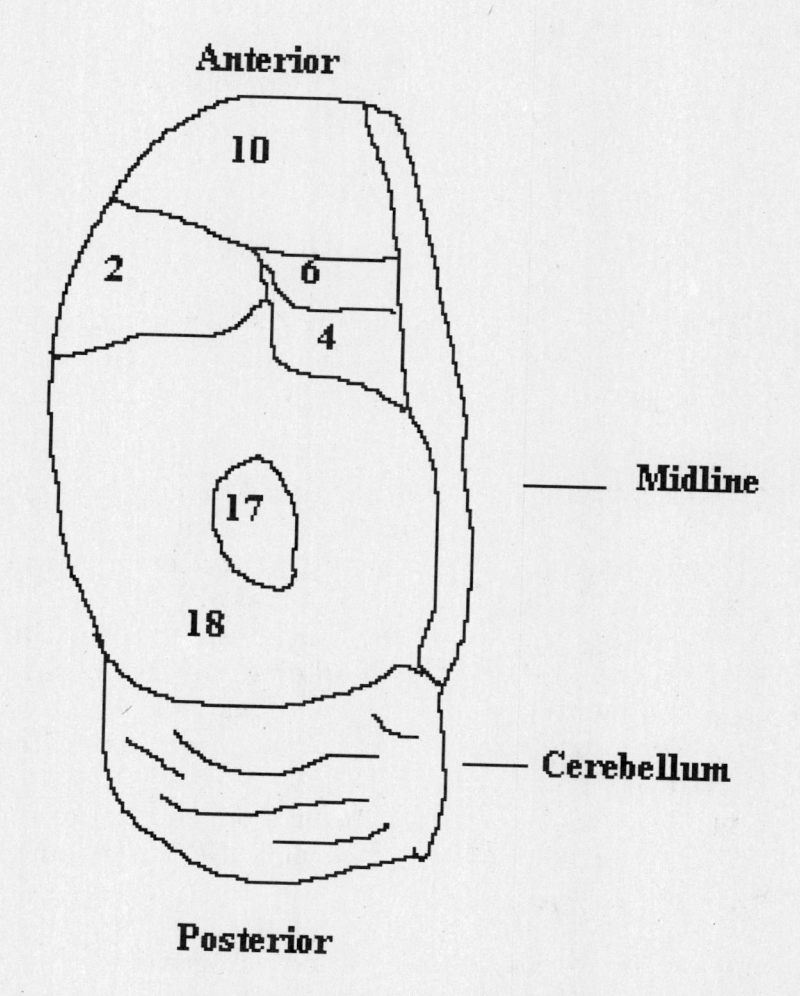

Figure E4.1. Dorsal view of the of the left hemisphere of the rat brain. The numbers within various areas refer to the Brodmann system of cortical classification. The sensorimotor cortex consists of Areas 4, 6 and 10.

Exercise 4: Motor Cortex

The purpose of this exercise is to map the organization of the anterior motor cortex of the rat. In addition, you will determine the current threshold for each point within the motor cortex of the rat, whether the stimulation induces excitation of motor groups on the same side as the site of stimulation (ipsilateral) or the opposite side (contralateral) and the stability of the motor response. The latter refers to the notion that the current intensity required to elicit a motor response may change over time or the nature of the motor response may change (Wilsoncroft and Law, 1967).

Materials
   Scalpel handle (#10) and blade (#3)
   Stereotaxic instrument with electrode holder
   Stereotaxic ear-bar plugs
   Bipolar electrode (Plastics One MS303/1 or equivalent: diameter=.010 inch, stainless
      steel)
   Electronic stimulator (AC, 60 hz, variable voltage)
   Mineral oil (about 1 oz) with cotton swabs
   Stereotaxic drill (variable speed) and medium drill bit
   Hemostatic forceps (2, small)
   Rongeurs (bone chippers)
   Electrode cable with connector
   Vaseline or mineral oil
   Electric hair clippers
   Saline and cotton balls
   Sharp needle

Procedure

Only one rat will be required for this exercise. To more easily map rat motor cortex, use an adult rat weighing 300-400 grams. Anesthetize your rat with sodium pentobarbital (42 mg/ml/kg, IP) 10 minutes after treating it with atropine sulfate (0.3 mg/ml/kg, IP). Shave the skull from a point just anterior to the eyes to a point just anterior to the neck muscles and the posterior skull ridge. Cut the tissue below the auditory meatus with sharp scissors to facilitate placing the skull in the earbars of the stereotaxic instrument. As described in Chapter 4, mount the rat's skull in the ear bars of the stereotaxic instrument using ear plugs. This will be a terminal exercise so that it will not be necessary to use aseptic surgical technique as described in Chapter 3.

Incise the scalp and scrape the periosteum from the center of the skull out to each lateral ridge. Retract the scalp using the hemostatic forceps and control any bleeding with pressure exerted via cotton swabs.

Cut the bipolar electrode to about 10 mm in length (excluding the base) and attach it to the carrier arm. The electrode should be firmly attached and should be parallel to the carrier arm and the stereotaxic instrument base. The latter can be checked using a 3x5 lined index card placed perpendicular to the stereotaxic base.

Exercise 4: Motor Cortex

After the skull surface is clean and dry, you should use the tip of the electrode to map the surface of the skull using the stereotaxic vernier coordinates. Position the electrode on the midsagittal suture above bregma and record the lateral and A/P coordinates. Then position the electrode tip along the midsagittal suture above lambda. Then repeat the measurements of A/P and lateral but now positioning the electrode tip out to the lateral ridge on each side of bregma and lambda. These 6 points should provide a coordinate system for the skull for any point lying between bregma and lambda and the midline and the lateral ridges. Make a sketch of the skull surface on graph paper (10 squares per inch) using a scale of 1 inch = 1 mm. Include in your sketch the position of bregma, lambda, the midline, and the lateral ridges (see Figure E4.2).

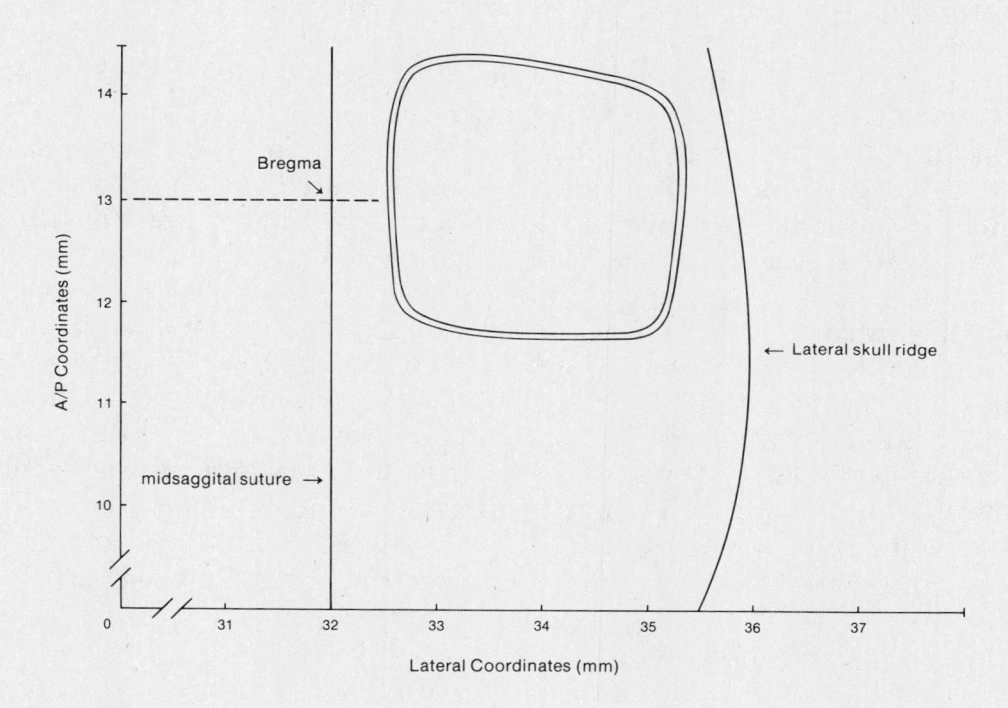

Figure E4.2. An example of the grid system of coordinates used to map the anterior and medial cortex of the rat brain for motor stimulation sites.

Exercise 4: Motor Cortex

Drill 3-4 holes, using a medium-sized drill bit, in an area at least 1 mm off the midline at the level of bregma. Extend these holes for 2 mm anterior and posterior to bregma. The purpose of these holes is to provide a "window" to the cortex through which you will stimulate the cortical tissue. Avoid cutting too close to the midline as your bur may cut the midsagittal sinus thereby producing profusive bleeding and compromising your experiment. Use the tips of the Rongeurs to enlarge the skull holes so as to expose a rectangular section of dura overlying the cortex. Use a sharp needle to cut the dura from the surface of the brain. Place a thin layer of mineral oil on the surface of the cortex; this layer will prevent the cortical tissue from dehydrating during your mapping session.

Connect the stimulator leads to the stimulating electrode via a connector cable. Your instructor should verify that these whether connections are correct. If your stimulator does not have a provision for electrical isolation, be certain that you are not touching either the stimulator, the cable, the stereotaxic unit or the rat while the stimulator is on. Ground currents returning through the animal can electrocute both the rat and you: thus, stimulus isolation and caution are important for this exercise.

Position the tip of the electrode just on the cortex of the rat at the most anterior and medial extent visible through the skull window. Record the coordinates of this position (lateral and A/P: height can be ignored in this exercise). Now, while observing the rat, deliver a brief (1 second) train of stimulation separated by at least 5 seconds and observe any motor contractions in your rat. Always start with the lowest possible voltage value and then systematically increase the voltage every 5 seconds until a contraction is noted. The voltage level at which a contraction is noted (the threshold), along with the body part that contracts in response to stimulation should be recorded along with the electrode coordinates. Now systematically repeat this process by moving the electrode in a posterior direction in 1 mm increments. At each point, record the coordinates and note the voltage at which a contraction, if any was noted. Your instructor should set a ceiling on the maximal voltage to be used (e.g. under no circumstances deliver more than 90 volts). As you reach the most posterior extent of the exposed cortex, move the electrode laterally 1 mm and repeat the process moving in an anterior direction. Continue this process until you have mapped the entire exposed cortex.

Data Summary and Interpretation

Refer to the map of the cortex you have drawn. If your scale is 10 squares per mm, you will easily be able to transfer your data to this cortical map. At each electrode coordinate, note the position and indicate the threshold voltage and the nature of the motor effect. Also note which part of the body showed contraction (i.e. ipsilateral? contralateral?).

If there is time after you have finished mapping the cortex for motor excitability, you may wish to return to one or more of the stimulation sites and examine the stability of the stimulation-elicited motor responses. In particular, you may wish to look for the following changes in excitability as noted by Wilsoncroft and Law (1967):

Exercise 4: Motor Cortex

REVERSAL: A site that formerly yielded flexion (limb moved in toward the body) now induces extension (the limb moves away from the body).

FACILITATION: The threshold voltage at which a motor response is observed decreases with repeated stimulations.

DEVIATION: A different muscle group is now excited by stimulation of a single motor cortex site.

INHIBITION: A site that formerly was responsive to cortex stimulation no longer responds.

Questions that you should address in your exercise summary include the following:

Does your cortical map show consistent organization of function? That is, are there systematic changes in the body parts that contract as you move along the cortex either laterally or in an A/P direction? Were the motor responses always observed on the opposite side of the body from the point of cortical stimulation? Finally, if you were able to retest any motor sites in your rat, was there any evidence of instability of the motor response? You may wish to speculate as to the factors that might produce such instability.

At the end of the exercise, remove your rat from the stereotaxic instrument and euthanize it with 60 mg/ml/kg (IP) sodium pentobarbital. Dispose of the carcass properly and then clean your work station.

REFERENCES AND SUGGESTED READINGS

Fritsch, G. and E. Hitzig. (1870). On the electrical excitability of the cerebrum. Archiv. f. Winenschaftlie Medizin, 300-332. Translated by D. Harriss in: K. H. Pribram (Ed) Brain and Behavior Books, 1969.

Wilsoncroft, W. E. and O.T. Law. (1967). Laboratory Manual for Physiological Psychology, Goleta, California: Psychonomic Press.

Exercise 4: Motor Cortex

Exercise 5
Apomorphine-induced Stereotypy in Rats

Background and Problem

Acute and chronic treatment of the rat with a catecholamine (CA) agonist such as amphetamine produces a bizarre motor state termed stereotypy. Stereotyped behavior in the rat consists of repetitive bouts of sniffing, licking or biting. Moreover, the incidence of normal behaviors, such as feeding, grooming and forward locomotion are greatly suppressed in rats exhibiting stereotypy. Especially striking is the intensity and invariance of stereotyped behavior.

Amphetamine-stimulated stereotypy is thought to result from release of the transmitter dopamine from central dopaminergic neurons. Stereotyped behavior induced by systemic amphetamine treatment is greatly reduced in rats following injections of dopamine synthesis inhibitors (AMPT), dopamine receptor blockers (haloperidol) or following lesions of dopamine neurons within the substantia nigra (Scheel-Kruger, 1971; Rolinski and Scheel-Kruger, 1973; Costal, Marsden, Naylor and Pycock, 1977).

There is a strong similarity between the stereotypy observed in rats and that observed in human amphetamine addicts. Rylander (1966) noted:

> "a rather curious phenomenon is that the addicts can, in an obsessive-compulsive manner, be plucking at the same objects for hours or engage themselves with some other meaningless activity, for example, polishing nails or dismantling and reassembling clocks or motors"

Interestingly, the stereotypic behavior associated with amphetamine abuse in humans is frequently associated with psychotic behavior which is virtually indistinguishable from that of a functional psychoses. Indeed, the link between stereotypic behavior and a dopaminergic mechanism of psychoses is further suggested by the observation that both states are antagonized by treatment with the dopamine receptor blocker haloperidol.

The purpose of this exercise is to demonstrate the stereotypy induced by apomorphine in normal rats. Although amphetamine is the typical agent used to induce stereotypy, the problems associated with access to and use of amphetamine in an undergraduate laboratory resulted in the choice of the dopamine agonist apomorphine (Costall, Marsden, Naylor and Pycock, 1977). In this exercise, you will become proficient at rating the behavior of rats treated with saline or 1.0 mg/kg apomorphine (sc) using a 9 point rating scale developed by Ellinwood and Balster (1974).

Exercise 5: Stereotypy

<u>Materials</u>
  Stop watch or electronic clock
  6 clear plastic enclosures (47 x 30 x 20 cm) with wire-mesh lid
  0.9% saline solution
  1 cc syringes with 27 gauge (0.5 inch) needles
  1.0 mg/ml apomorphine hydrochloride (Sigma Chemical)

<u>Method</u>
   The subjects for this experiment will be 6 female Sprague-Dawley rats weighing between 150 and 200 grams at the beginning of the experiment. The rats should be housed singly with free access to food and water throughout the experiment. Weigh your rats daily to the nearest gram to accustom them to routine handling.

   Table E5.1 presents the behavioral rating schedule devised by Ellinwood and Balster (1974) to quantify the effect of amphetamine on behavior in the rat. This rating scale is used to simultaneously rate the behavior exhibited by each of 6 rats during a 60 minute test trial. Therefore, you will need 6 clear (Plexiglass) enclosures, each provided with a wire-mesh lid and a floor covered with sawdust bedding. You should arrange the cages in a half-circle around you so that you can easily observe and rate the behavior of each cage occupant. On each of 3 days, place a rat into each of the test cages and allow the rats to habituate to this test environment for 15 minutes. You should always place the same rat into the same enclosure over the test days.

   On the 4th day, place the rats into the observation cages for the 15 minute adaptation period. You should leave the room and another experimenter should enter for the purpose of removing each rat from it's observation cage and injecting each with either 0.9% saline (1.0 ml/kg, IP) (n=3) or 1.0 mg/ml/kg apomorphine hydrochloride (ip; n=3). Prepare the apomorphine solution by dissolving apomorphine hydrochloride into sterile distilled water containing 0.1% sodium metabisulphite (Costall et al., 1977). The experimenter should replace each rat into the proper test cage and you should then reenter the room to begin 60 minutes of observation. In this way, your ratings of the behaviors of these rats will be blind to their injection history. Rate the behavior of each rat for 20 seconds every 10 minutes (at 0, 10, 20, 30, 40, 50 and 60 minutes post-injection). The behavioral score, ranging between 1 and 9, assigned to each rat will be the dominant (most frequent) behavior exhibited by that rat during each 20 second observation interval.

<u>Data Summary and Interpretation</u>
   The data set you have collected consists of a series of behavioral rating scores for each rat during a 60 minute period after saline or apomorphine injection. For each drug treatment group, average the group ratings at each time period. Thus, if the rats in the apomorphine group had ratings scores of 7, 8 and 9 at 40 minutes following injection, then the average behavioral rating score for this group at this time period would be 8. Use the graphic axes provided in Figure E5.1 to depict the effect of apomorphine on stereotypy in the rat.

Exercise 5: Stereotypy

You should describe the changes in behavior produced by apomorphine in your summary report. In particular, you should describe the varieties of behaviors observed in rats treated with apomorphine. Were certain classes of behavior observed in greater frequency while others became less frequent? What was the time course of these changes? Was there evidence of circling or rotational behavior in your rats? If so, you may wish to read the report of Jerussi and Glick (1975) and compare their results with yours. Finally, you should comment on the use of dopamine stimulants to markedly alter behavior. For example, Gambill and Cornetsky (1976) demonstrated that although 8 mg/kg amphetamine produced reliable stereotypy in rats, there were clearly large individual differences as to the effect of amphetamine on social behavior, including fighting. Interestingly, dominant rats became oblivious of others while amphetamine-treated subordinate rats retreated to defensible locations and over-reacted to approach by other rats by either fleeing or engaging in stereotypic boxing-like aggression.

Table E5.1. Rating scale for the stereotypic action of apomorphine in the rat.

Score:	Category:	Behavioral Description:
1	Asleep	Lying down, eyes closed
2	Inactive	Lying down, eyes opened
3	Grooming	Grooming
4	Normal Activity	Moving about cage, sniffing, rearing
5	Hyperactive	Running movements characterized by rapid changes in position (jerky)
6	Slow patterned	Repetitive exploration of the cage at normal level of activity
7	Fast Patterned	Repetitive exploration of the cage with hyperactivity
8	Restricted	Rat remains stationary with fast, repetitive head and/or forelimb movements
9	Dyskinetic	Backing up, jumping, seizures, abnormal postures

Exercise 5: Stereotypy

REFERENCES AND SUGGESTED READINGS

Costall, B., C.D. Marsden, R.J. Naylor and C.J. Pycock (1977). Stereotyped behaviour patterns and hyperactivity induced by amphetamine and apomorphine after discrete 6-hydroxydopamine lesions of extrapyramidal and mesolimbic nuclei. Brain Research, 123, 89-111.

Ellinwood, E.H. and R.L. Balster. (1974). Rating the behavioral effects of amphetamine. European Journal of Pharmacology, 28, 35-41.

Gambill, J.D. and C. Kornetsky. (1976). Effects of chronic d-amphetamine on social behavior of the rat: Implications for an animal model of paranoid schizophrenia. Psychopharmacology, 50, 215-223.

Jerussi, T.P. and S.D. Glick. (1975). Apomorphine-induced rotation in normal rats and interaction with unilateral caudate lesions. Psychopharmacology, 40, 329-334.

Rolinski, Z.and J. Scheel-Kruger. (1973). The effect of dopamine and noradrenaline antagonists on amphetamine-induced locomotor activity in mice and rats. Acta Pharmacologia et Toxicologica, 33, 385-399.

Rylander, G. (1966). Addiction to Preludin intravenously injected. In: Proceedings of the Fourth World Congress of Psychiatry, Madrid, Amsterdam: Excerpta Medica Foundation.

Scheel-Kruger, J. (1971). Comparative studies of various amphetamine analogues demonstrating different interactions with the metabolism of the catecholamines of the brain. European Journal of Pharmacology, 14, 47-59.

Exercise 5: Stereotypy

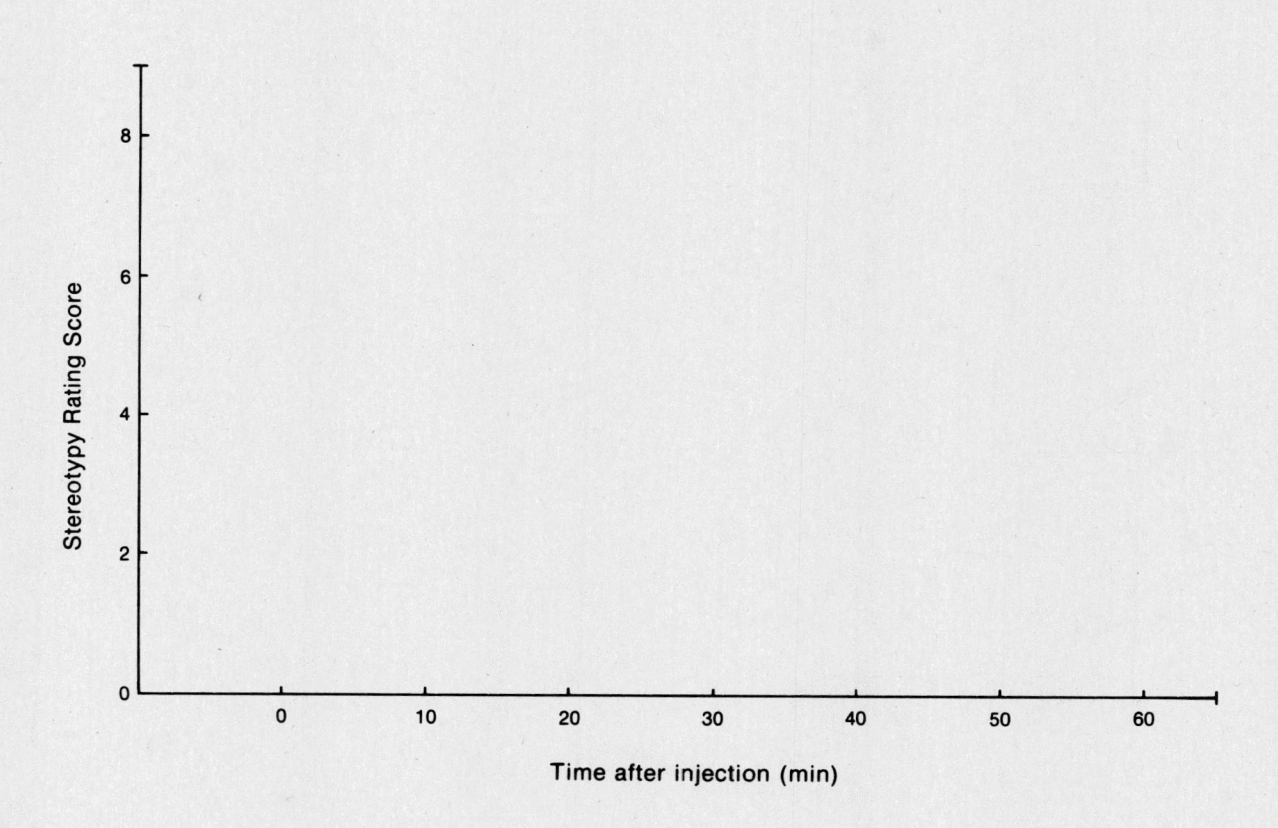

Figure E5.1. Graphic axes used to depict the stereotypy data of Exercise 5.

Exercise 5: Stereotypy

Exercise 6
Morphine-induced Analgesia in Rats

Background and Problem

Pain is an important, albeit aversive, stimulus that communicates to the brain the onset of tissue destruction. Considerable research during the last two decades has established that Substance P is the probable neurotransmitter for first order pain neurons that synapse onto ascending neurons within the spinal cord. Substance P is found within the dorsal horn of the cord, painful stimuli release Substance P and local application of substance P within the spinal cord induces a marked apparent state of pain in rats (Yaksh, Farb, Leeman and Jessell, 1979). In opposition to the ascending pain system is an inhibitory endogenous opiate system that serves to reduce the perception of pain, an effect termed analgesia. Most opiates (morphine, heroin) are exogenous compounds, derived from the poppy, that reduce pain. Hughes (1975) demonstrated the existence of endogenous opiates, later termed "endorphins" and enkephalins, that reside within the brain. The neurons that contain endorphins are found within the periacqueductal gray (PAG), the hypothalamus and the limbic system (Koyabashi, 1978). These fiber systems project to the medulla and eventually make contact onto ascending pain fibers in the dorsal horn of the spinal cord (Fields, Heinricher and Mason, 1991). Low-level electrical stimuation of the PAG produces prolonged analgesia that is partly reversed by pretreatment with naloxone, a narcotic antagonist. The partial inability of PAG stimulation to induce analgesia in rats treated with naloxone is significant in that naloxone is thought to act by binding to opiate receptors thereby preventing the opiate from activating the receptor. Interestingly, several analgesic phenomena are at least partially reversible with naloxone. These include analgesia associated with "placebo" treatments, pregnancy, stress, and acupuncture (Akil et al. 1976; Levine, Gordon and Fields, 1979; Mayer and Hayes, 1975). Presumably, these treatments induce analgesia by causing the release of endogenous opiates.

The present exercise introduces the measurement of analgesia induced by morphine and its reversal by pretreatment with naloxone. The index of pain sensitivity used herein is the latency from the onset of the thermal stimulus to a paw lick response. The latency to paw lick is a measure of pain sensitivity in that normal rats exhibit latencies around 2-3 seconds whereas the opiate morphine can greatly lengthen the paw lick latency to more than 20 seconds. Rats pretreated with naloxone and then treated with morphine ought to exhibit normal pain sensitivity.

This exercise will require ethical justification. The experimental study of pain is an important area but you should be aware of the ethical implications of subjecting animals to experimental pain. The Committee for Research and Ethical Issues of the International Association for the Study of Pain has published important guidelines for the conduct of research involving pain (Author, 1980). Briefly, these state that the

Exercise 6: Morphine-Induced Analgesia

procedures for a pain study should be reviewed carefully by peers and laypersons and that the experimenter should verify the nature of the pain stimulus by personal experience. To understand the magnitude of the pain stimulus, you should measure your response to the hot-plate (you need not lick your hand but you might time the duration that you can maintain your hand on the plate surface). In addition, your instructor will need approval of the local animal care committee to conduct this exercise.

Materials
1 cc syringe with 27 gauge (0.5 inch needle)
5 mg/ml morphine sulfate (Sigma Chemical or local veterinarian)
0.9 % saline
1.0 mg/ml naloxone hydrochloride (Sigma Chemical)
Thermometer
Timer (stop-watch)
Paw-lick apparatus (see description below)
Tape
Small desk lamp
Damp sponge

Method

The subjects for this experiment should be 12 male hooded rats approximately 280-320 grams in body weight. The design of this experiment is a 2 X 2 factorial. The pretreatment factor consists of injection of either saline or 1 mg/kg naloxone hydrochloride 30 minutes prior to the analgesia test. The treatment factor consists of injection of either saline or morphine 15 minutes prior to the test. These combinations produce 4 groups (n = 3 each): Saline-Saline, Saline-Morphine, Naloxone-Saline and Naloxone-Morphine. Your lab group should randomly assign the rats to the treatment groups and then decide upon an injection schedule: that is, when and who will perform the injections and when and who will perform the analgesia test. The person collecting the analgesia data should be kept blind as to the injection condition of each rat.

The paw-lick apparatus used to assess pain sensitivity consists of a clear Plexiglass enclosure that is open at the bottom and outfitted with a hinged lid at the top. The enclosure is placed onto the surface of the slide warmer. The temperature of the plate should be maintained at 50 degrees C. Plate temperature should be monitored using a mercury thermometer taped to the plate surface. Temperature control using the slide warmer thermostat is often imprecise. To precisely maintain the plate temperature, set the slide warmer at its highest thermostatic setting and then plug the power cord of the plate into a variable ac power supply (VARIAC: Standard Electrical Company, 300 BU). The variac can then be adjusted so as to maintain a constant plate temperature. The temperature tests should be conducted in a quiet room with dim or no overhead lighting. A small office lamp suspended above the test apparatus is used to provide illumination for the chamber.

Exercise 6: Morphine-Induced Analgesia

After injecting each rat with either saline or naloxone (30 min prior to the test) and then with either saline or morphine (15 min prior to the test), reset the timer to zero and open the test chamber lid. Grasp the rat around the neck and gently place it into the test chamber. Always place the rat onto the plate surface facing the same direction and begin timing when all four paws are on the plate surface. Close the lid and observe the rat's behavior for a paw-lick response (the rat licks either a front or rear paw). When you observe a paw lick or when 25 seconds have gone by, terminate the timing and immediately remove the rat from the plate. Under no circumstance should you leave the rat on the plate for longer than 25 seconds. After each trial, you should clean the plate surface of urine and any feces (hence the damp sponge) and then verify that the plate temperature returns to 50 degrees C prior to beginning the next trial.

Data Summary and Interpretation

This experiment represents a 2 X 2 factorial design with saline and naloxone as the pretreatment factor and saline and morphine as the treatment factor. For each group of 3 rats, calculate the mean paw lick latency for each of the groups after injection. These values should be depicted using the axes provided in Figure E6.1. Analgesia will be evident in the comparison of the paw lick latencies of the saline-morphine group relative to the saline-saline group. You should assess the influence of naloxone on pain sensitivity in the saline-treated rats and the morphine-treated rats. Although one might easily explain the reversal of morphine analgesia in the naloxone-morphine group, how would you interpret a decline in paw lick latency in the naloxone-saline group relative to the saline-saline group?

REFERENCES AND SUGGESTED READINGS

Akil, H., J. Madden, R.L. Patrick and J.D. Barchas. (1976). In: H.W. Kosterlitz (Ed) Opiates and Endogenous Opioid Peptides, Amsterdam: North-Holland, p. 63.

Akil, H., D. Mayer and J. C. Liebeskind. (1976). Antagonism of stimulation-produced analgesia by naloxone, a narcotic antagonist. Science, 191, 961-962.

Author. (1980). Guidelines for the experimental investigation of pain. Pain, 9, 141-143.

Bardo, M.T., P.J. Wellman and R.A. Hughes. (1981). Role of hotplate and general environmental stimuli in morphine analgesic tolerance. Pharmacology, Biochemistry and Behavior, 23, 343-348.

Fields, H.L., M.M. Heinricher and P. Mason. (1991). Annual Review of Neuroscience, 14, 219-245.

Hughes, J., T.W. Smith, H.W. Kosterlitz, L.A. Fothergill, B.A. Morgan and H.R. Morris. (1975). Identification of two related pentapeptides from the brain with potent opiate agonist activity. Nature, 258, 577-579.

Exercise 6: Morphine-Induced Analgesia

Koyabashi, L. (1978). Brain peptides. Life Sciences, 22, 379-389.

Levine, J.D., N.C. Gordon, and H.L. Fields. (1979). The role of endorphins in placebo analgesia. In: Advances in Pain Research and Therapy, (Ed). J. Bonica, J.C. Liebeskind, and D. Albe-Fessard. New York: Raven Press.

Mayer, D.J. and R. Hayes. (1975). Stimulation-produced analgesia: Development of tolerance and cross-tolerance to morphine. Science, 188, 941-943.

Mayer, D.J. and J.C. Liebeskind. (1974). Pain reduction by focal electrical stimulation of the brain: An anatomical and behavioral analysis. Brain Research, 68, 73-93.

Exercise 6: Morphine-Induced Analgesia

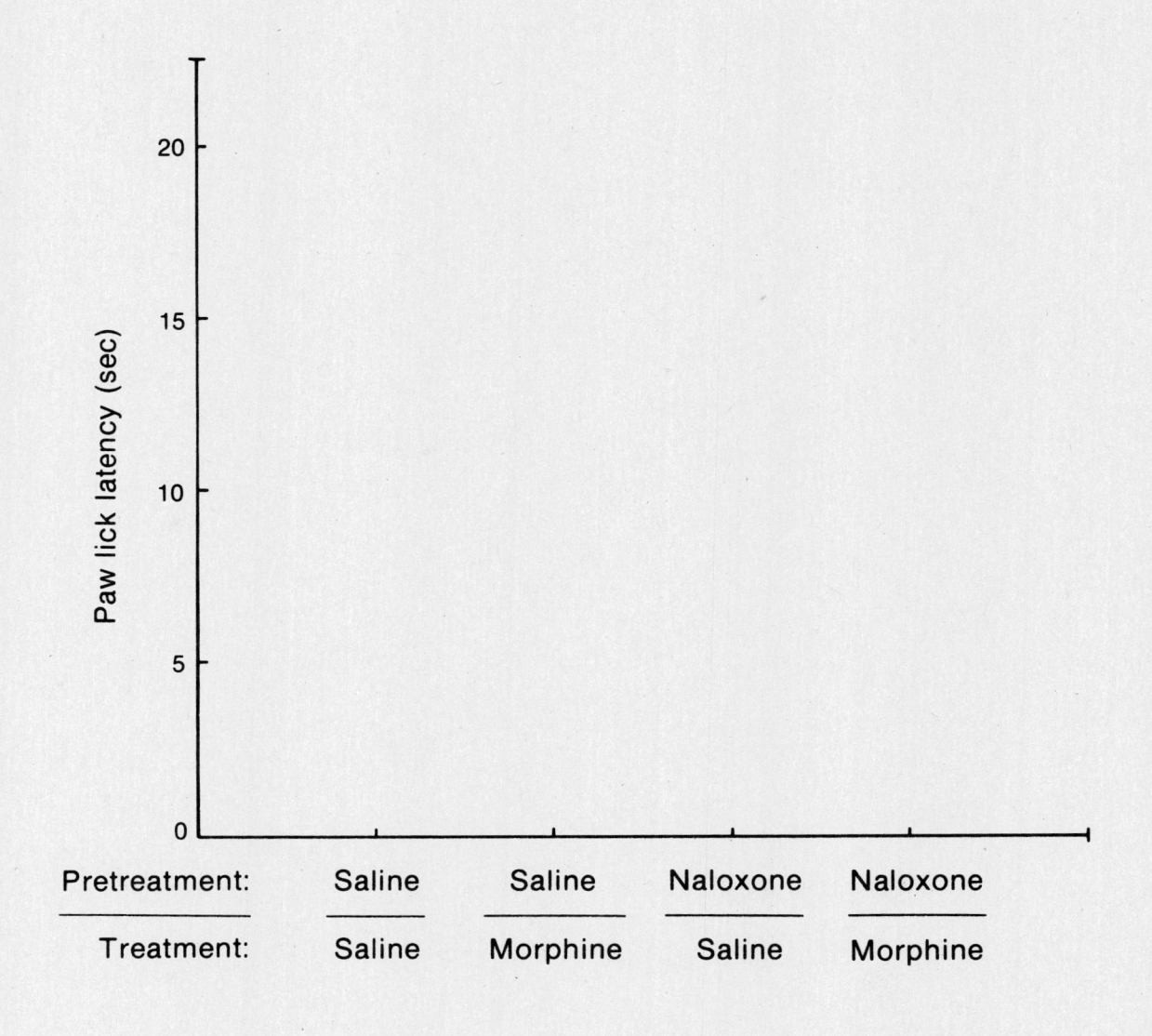

Figure E6.1. Graphic axes used to depict the mean group paw lick latencies (sec) for saline- and morphine-treated animals tested using a 50 degree C hot plate.

# Exercise 6: Morphine-Induced Analgesia

Exercise 7
Pain Perception in Humans

Background and Problem

As noted in Exercise 6, animal research has provided a considerable knowledge base as to the afferent and efferent fiber systems that modulate pain. This knowledge has been used by clinical pain researchers to examine the modulation of pain in humans. In this exercise, we will examine how to assess pain perception in humans and we will examine some of the variables that result in alteration of pain perception.

There are a variety of stimuli that can be acutely administered which result in the perception of pain (Naliboff and Cohen, 1989). A common stimulus involves immersing the arm in a bath of ice water (termed the "cold pressor" test). In the cold pressor test, the subject's hand or arm is left in the ice water for a fixed duration. The subject can be asked to indicate when pain is first felt (threshold), can be asked to rate the intensity of the pain during the test (every 20 seconds over 4 minutes) and can be allowed to terminate the test by raising their hand from the ice water (termed pain tolerance). . Hilgard et al., (1974) provide background information regarding the scaling of the cold pressor test whereas Walsh et al (1989) provide empirical norms for subjects undergoing the cold pressor test.

In this exercise, you and your lab partners will examine how several variables may interact with pain transmission to increase or decrease the degree of perceived pain. In Exercise 6, morphine was used to produce analgesia (more specifically, hypoalgesia). In this exercise, you will examine the effects on pain perception of variables including attention/distraction, and exercise. Your instructor will decide which of these manipulations to include in this exercise and will seek approval from your Institutional Human Review Board (the human ethics committee).

Materials
- Ice chest
- Thermometer (calibrated in degree C)
- Fish tank aerator
- Stop watch or timer
- Exercise bike

Procedures

This exercise requires a minimum amount of equipment and setup. You should obtain an ice chest and fill it with water maintained at 7 degrees C. The thermometer should be mounted on the inside of the chest with its tip halfway into the water. The aerator is mounted on the bottom of the chest and is used to recirculate the ice water. The chest should be positioned on low table such that a subject sitting in a chair can easily maintain their hand in the water.

Exercise 7: Pain Perception

The following description is a general procedure to be used for each of the specific manipulations. Your tests of pain perception will be done using a pre-test post-test design. That is, for each subject, you will first record the various measures of pain perception while the hand is maintained in the ice water bath. Each subject will have a minimum of 15 minutes to recover from the pre-test. The specific manipulation will be administered and post-test measures of pain perception will be recorded.

Each test will be 4 minutes in duration. The specific measures to be recorded during each test include the following:

1. Threshold: at what time point after immersion does the subject state that this is painful?

2. Pain ratings: every 30 seconds, have the subject rate the degree of pain using a scale ranging from:

    "1" -"This just bothers me"

    to

    "10"- "This is unbearable".

3. Pain tolerance: this measure is defined as the latency from immersion in water until the subject voluntarily removes their hand from the water. Note that this measure of pain sensitivity is similar to that employed in rats in Exercise 6.

Specific Manipulations:

Distraction. McCaul and Haugtvedt (1982) reported that distraction from painful stimuli reduced responsivity to pain produced in the cold pressor test. Various means have been used to distract subjects during the cold pressor test. Subjects have been asked to look at slides on a projection screen, to imagine a favorite vacation spot or have been asked to do mental tasks such as addition or subtraction (Hodes et al., 1990). In this procedure, you should decide on a specific mental task that your subject will perform during the second pain perception procedure. The effect of the distraction manipulation will be judged by the difference between the pre-test and post-test scores. Note that in the procedure, the subjects will be engaged in a difficult math procedure (start at 100, subtract 7, add 2, and then repeat steps 2 and 3) throughout the 4 minute post-test or will not be asked to do so. Your instructor will provide details as to how many subjects will be used in the distraction/no distraction groups.

Exercise 7: Pain Perception

Exercise

Long-distance runners often report a positive emotional state after a run that has been likened to drug-induced euphoria. Exercise per se may induce the release of endorphins which reduce pain perception and which induce a positive mood. Yet, experimental studies of the effects of exercise on pain perception have yielded conflicting findings. Padawer and Levine (1992) reviewed the exercise and pain perception literature and suggested that exercise does not always alter pain perception in the cold pressor test. One interesting aspect of these studies is that these tests are rarely conducted in active athletes. The intent of this manipulation is to examine the effects of an exercise task on pain perception and to determine whether active versus non-active subjects show a difference in their pain sensitivity after the exercise task.

In the exercise task, you will first attempt to identify subjects who have an active exercise history (i.e. jog regularly, play racquetball etc.) and subjects who are relatively inactive. Conduct a pre-test of pain perception. Note whether active vs inactive subjects show initial differences in pain sensitivity in the cold pressor test. Then have each subject ride the exercise bike for 10 minutes at a moderate work load. Allow 3 minutes for recovery from the exercise task and then conduct a post-test assessment of pain perception.

Issues to Address in the Laboratory Report

It is likely that you will conduct only one of the manipulations of pain perception using the cold pressor test. In each writeup, describe the specific details of the manipulation that you used. Indicate whether there were initial differences between your groups. In the distraction manipulation, were the distraction subjects equivalent to the controls in terms of pain threshold, overall pattern of pain ratings and in pain tolerance? Similarly, were these pre-test measures equivalent in the exercise vs inactive subjects?

For each manipulation, note whether the manipulation altered threshold, pain ratings and pain tolerance during the post-test period. If you noted an effect of either distraction or exercise, when did the effect occur during the 4 minute post-test period? Was the effect specific to pain ratings or to pain tolerance?

Finally, you should speculate in your report as to how these manipulations alter pain perception. Do they alter the stimulus or central processing of pain perception?

REFERENCES AND SUGGESTED READINGS

Hilgard, E.R., J.C. Ruch, A.F. Lange, J.R. Lenox, A.H. Morgan, and L.B. Sachs. (1974). The psychophysics of cold pressor pain and its modification through hypnotic suggestion. American Journal of Psychology, 87, 17-31.

Exercise 7: Pain Perception

Hodes, R.L., E.W. Howland, N. Lightfoot and C.S. Cleeland (1990). The effects of distraction on responses to cold pressor pain. Pain, 41, 109-114.

McCaul, K.D. and C. Haugtvedt. (1982). Attention, distraction and cold-pressor pain. Journal of Personality and Social Psychology, 43, 154-162.

Naliboff, B. and M.J. Cohen. (1989). Psychophysical laboratory methods applied to clinical pain patients. In: C.R. Chapman and J.D. Loeser (Eds)., Issues in Pain Measurement, New York: Raven Press.

Padawer, W.J. and F.M. Levine. (1992). Exercise-induced analgesia: Fact or artifact? Pain, 48, 131-135.

Walsh, N.E., L. Schoenfeld, S. Ramamurthy and J. Hoffman. (1989). Normative model for cold pressor test. American J. Physical Medicine and Rehabilitation, 68, 6-11.

Exercise 8
Sexual Receptivity in the Rat after Ovariectomy

Background and Problem

Beach (1976) identified 3 components that comprise sexual behavior in the female rat: attractivity, proceptivity and receptivity. Attractivity refers to the effect of odor cues on the proximity of a male rat to the female, proceptivity refers to the mechanisms (ultrasound signals) by which a female in heat invites the approach of male whereas receptivity refers to the responses that female rats exhibit in response to contact with the male. The best example of the latter category is the receptive behavior termed lordosis in which a female rat arches her back and presents the perineum to the male rat.

Experiments in behavioral endocrinology (Feder, 1984; Leshner, 1978; Pfaff, 1982) have described the hormonal bases of receptive behavior in the rat. The female rat exhibits 4-5 day cycles of estrogen secretion from the ovaries. Estrogen secretion peaks just prior to sexual receptivity (estrus) whereas declines in estrogen secretion precede dietrus (a decline in sexual receptivity). Surgical removal of the ovaries (ovariectomy: OVX) reduces receptive sexual behavior in the female rat. Replacement of estrogen, employing exogenous injections, reverses the anestrus observed in the ovariectomized female rat (Davidson, Rogers, Smith and Bloch, 1968). Progesterone alone does not return receptivity to an ovariectomized rat but does facilitate the effect of estrogen on sexual receptivity. Typical replacement regimens call for estrogen to be given followed by progesterone. The purpose of the present exercise is to demonstrate the decrement in sexual receptivity exhibited by rats after ovariectomy and the influence of estrogen and progesterone replacement on sexual receptivity.

Materials
9 mm wound clips and applicator
Suture (Cat-gut) with traumatic needle
Scalpel handle (#3) with #10 blade
Hemostatic forceps
0.3 mg/ml atropine sulfate
42 mg/ml sodium pentobarbital (or anesthetic equivalent)
Iris scissors
Electric hair clippers
10 % alcohol solution
Watch or electronic clock
Small glass aquarium (lined with sawdust bedding)

Procedure

This exercise requires 2 adult (at least 90 days of age) female rats and 2 adult male rats each with prior sexual experience. You may wish to verify that both male and female rats are successful copulators a few days prior to beginning this experiment; this

Exercise 8: Sexual Receptivity

will also allow you to become familiar with the form of male and female sexual behavior in rodents (see description below). The female rats will then undergo bilateral surgical removal of the hormone-secreting ovaries.

Prepare each female rat for aseptic surgery. Atropinize each rat (0.3 mg/ml/kg atropine sulfate, ip) and then anesthetize each with 42 mg/ml/kg (ip) sodium pentobarbital (or anesthetic equivalent). Use the electric hair clippers to shave the fur on the abdomen and on each side of the body. Clean the incision sites using Betadyne and 10% alcohol. Position each rat on its side and make a 4 cm longitudinal incision of the skin using a sterile scalpel blade at a point 2-3 cm's off the midline and 1-2 cm's below the ribcage. Then use blunt dissection using the iris scissors to make a 3 cm long incision through the body wall and expose the peritoneal cavity. The ovaries of the rat are found laterally in the peritoneal cavity. Each ovary lies at the distal end of the Fallopian tube in a pocket of fat (refer to Figure E8.1). An aid to identifying the ovary is the identification of the ovarian artery and vein that run along the Fallopian tube. Use blunt forceps to gently extract the ovary from the peritoneal cavity. Use forceps and cat-gut suture material to tie a square-knot around the Fallopian tube and blood vessel just below the ovary. This knot must be tight as you will be cutting the ovarian blood vessels as you excise the ovary with the scalpel blade. Then cut the ovary from the Fallopian tube and check for bleeding; if any, tie another knot around the tube and then replace the Fallopian tube into the peritoneal cavity. Use suture to close the body wall (thereby preventing a hernia) and then use either suture or 9 mm wound clips to close the skin. Repeat the ovariectomy procedure on the other side of the body and then give the rat post-operative care. Upon recovery, return each rat to a home cage supplied with both food and water. Allow 3-5 days for the ovariectomized rats to recover from the surgery.

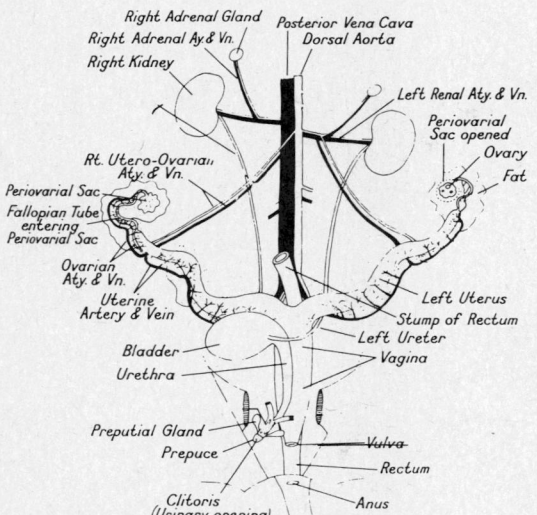

Figure E8.1. Location of the ovaries and the Fallopian tube within the abdominal cavity of the female rat. (Figure reprinted with permission from Wells, T.A.G. (1964). <u>The Rat, New York: Dover Publications.</u>)

Exercise 8: Sexual Receptivity

In the absence of ovarian hormones, the female rat exhibits diestrus, a state characterized by lack of receptivity to male sexual advances. Lordosis refers to the stereotyped arching of the back by a female (so as to elevate and expose the perineal area) in response to a male rat grasping the female's flanks from the rear (see Figure E8.2). An ovariectomized rat does not exhibit lordosis to flank stimulation; indeed, the female frequently does not allow the male to come close enough to stimulate the flanks.

To asssess the lordotic response of an ovariectomized female rat to a sexually experienced male rat, you will need to provide a quiet, dim test environment. Testing should be done in a glass aquarium provided with sawdust bedding on the floor. Always place the male rat into the test cage for 10 minutes prior to testing to allow for adaptation to the novel cues associated with a new environment. Then place an ovariectomized female into the test chamber with the male and start a 30 minute timer. During this period, you should quietly note the following:

a: the number of mounts exhibited by the male (a mount refers to the male approaching the female from the rear, grasping her flanks and then performing one-to five quick thrusts of the pelvis against the female's perineum).

b: the number of intromissions exhibited by the male. If the male succeeds in penetrating the vagina (intromission), he typically makes a single deep thrust and then, in a very non-human fashion, quickly dismounts from the female. This dismount is in fact a clinical sign that intromission has occurred. Following intromission, the male rat will engage in genital grooming (both his and hers) and then, after a few seconds, perform another mount and intromission (refer to Figure E8.2)

c: the number of ejaculations exhibited by the male. A male rat will frequently intromit 8-15 times prior to ejaculation. The clinical signs of ejaculation in the male rat include spasmodic quivering of the hindquarters, a very deep pelvic thrust and no dismount. Rather, the male rat will tightly grasp and lay quietly on the female for 1-3 seconds (refer to Figure E8.2). Following ejaculation, the male rat is refractory to further sexual stimulation for approximately 5 minutes.

d: the number of lordosis responses exhibited by the female during the 30 minute test period.

For a further description of male and female rodent sexual behavior, see the excellent descriptions by Bermant (1967) and Pfaff and Lewis (1974).

After verifying that the ovariectomized rats exhibit minimal sexual receptivity, an additional receptive test will follow replacement of the ovarian hormones. Your laboratory instructor will set a test day; you will inject your ovariectomized rats with 0.5 mg estradiol benzoate (intramuscular) 40 hours prior to the test. In addition, give an intramuscular injection of progesterone (1.0 mg in 0.4 ml peanut oil) five hours prior to

Exercise 8: Sexual Receptivity

the receptivity test. The oil serves to suspend the progesterone and to prolong absorption. The procedures used during this receptivity test should be identical to those of the baseline receptivity test.

Data Summary and Interpretation

Average the data from the two ovariectomized females prior to and following estrogen/progesterone replacement and depict in Table E8.1. Average the number of mounts by the male, the number of intromissions by the male, the number of ejaculations by the male and the number of lordotic responses by the female. In your experimental summary, contrast the sexual behavior exhibited by the females prior to and following estrogen replacement. How closely was the sexual behavior of the female tied to her hormonal state? In a similar vein, how closely was the sexual behavior of the male rat tied to the hormonal state of his female partner?

Table E8.1. Effect of estrogen/progesterone replacement on sexual behavior.

Replacement Hormone:	Lordosis #:	# Mounts	#Intromissions	#Ejaculations
None				
Estrogen/ Progesterone				

REFERENCES AND SUGGESTED READINGS

Beach, F.A. (1976). Sexual attractivity, proceptivity and receptivity in female mammals. Hormones and Behavior, 7, 105-138.

Bermant, G. (1967). Copulation in rats. Psychology Today, 1, 52-60.

Davidson, J.M., C.H. Rodgers, E.D. Smith and G.H. Bloch. (1968). Relative thresholds of behavior and somatic responses to estrogen. Physiology and Behavior, 3, 227-229.

Feder, H.H. (1984). Hormones and sexual behavior. The Annual Review of Psychology,, 35, 165-200.

Leshner, A.I. (1978). An Introduction to Behavioral Endocrinology, New York: Oxford University Press.

Pfaff, D.W. (1982). Neurobiological mechanisms of sexual motivation. In: Pfaff, D.W. (Ed). The Physiological Mechanisms of Motivation , New York: Springer-Verlag.

Pfaff, D.W. and C. Lewis. (1974). Film analyses of lordosis in female rats. Hormones and Behavior, 5, 317-335.

Exercise 8: Sexual Receptivity

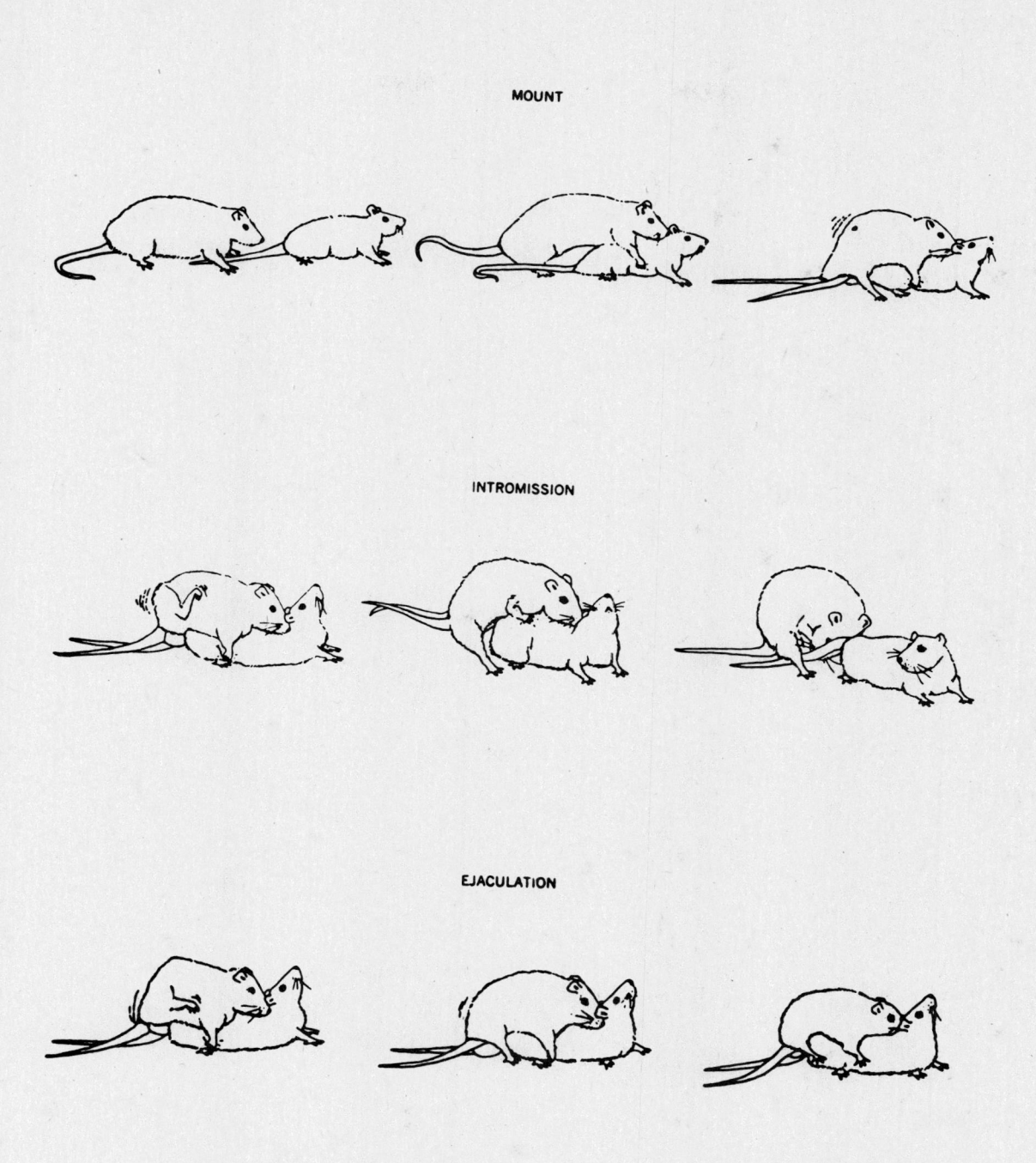

Figure E8.2. Sexual behavior of the female rat including lordosis (center) and of the male rat including mount (top), intromission (center) and ejaculation (bottom). (Reprinted with permission from Bermant, G. (1967). Copulation in rats. Psychology Today, 1, 52-60.)

Exercise 8: Sexual Receptivity

Exercise 9
Thirst Induced by Intraventricular Angiotensin II in Rats

<u>Background and Problem</u>

Depletion of extracellular volume (hypovolemia) results in thirst and consequently, the restoration of vascular volume. The neural and hormonal events that produce hypovolemic thirst include stimulation of left atrial baroreceptors and the release of renin from the kidneys. Renin is the substrate which converts plasma angiotensinogen into Angiotensin I which is then converted to Angiotensin II (AII). The latter peptides are known to produce drinking when infused either intravenously or into the ventricles of the brain (Phillips, 1978).

The precise location of the receptors for AII is controversial. That AII receptors reside within the brain is supported by the fact that the dose of AII required to induce drinking is a thousand fold higher for intravenous infusion than when infused into the ventricles of the brain (Phillips, 1978). Two ventricular sites have been indicated as possible locations that may contain AII receptors. These sites, the subfornical organ (SFO) and the organum vasculosum, lamina terminalis (OVLT), have an incomplete blood-brain barrier. Peripherally circulating AII might therefore stimulate central receptors via one or both of these ventricular organs. Current evidence seems to favor the suggestion that AII receptors reside within the subfornical organ (Lind et al., 1984; Simpson et al., 1976).

The purpose of the present exercise is to demonstrate the drinking response induced by unilateral infusion of AII. The target site for AII in this exercise will be the anterior lateral ventricle (refer to Figure E9.1). Although the anteroventral third ventricle is

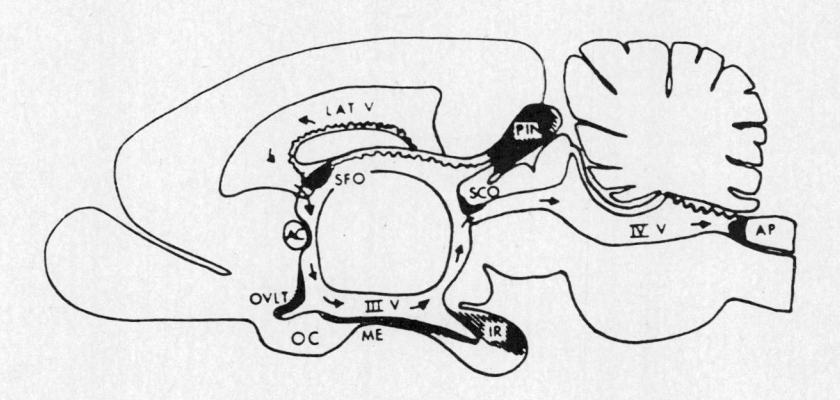

Figure E9. 1. The rat ventricular system. Depicted are the lateral ventricle (Lat V.), the subfornical organ (SFO), the organum vasculosum lamina terminalis (OVLT), the third ventricle (IIIV) and the 4th ventricle (IV V). (Figure reprinted with permission from Phillips, M.I. (1978). Angiotensin in the brain. <u>Neuroendocrinology</u>, 25 354-377).

Exercise 9: Angiotensin and Thirst

reportedly more sensitive to AII than the lateral ventricle, the former site involves implanting the cannula near the midline thereby damaging the midsaggital sinus. In this procedure you will stereotaxically implant a cannula within the rat brain and then assess the effects of AII injections into the ventricle on thirst. Variables of interest here will be the latency to drink (in seconds) following AII infusion and the determination of the dose-response curve for AII drinking.

Materials
  Electric hair clippers
  Vaseline or mineral oil
  #3 scalpel with #10 blade
  22 gauge guide cannula (Plastics One C313-G)
  28 gauge internal injection cannula (Plastics One C313-GC)
   10-microliter syringe (Hamilton #701)
  Cannula connector cable (Plastics One C313-C)
  Dental acrylic powder and liquid
  Spatula and watchglass
  Jewelers screws
  Curved forceps
  Scissors (5 inch)
  Hemostatic forceps
  Medium drill bit and variable-speed drill
  Stereotaxic unit with ear plugs
  Furacin powder
  0.3 mg/ml atropine sulfate
  42 mg/ml sodium pentobarbital
  Cotton balls
  9 mm wound clips and applicator
  Calibrated drinking tubes individual drinking test cages
  AII solutions (Sigma Chemical: 1, 10 50 and 100 nanograms/microliter)
  Cyanoacrylate glue (Superglue)
  Stop watch or electronic clock

Procedure
    This exercise will require two male rats each weighing approxmiately 300 grams. Prepare each rat for aseptic surgery. On the day of surgery, weigh each rat, inject it with 1.0 mg/ml/kg (ip) atropine sulfate and anesthetise it with sodium pentobarbital (42 mg/ml/kg, ip). Shave the scalp and around the ears and then cut the membrane below the external auditory meatus. Place Vaseline or mineral oil over the eyes and identify each rat with tape around the base of the tail.

    The surgical procedure of implanting a cannula is described in Chapter 4 and should be performed on each rat. Mount the rat's head in the earbars of the stereotaxic instrument and center the ear bars. Clean and incise the scalp and scrape the skull free of periosteum. Clean and dry the skull using cotton balls. Skull bleeding can be

Exercise 9: Angiotensin and Thirst

controlled using pressure from a forceps wrapped in cotton.

Mount the cannula in the stereotaxic carrier arm and verify that the cannula is parallel to the carrier arm. Because this exercise will use coordinates derived from the Pellegrino, Pellegrino and Cushman (1979) atlas, the instrument zero readings will be those of bregma. Before you determine the coordinates for height, verify that the upper incisor bar of the instrument is set at +5.0 mm above the interaural line. The atlas coordinates will be:

AP= 1.0 mm anterior to bregma
L= 1.6 mm lateral from the midline
H= 5.5 mm below the skull

Now choose the side of the brain within which you will implant the cannula. Roughen the skull by drilling a number of half-holes into the skull. Determine the coordinates at which you will position the cannula. Mark the entry site for the cannula on the skull using the sharp tip of a pencil. Drill a hole through the entry site and then complete four holes near the entry site into which support screws can be secured. Control any fluid exiting from the skull holes using cotton swabs. Place a thin layer of cyanoacrylate glue over the clean skull and screws. After this layer has dried, begin the dental acrylic pedestal. Place the cannula at the final coordinates within the brain and finish building the pedestal around the cannula. Smooth the pedestal base so that rough edges do not irritate the rat's skin. After the pedestal is dry, remove the carrier arm and place the obdurator into the guide cannula so to keep the inner barrel of the cannula free of any obstruction.

Remove the hemostatic forceps and clean the scalp using sterile cotton swabs and saline. Apply Furacin to the scalp and then close the scalp around the pedestal using 9 mm wound clips. Check respiration and temperature frequently until the rat is conscious and moving. Allow 4-5 days of recovery from surgery with continuous access to food and water. You should handle your rat daily and check the healing of the wound around the pedestal. If signs of an infection appear, apply Furacin to the edges of the scalp and you may wish to give 2-3 days of penicillin treatment (120,000 units daily, IM).

The drinking test sequence will consist of daily tests 60 minutes in length. Remove each rat from the home cage. Lightly restrain the rat's head against your chest with your left hand and remove the cannula obdurator. Clean the obdurator and set it aside. During the first 3 tests, insert the injection cannula into the implanted cannula and infuse 1.0 microliter of .9% sterile saline into the ventricle over a 10 second period. Remove the injection cannula and replace the obdurator into the cannula. Place the rat into the home cage and note the fluid level in the calibrated drinking tube. A clock should be started when each rat is placed into the cage. Latency to drink is defined here as the time interval between placement into the cage and the appearance of the first bubble in the drinking tube. At the end of the 60 minute period, again note the fluid level and calculate the amount of fluid consumed. These values, when averaged across

Exercise 9: Angiotensin and Thirst

the 3 days, will serve as the baseline values against which you will compare your AII infusion results.

The procedures for the AII tests will be identical to those of saline except that a 1.0 microliter infusion (over 10 seconds) of one of the AII doses will be given in place of saline. Because you wish to construct a dose-response curve but will be giving each rat each of the doses, you must assess whether there are any carryover effects of AII from day to day. One technique is to alternate drug and saline tests as in the following:

AII-Sal-AII-Sal-AII

On each drug test day, each rat will receive an infusion of one of AII doses (1, 10, 50 and 100 nanogram/microliter). Note that each rat will receive all doses of AII. These solutions are prepared by dissolving either 1, 10, 50 or 100 milligrams of AII into 1 microliter of sterile 0.9% saline. Fill a 10 microliter syringe with one of the solutions; always flush the syringe several times with distilled water before using a different dose level in the syringe. You should randomly determine the order of dose infusion. On the intervening days, again infuse saline and note whether baseline latency to drink and the amount consumed during a 60 minute period are different from the baseline measures collected prior to the AII sequence. Finally, you should note that in these tests, you are assessing the effect of AII on drinking behavior in a satiated rat. Thus, each rat should have free access to food and water between the tests. Only water should be available in the test cage during the daily 60 minute test.

As always, your data are not meaningful until you have verified the placement of your cannula in the brain. A simple technique for this is to inject 1.0 ul of cresyl violet (5% solution) into the cannula. Immediately thereafter, sacrifice each rat with an overdose of sodium pentobarbital and remove the brain (after perfusion) for histology. If the cannula was properly positioned within the lateral ventricle, you should observe the presence of cresyl violet within the lateral ventricle at histology.

<u>Data Summary and Interpretation</u>
Calculate the average latency to drink (in seconds) and the average amount of fluid consumed (in mls) during a 60 minute session for the saline tests and for each of the AII tests. Graph these data using figures similar to those depicted in Figure E9.2. What was the threshold dose for drinking to AII? (i.e. at what dose level did drinking to AII exceed that observed after saline?). Another measure of threshold is the latency to drink; here, the threshold would refer to that dose at which the latency to drink after AII is shorter than that after saline. To compare the sensitivity of your preparation, compare your data with the curve provided by Phillips (1978: Figure 4).

Exercise 9: Angiotensin and Thirst

REFERENCES AND SUGGESTED READINGS

Johnson, A.K. (1975). The cerebral ventricles as the avenue for the dipsogenic action of intracranial angiotensin. Brain Research, 86, 339-418.

Lind, R.W., R.L. Thunhorst and A.K. Johnson. (1984). The subfornical organ and the integration of multiple factors in thirst. Physiology and Behavior, 32, 69-74.

Phillips, M.I. (1978). Angiotensin in the brain. Neuroendocrinology, 25, 354-377.

Simpson, J.B., A.N. Epstein and J.S. Camardo. (1978). The localization of dipsogenic receptors for angiotensin II in the subfornical organ. Journal of comparative and physiological Psychology, 92, 581-608.

Exercise 9: Angiotensin and Thirst

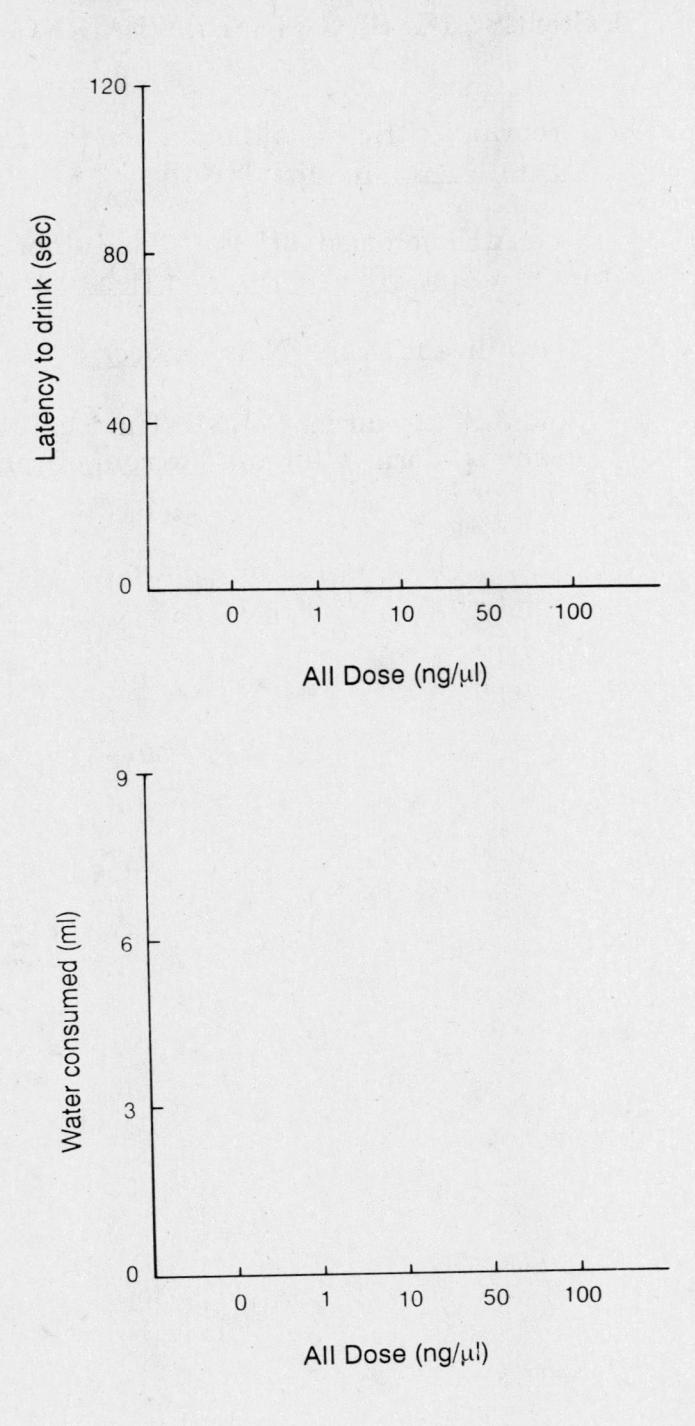

Figure E9.2. Graphic axes for the data of Exercise 9. Top panel: latency to drink (seconds) after infusion into the lateral ventricle of various concentrations of angiotensin II (AII). Bottom panel: volume of water consumed (mls) after angiotensin II.

Exercise 9: Angiotensin and Thirst

Stereotaxic Surgery Record Sheet

Student Name: _____

Animal Number:

Strain:

Age:

Sex:

Weight:

   Preoperative:
   Operative:
   Post-operative

Operation Date:

Anesthesia:

   Volume:
   Type:

Atlas Coordinates: AP: H: L:

Instrument Zero: AP: H: L:

Final Coordinates: AP: H: L:

Surgery Comments:
   Type:
   Upper Incisor Bar at: _____ mm
   Intended Structure-
   Stereotaxic Atlas:

Sacrifice date :

Histology Results:

Exercise 9: Angiotensin and Thirst

Stereotaxic Surgery Record Sheet

Student Name: _____

Animal Number:

Strain:

Age:

Sex:

Weight:

    Preoperative:
    Operative:
    Post-operative

Operation Date:

Anesthesia:

    Volume:
    Type:

Atlas Coordinates: AP: H: L:

Instrument Zero: AP: H: L:

Final Coordinates: AP: H: L:

Surgery Comments:
    Type:
    Upper Incisor Bar at: _____ mm
    Intended Structure-
    Stereotaxic Atlas:

Sacrifice date :

Histology Results:

Exercise 10
Hypothalamic Adrenergic Receptors and Feeding in Rats

Background and Problem

Grossman (1962) noted that the introduction of exogenous norepinephrine (NE) into the brain was sufficient to stimulate feeding whereas introduction of acetylcholine would stimulate drinking. Further studies of the effects of NE on the stimulation of feeding noted that the paraventricular nucleus of the hypothalamus (PVN: see Figure E10.1) is a focal point for this effect. Injections of NE into the PVN stimulate feeding in a dose-dependent fashion (Leibowitz, 1978). Moreover, NE is believed to stimulate feeding by activating $\alpha 2$-adrenergic receptors located on post-synaptic membranes of neurons within the PVN. NE as well as other drugs which activate the $\alpha 2$ receptor stimulate feeding when injected into the PVN. In contrast, drugs that inactivate the $\alpha 2$-adrenergic receptor prevent the feeding stimulatory effects of injecting NE in the PVN (Leibowitz, 1988; Goldman et al., 1985).

Norepinephrine is an inhibitory neurotransmitter which acts by producing an inhibitory post-synaptic potential (Kow and Pfaff, 1989). An interesting issue in understanding its effects on feeding is to suppose that NE inhibits an inhibitory feeding system in order to stimulate food intake (Hoebel and Leibowitz, 1981). Support for this idea comes from studies in which lesions of the PVN produce overeating and obesity (Leibowitz, Hammer and Chang, 1981). If NE acts to inhibit PVN cells, what would excitation of these cells do to feeding? The PVN also contains $\alpha 1$-receptors (Leibowitz et al., 1982). These receptors are activated by drugs such as phenylephrine or methoxamine. Injection of these $\alpha 1$-adrenergic agonists into the PVN results in the suppression of feeding (Wellman, et al., 1993).

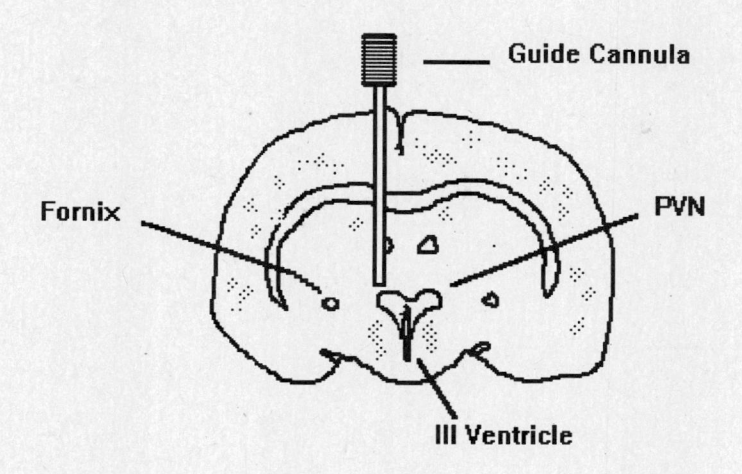

Figure E10.1. A coronal section through the hypothalamus illustrating the position of a guide cannula which terminates above the paraventricular nucleus (PVN).

Exercise 10: Norepinephrine and Feeding

The purpose of the present exercise is to explore the effects of injections of various α-adrenergic agonists into the rat PVN on feeding. You will prepare two rats with a unilateral cannula aimed at the PVN. You will assess the feeding stimulatory effects of NE when injected into the PVN (an α2-adrenergic receptor effect) and the inhibitory effects on feeding of phenylephrine when injected into the PVN (an α1-adrenergic receptor effect). Additional information regarding drug injection procedures can be found in Routtenberg, 1972) and in Leibowitz and Myers, (1987).

Materials
   Electric hair clippers
   Vaseline or mineral oil
   #3 scalpel with #10 blade
   22 gauge guide cannula (Plastics One C313-G)
   28 gauge internal injection cannula (Plastics One C313-GC)
   10-microliter syringe (Hamilton #701)
   Cannula connector cable (Plastics One C313-C)
   Dental acrylic powder and liquid
   Spatula and watchglass
   Jewelers screws
   Curved forceps
   Scissors (5 inch)
   Hemostatic forceps
   Medium drill bit and variable-speed drill
   Stereotaxic unit with ear plugs
   Furacin powder
   0.3 mg/ml atropine sulfate
   42 mg/ml sodium pentobarbital
   Cotton balls
   9 mm wound clips and applicator
   NE solutions (Sigma Chemical: 2, 4 and 6 mg/ml)
   Phenylephrine solutions (Sigma Chemical: 10, 20 and 40 mg/ml).
   Cyanoacrylate glue (Superglue)
   Stop watch or electronic clock

Procedure
   Surgery. This exercise will require two male rats each weighing approximately 300 grams. Prepare each rat for aseptic surgery. Inject each rat with 0.3 mg/ml/kg (ip) atropine sulfate and anesthetize it with sodium pentobarbital (42 mg/ml/kg, ip). Shave the scalp and around the ears and then cut the membrane below the external auditory meatus. Place Vaseline or mineral oil over the eyes and identify each rat with tape around the base of the tail.

   Each rat will undergo a surgical procedure in which a guide cannula is implanted above the PVN using stereotaxic procedures described in Chapter 4. Mount the rat's

Exercise 10: Norepinephrine and Feeding

head in the earbars of the stereotaxic instrument and center the ear bars. Clean and incise the scalp and scrape the skull free of periosteum. Clean and dry the skull using cotton swabs. Skull bleeding can be controlled using pressure from a forceps wrapped in sterile cotton.

You will be using a metal cannula 10 mm in length (tip to base of cannula). The cannula should be cut in such a way that the injector extends 1.0 mm beyond the cannula tip. The coordinates were chosen in such a way that the cannula tip will be positioned in the brain 1.0 mm above the PVN. The obdurator should be cut so that it is flush with the cannula tip.

Mount the cannula in the stereotaxic carrier arm and verify that the cannula is parallel to the carrier arm. Because this exercise will use coordinates derived from the Pellegrino, Paxinos and Watson (1986) atlas, the instrument zero readings will be those of bregma. Before you determine the coordinates for height, verify that the upper incisor bar of the instrument is set at 5.0 mm above the interaural line. The atlas coordinates will be:

> AP= 0.4 mm posterior to bregma
> L= 0.3 mm lateral from the midline
> H= 7.8 mm below the skull

Now choose the side of the brain within which you will implant the cannula. Roughen the skull by drilling a number of half-holes into the skull. Determine the coordinates at which you will position the cannula. Mark the entry site for the cannula on the skull using the sharp tip of a pencil. Drill a hole through the entry site and then complete four holes near the entry site into which support screws can be secured. Control any fluid exiting from the skull holes using sterile cotton swabs. Place a thin layer of cyanoacrylate glue over the clean skull and screws. After this layer has dried, build up the dental acrylic pedestal in a circle around the skull hole. Lower the cannula through the skull hole and position it at the final height coordinates within the brain. Now encase the cannula with dental acrylic and complete the pedestal around the cannula. Smooth the pedestal base so that rough edges do not irritate the rat's skin. After the pedestal is dry, remove the carrier arm from the guide cannula and place the obdurator into the guide cannula so to keep the inner barrel of the cannula free of any obstruction.

Remove the hemostatic forceps and clean the scalp using sterile cotton swabs. Apply Furacin to the scalp and then close the scalp around the pedestal using 9 mm wound clips. Check respiration and temperature frequently until the rat is conscious and moving. Allow 4-5 days of recovery from surgery with continuous access to food and water. You should handle your rat daily and check the healing of the wound around the pedestal. If signs of an infection appear, apply Furacin to the edges of the scalp and you may wish to give 2-3 days of penicillin treatment (120,000 units daily, im).

Exercise 10: Norepinephrine and Feeding

Food Intake Tests.

The feeding test sequence will consist of daily tests 30 minutes in length. To avoid having to food deprive the rats in order to have a reasonable amount of food consumption during baseline procedures, you should conduct your tests in the late afternoon prior to lights off (Davies and Wellman, 1992). At this time of day, the rats spontaneously consume 0.5-1.5 g meals when offered fresh food. This baseline value is important because in these tests you will be examining drug effects which both increase (NE) and suppress (phenylephrine) food intake.

Remove each rat from the home cage. Lightly restrain the rat's head against your chest with your left hand and remove the cannula obdurator. Clean the obdurator and set it aside. During the first 3 tests, insert the injection cannula into the implanted cannula and infuse 1.0 microliter of 0.9% sterile saline into the PVN over a 10 second period. Leave the injector in place for 50 seconds before removing; this will allow time for the solution to diffuse away from the cannula tip. Remove the injection cannula and replace the obdurator into the cannula. Place the rat into the home cage and note the fluid level in the calibrated drinking tube. A clock should be started when each rat is placed into the cage. Place the rat in a clean cage and provide the rat with about 15 grams of food placed on the cage floor 5 minutes after the end of the injection. Water should be available during the feeding test. At the end of the 30 minute period, remove the food pellets and any spillage from the cage floor and subtract this amount from the value recorded at the start of the trial. These values, when averaged across the 3 days, will serve as the baseline values against which you will compare your NE and phenylephrine infusion results.

The procedures for the NE tests and phenylephrine tests will be identical to those of the saline tests except that a 1.0 microliter infusion (over 10 seconds) of one of the NE or phenylephrine doses will be given in place of saline. For one rat, give the NE test series first, with the other rat receiving the phenylephrine test series. Each rat will receive all doses of each drug. For each rat, randomly select the dose order for each drug. To avoid carryover effects, place a non-drug trial between each drug trial. An example of a drug test sequence might look like that depicted in Table E10.1.

On each drug test day, prepare fresh drug solutions. This is particularly important for NE which will oxidize and lose potency over several days. The NE solutions are prepared by dissolving 2, 4 or 6 mg NE into 1 milliliter of sterile 0.9% saline. The phenylephrine solutions are similarly prepared using 10, 20 and 40 mg in 1 ml of saline. Fill a microliter syringe with one of the solutions; always flush the syringe several times with distilled water before using a different dose level in the syringe. Note that when you prepare a solution of 2 mg/ml and then inject 1.0 uL into brain, there will be 2 ug in each uL injected. Remember to allow a 5 minute interval between the end of the drug injection and the start of the drug trial.

Exercise 10: Norepinephrine and Feeding

Finally, you should note that in these tests, you are assessing the effect of NE and phenylephrine on feeding behavior in a satiated rat. Thus, each rat should have free access to food and water between the tests.

Table E10.1. A tentative schedule of drug injection for Exercise 10.

Days:	Rat 1	Rat 2
1	NE-2	PHEN-20
2	NO DRUG	NO DRUG
3	NE-4	PHEN-10
4	NO DRUG	NO DRUG
5	NE-6	PHEN-40
6	NO DRUG	NO DRUG
7	PHEN-10	NE-6
8	NO DRUG	NO DRUG
9	PHEN-20	NE-4
10	NO DRUG	NO DRUG
11	PHEN-40	NE-2

As always, your data are not meaningful until you have verified the placement of your cannula. After the last trial, sacrifice each rat with an overdose of sodium pentobarbital and remove the brain (after perfusion) for histology. Note whether the cannula was properly positioned above the PVN.

Data Summary and Interpretation

Calculate the average amount of food consumed (in grams) during a 30 minute session for the saline tests and for each of the α1- and α2-adrenergic agonists. Average the food intake values for each of the drug trials and depict these averages in the figure (E10.2) provided for this exercise. Describe the effects of these agonists on food intake. Did NE stimulate feeding? What was the threshold dose for this effect? Did phenylephrine suppress feeding? What was the threshold dose for this effect? Was it possible to calculate an ED50 value for these effects (i.e. the dose required to produce a half-maximal stimulation of feeding or to supress feeding by 50%).

Exercise 10: Norepinephrine and Feeding

REFERENCES AND SUGGESTED READINGS

Davies, B.T., P.J. Wellman, B. DiCarlo. (1992). Microinjection of the α1-agonist methoxamine into the paraventricular induces anorexia in rats. Brain Research Bulletin, 28, 633-635.

Davies, B.T., and P.J. Wellman. (1992). Effects on ingestive behavior in rats of the α1-adrenoceptor agonist cirazoline. European Journal of Pharmacology, 210, 11-16.

Goldman, C.K., L. Marino and S.F. Leibowitz (1985). Postsynaptic alpha2-adrenergic receptors in the paraventricular nucleus mediate feeding induced by norepinephrine and clonidine. European Journal of Pharmacology, 115, 11-19.

Grossman, S.P. (1962). Direct adrenergic and cholinergic stimulation of hypothalamic mechanisms. American J. Physiology, 202, 872-882.

Hoebel, B.G. and S.F. Leibowitz (1981). Brain monoamines in the modulation of self-stimulation, feeding and body weight. In: H. Weiner, M.A. Hofer and A.J. Stunkard (Eds)., Brain, Behavior and Disease, New York: Raven Press.

Kow, L.M. and D.W. Pfaff. (1989). Responses of hypothalamic parventricular neurons in vitro to norepinephrine and other feeding-relevant agents. Physiology and Behavior, 46, 265-271.

Leibowitz, S.F. (1978). Paraventricular nucleus: A primary site mediating adrenergic stimulation of feeding and drinking. Pharmacology, Biochemistry and Behavior, 8, 163-175.

Leibowitz, S.F. (1988). Hypothalamic paraventricular nucleus: Interaction between α2--noradrenergic system and circulating hormones and nutrients in relation to energy balance. Neurosciencce and Biobehavioral Reviews, 12, 101-109.

Leibowitz, S.F., N.J. Hammer and K. Chang. (1981). Paraventricular nucleus lesions produce overeating and obesity in the rat. Physiology and Behavior, 27, 1031-1040.

Leibowitz, S.F., M. Jhanwar-Uniyal, B. Dworkin, and M.H. Makman. (1982). Distribution of α-adrenergic, ß-adrenergic and dopaminergic receptors in discrete hypothalamic areas of rat. Brain Research, 233, 97-114.

Leibowitz, S.F. and R.D. Myers. (1987). The neurochemistry of ingestion: Chemical stimulation of the brain and in vivo measurement of transmitter release. In: F.M. Toates and N.E. Rowland (Eds.), Feeding and Drinking, Amsterdam: Elsevier.

Routtenberg, A. (1972). Intracranial chemical injection and behavior: A critical review. Behavioral Biology, 1, 601-641.

Exercise 10: Norepinephrine and Feeding

Wellman, P.J. and B.T. Davies, (1991), Suppression of Feeding Induced by phenylephrine microinjections within the paraventricular hypothalamus in rats. Appetite, 17, 121-128.

Wellman, P.J., B.T. Davies, A. Morien and L. McMahon (1993). Modulation of feeding by hypothalamic paraventricular nucleus α1- and α2-adrenergic receptors. Life Science, 53, 699-680.

Exercise 10: Norepinephrine and Feeding

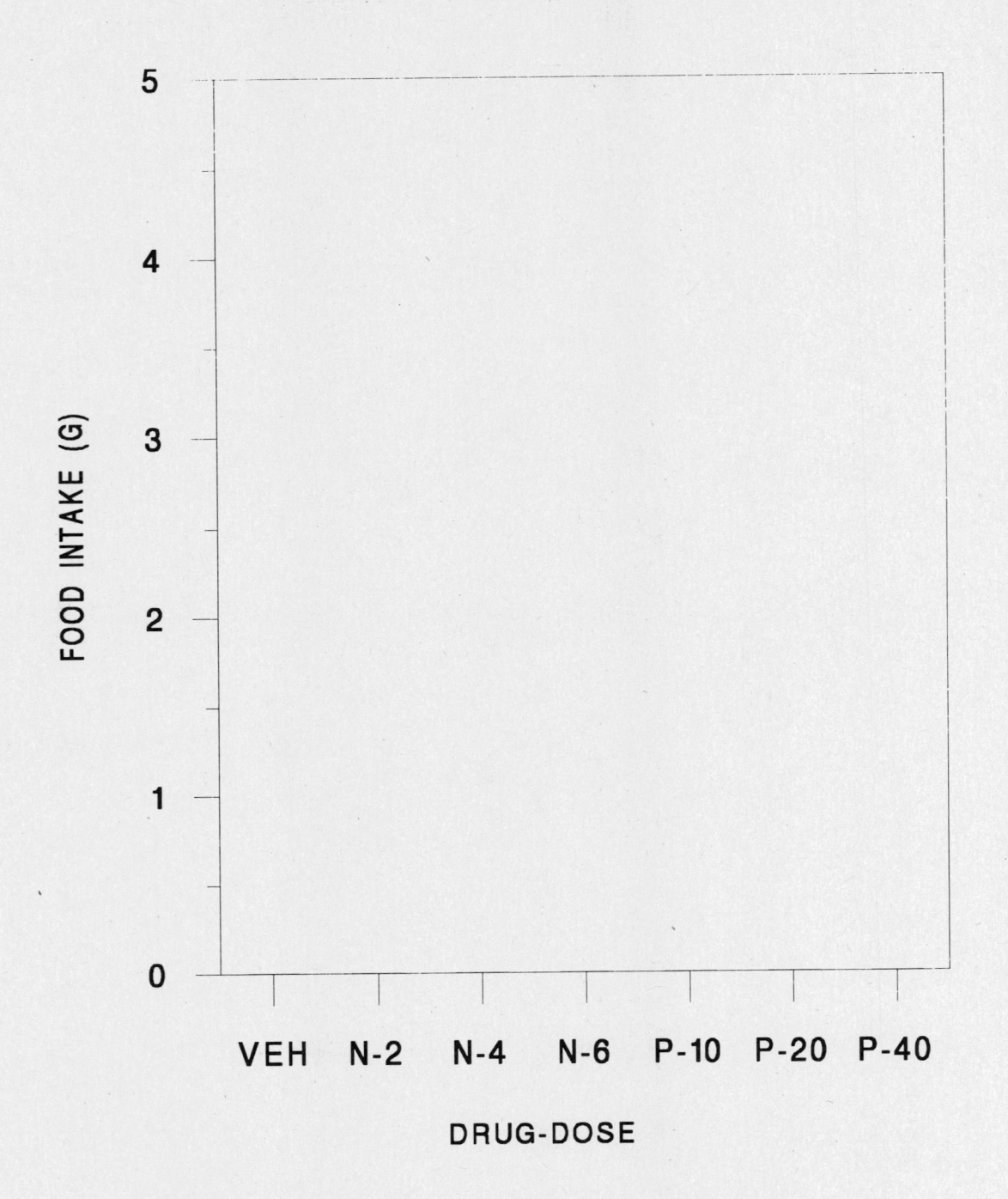

E10.2. Graphic axes used to depict the effects of intra-PVN injection of norepinephrine (N: 2, 4 and 6 ug/uL) and of phenylephrine (P: 10, 20 and 40 ug/uL).

Exercise 10: Norepinephrine and Feeding

Stereotaxic Surgery Record Sheet

Student Name: _____

Animal Number:

Strain:

Age:

Sex:

Weight:

   Preoperative:
   Operative:
   Post-operative

Operation Date:

Anesthesia:

  Volume:
  Type:

Atlas Coordinates: AP: H: L:

Instrument Zero: AP: H: L:

Final Coordinates: AP: H: L:

Surgery Comments:
   Type:
   Upper Incisor Bar at: _____ mm
   Intended Structure-
   Stereotaxic Atlas:

Sacrifice date :

Histology Results:

Exercise 10: Norepinephrine and Feeding

Stereotaxic Surgery Record Sheet

Student Name: _____

Animal Number:

Strain:

Age:

Sex:

Weight:

   Preoperative:
   Operative:
   Post-operative

Operation Date:

Anesthesia:

  Volume:
  Type:

Atlas Coordinates: AP: H: L:

Instrument Zero: AP: H: L:

Final Coordinates: AP: H: L:

Surgery Comments:
  Type:
  Upper Incisor Bar at: _____ mm
  Intended Structure-
  Stereotaxic Atlas:

Sacrifice date :

Histology Results:

Exercise 10: Norepinephrine and Feeding

Stereotaxic Surgery Record Sheet

Student Name: _____

Animal Number:

Strain:

Age:

Sex:

Weight:

   Preoperative:
   Operative:
   Post-operative

Operation Date:

Anesthesia:

  Volume:
  Type:

Atlas Coordinates: AP: H: L:

Instrument Zero: AP: H: L:

Final Coordinates: AP: H: L:

Surgery Comments:
   Type:
   Upper Incisor Bar at: _____ mm
   Intended Structure-
   Stereotaxic Atlas:

Sacrifice date :

Histology Results:

Exercise 10: Norepinephrine and Feeding

Stereotaxic Surgery Record Sheet

Student Name: _____

Animal Number:

Strain:

Age:

Sex:

Weight:

    Preoperative:
    Operative:
    Post-operative

Operation Date:

Anesthesia:

    Volume:
    Type:

Atlas Coordinates: AP: H: L:

Instrument Zero: AP: H: L:

Final Coordinates: AP: H: L:

Surgery Comments:
    Type:
    Upper Incisor Bar at: _____ mm
    Intended Structure-
    Stereotaxic Atlas:

Sacrifice date :

Histology Results:

Exercise 11
Effects of Bombesin on Feeding and Drinking

Background and Problem
   Peptides which consist of short chains of amino acids are found within the brain and the gut and are believed to influence neuron function (cf. Kreiger, 1983). Within the last 15 years, an ever-increasing number of peptides have been identified within discrete brain areas and most importantly, have been found to exert control over behavior. The purpose of the present exercise is to examine the effect of a peptide termed Bombesin on behavior. Bombesin (BBS) was first isolated from frog skin and subsequently was found both within the gut and the brain.

   Bombesin has dramatic effects on lowering both blood pressure and body temperature (Brown, Rivier and Vale, 1977). Moreover, infusion of bombesin into rat gut causes a reduction of feeding (anorexia) as does bombesin infusion within the rat lateral hypothalamus (LH) (Gibbs et al., 1979; Gibbs, Kulkosky and Smith, 1981; Stuckey and Gibbs, 1982). The anorexic action of bombesin has been observed in humans (Lieverse et al., 1993) and infusion of specific bombesin receptor antagonists produce an increase in feeding (Merali, Moody and Coy, 1993). These effects suggest that bombesin may serve to limit human appetite (Smith and Gibbs, 1992).

   The purpose of this exercise is to document the anorexic action of BBS when injected into the intraperitoneal cavity of the rat. An anorexic effect may reflect a true reduction of hunger (a motivational state referred to as "satiety") or may reflect nausea, discomfort or disablity (recall your lack of motivation to eat or drink when you suffered from motion sickness...). In the present exercise, you will measure feeding and drinking behaviors in rats treated with saline and with several doses of bombesin (4, 8 ug/kg) to determine whether the action of bombesin is specific to the suppression of feeding.

Materials
   Individual rodent cages with wire floors
   Paper towels (used to collect spillage under each cage floor)
   Rodent chow (pellet form)
   Drinking tubes (calibrated to 1.0 ml)
   1 cc tuberculin injection syringes with 27 gauge needles
   0.9% saline solution
   0, 4 and 8 ug/ml Bombesin solutions (Sigma Chemical; prepare
       prior to injection)
   Laboratory balance (capable of weighing food to 0.1 gram)

Procedure
   Your lab instructor will provide you with 3 rats for this exercise. The rats will be comparable in terms of age, sex, body weight and prior experimental experiences. You

Exercise 11: Bombesin and Ingestion

should weigh each rat daily throughout the study. Each rat will be tested in an individual cage supplied with a weighed amount of food pellets placed on the cage floor and a drinking tube (filled with tap water) positioned so that the drinking spout extends into the test cage. Position a paper towel beneath the test cage to catch both excreta (to be discarded) and food crumbs (to be weighed). On each of the 7 baseline test days (see schedule below), weigh each rat and then place it in the test cage for 30 minutes. You should record the beginning volume of the drinking tube to the nearest 1.0 ml (be sure that you read the bottom of the meniscus of the water level). At the end of the test period, return the rat to the home cage and then weigh the food remaining in the cage and the spillage beneath the cage for each rat. The difference between the initial weight of the food and leftover food and spillage is the amount of food consumed. Record the final volume of the water tube: the difference between the initial and final volume is the water consumed. Food and water are only available during the daily 30 minute feeding test. You should make certain that the rats are given bedding but neither food nor water during the 23.5 hour interval between tests. To accustom the rats to the injection procedures, baseline food intakes are recorded on Days 5, 6 and 7 as before except that each rat should be injected with 1.0 ml/kg 0.9% saline (ip) 30 minutes prior to each intake test.

In this study, you will test the effect of various dose levels of bombesin on feeding and drinking in these rats. There are two designs one could use in this study: a between-group design or a within-group design (for a discussion of these designs, refer to Christensen, 1994). In a between-group design, you would inject different groups of rats with the different dose levels. The between-group design involves only one drug test day but uses a large number of animals (i.e. a test with 3 doses and 3 rats per group would require 9 rats). In contrast, a within-group design uses fewer animals but more tests. That is, rather than testing separate groups of animals, each rat receives each test injection. Here you would use only 3 rats but would examine their behavior in 3 different tests (saline, 4, 8 ug/kg bombesin). To prevent problems associated with drug order (i.e. the effect of a drug dose depends on what drug dose was given on the preceding day), you will randomly administer the drug levels. To reduce the problem of drug carryover effects (i.e. the drug effect spans one or more days), you will interpose several saline test days (Days 9,10) between the bombesin tests (Day 8 and Day 11). The test sequence is summarized below:

Trials: Test Treatments/Measurements:

Trials	Test Treatments/Measurements
1, 2, 3, 4	Baseline Food/Water Measurements
5, 6, 7	Saline injected before each test
8	Bombesin test
9, 10	Saline injected before each test
11	Bombesin test

Exercise 11: Bombesin and Ingestion

Each rat will receive one of the BBS injection conditions (4 or 8 ug/kg BBS) on the drug test days. The intake procedures will be as before except that each rat will be injected with one of BBS dosages 30 minutes prior to the 30 minute test period.

Data Summary and Interpretation

Food intake: Calculate the mean group food intake (to the nearest 0.1 gram) for each injection condition for the three rats. The saline value can be calculated as the average of all saline tests (before the drug sequence and within the drug sequence). These values can be depicted using the graphic axes provided in Figure E11.1; use the left side of the figure to plot the food intake values and choose a symbol (e.g. o) to represent the food intake values. Your instructor will provide information on how to perform the statistical analyses of these data.

Water intake: Calculate the mean group water intake (to the nearest 1.0 ml) for each injection condition for the three rats. These values can be depicted using the right side of the graphic axes provided in Figure E11.1. Use a different symbol (e.g. X) to represent the water intake values.

The following discussion points should be addressed in your experiment summary:

Describe the effect of bombesin on food intake in rats. Relative to the food intake observed in the saline-treatment condition, did any of the BBS doses cause a reduction in food intake? If so, was the effect statistically significant? Was the effect related to the dose of BBS used (that is, did the effect become greater with a larger dose of bombesin?). You may wish to compare your results with those of Gibbs, Kulkosky and Smith (1981). Describe the action of bombesin on water intake and evaluate the results. Is the action of bombesin specific to feeding? If not, how would you explain the non-specific action of this peptide?

REFERENCES AND SUGGESTED READINGS

Brown, M., J. Rivier and W. Vale (1977). Bombesin: Potent effects on thermoregulation in the rat. Science, 196 , 998-1000.

Christensen, L. (1994). Experimental Methodology . Boston: Allyn and Bacon.

Gibbs, J., D.J. Faurer, E.A. Rowe, B.J. Rolls, E.T. Rolls and S.P. Maddison. (1979). Bombesin suppresses feeding in rats. Nature, 282, 208-210.

Gibbs, J., P.J. Kulkosky and G.P. Smith. (1981). Effects of peripheral and central bombesin on feeding behavior in the rat. Peptides Supplement 2, 179-183.

Kreiger, D.T. (1983). Brain peptides: What, Where and Why? Science, 222, 975-985.

Exercise 11: Bombesin and Ingestion

Lieverse, R.J., J.B. Jansen, A. van de Zwan, L. Samson, A.A. Masclee, L.C. Rovati, and C.B. Lamers. (1993). J. Clinical Endocrinology and Metabolism, 76, P1495-1498.

Merali, Z., T.W. Moody and D. Coy. (1993). Blockade of brain bombesin/GRP receptors increases food intake in satiated rats. American Journal of Physiology, 264, R1031-1034.

Smith, G.P. and J. Gibbs (1992). Are gut peptides a new class of anorectic agents? American J. Clinical Nutrition, 55, 283s-285s.

Stuckey, J.A. and J. Gibbs (1982). Lateral hypothalamic injection of bombesin decreases food intake in rats. Brain Research Bulletin, 8, 617-621.

Exercise 11: Bombesin and Ingestion

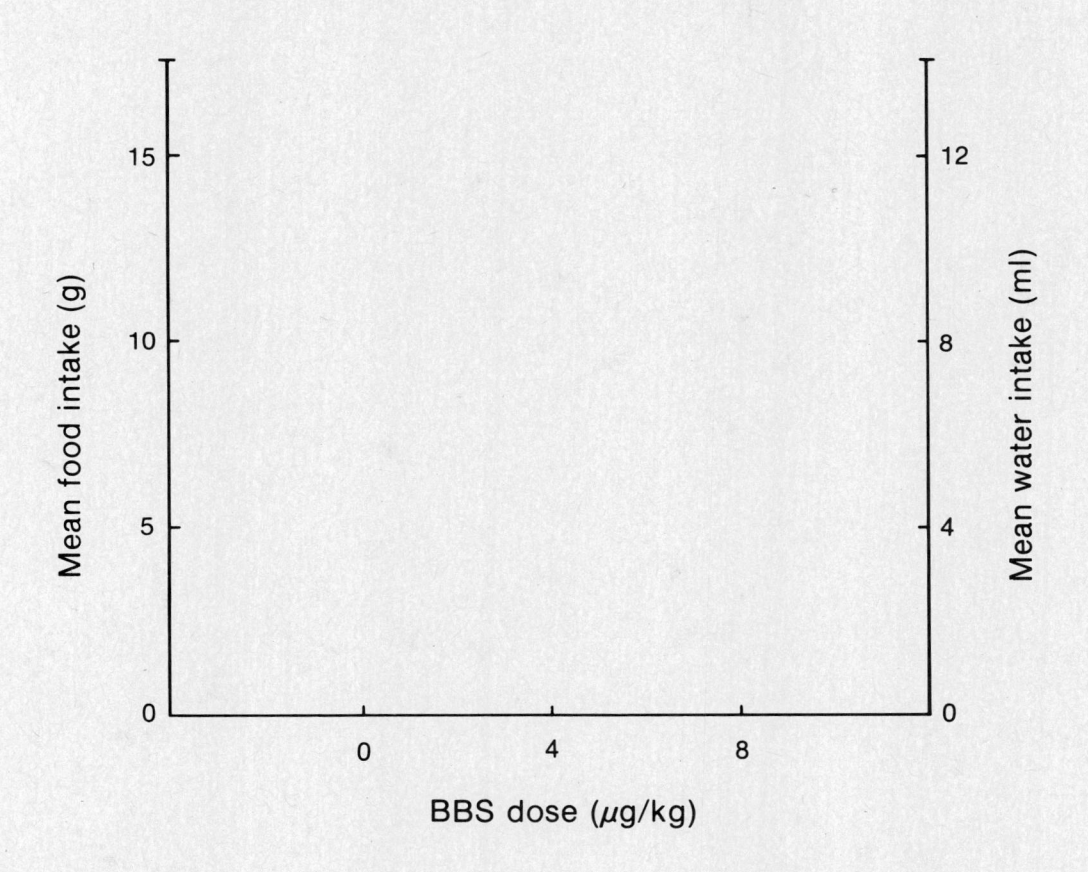

Figure E11.1: Graphic axes used to depict the effects of bombesin (BBS) on mean group food intake (left axis) and mean group water intake (right axis). The 0 dose of bombesin represents the saline treatment.

Exercise 11: Bombesin and Ingestion

Exercise 12
Emotional Behavior in the Septal Rat

Background and Problem

Rats sustaining electrolytic lesions of the medial and lateral septal nuclei exhibit a remarkable range of behavioral changes. These include: "freezing" in an open field, "rage" behavior when handled by human experimenters (Brady and Nauta, 1955), a sharp reduction in body weight (Beatty and Schwartzbaum, 1968), excessive reactivity to palatable saccharin solutions and bitter quinine solutions (Beatty and Schwartzbaum, 1968), hyperdipsia (Harvey and Hunt, 1965). Perhaps the most remarkable and unexpected behavioral change induced by septal lesions is the so-called "social cohesiveness" effect (Meyer, Ruth and LaVond, 1978). Although individual septal rats are frequently vicious when handled by a human experimenter, placement of a pair of septal rats into an arena results in vigorous and prolonged clinging of one septal rat to another rather than fighting as one would expect given the vicious reputation of these rats. This observation suggests that the septal region cannot simply be viewed as having inhibitory effects on emotional behavior.

The purpose of this exercise is to document the variety of behavioral changes that follow electrolytic damage to the septal nuclei in the rat. In particular, you will examine the effects of septal lesions on body weight, fluid intake (water, saccharin, and quinine) freezing in an open field (the tendency to remain motionless in an open field), and the so-called cohesiveness effect. You should review the material on stereotaxically-placed electrolytic lesions described in Chapter 4 prior to coming to the laboratory.

Materials
  Stereotaxic instrument and ear plugs
  Unipolar insulated electrode and electrode carrier
  1.0 mg/ml atropine sulfate
  42 mg/ml sodium pentobarbital or anesthetic equivalent
  Scissors (5 inch)
  Hemostatic forceps
  Scalpel blade (#3) with handle (#10)
  cotton balls
  9 mm wound clips and applicator
  Furacin powder
  bonewax and metal spatula
  dental drill and medium burr
  100 ml calibrated (1.0 ml gradations) drinking tubes
  individual drinking testing cages
  0.025% quinine hydrochloride solution (Sigma: 2.5 g per 1000 ml water)
  0.13% sodium saccharin (Sigma: 13 g per 1000 ml water)
  open field (see description below)
  stop watch or electronic clock

Exercise 12: Septum and Emotionality

Method

This exercise will require 8 rats (4 lesioned and 4 sham-surgery controls). The rats should be of the same sex and should weigh approximately 175 grams at the beginning of the experiment. Prepare the rats for aseptic stereotaxic surgery. Weigh each rat to the nearest gram on the day prior to surgery and the day of surgery. Each rat should be atropinized (0.3 mg/ml/kg, ip) and then anesthetized 10 minutes later with 42 mg/ml/kg (ip) sodium pentobarbital. Shave the scalp, cut the flap of tissue beneath the auditory meatus and then identify each rat using labelled tape wrapped around the tail.

The upper incisor bar of the stereotaxic instrument should be set to 2.4 mm below the interaural line such that the skull is level. Mount the skull in the stereotaxic frame using the ear plugs and then verify that the ear bars are centered. Clean and incise the scalp and retract the periosteum and scalp from the skull using the hemostatic forceps. The coordinates for the septal nuclei, as adapted from Thorne, Lin and Weaver (1983), are:

$$AP = 1.0 \text{ mm anterior to bregma}$$
$$H = 5.2 \text{ mm ventral to the surface of the skull}$$
$$L = 0.5 \text{ mm lateral from the midsagittal suture}$$

Record the coordinates for bregma, and then bring the electrode to the proper AP and lateral positions and mark the entry holes on the skull using the tip of a pencil. Drill the skull holes and verify that the electrode will clear both holes. Lower the electrode to the proper height and then connect the electrode to the lesion maker anode terminal. Insert a plug connected to the lesion maker cathode terminal into the rectum and pass 2.0 mA anodal current for 20 seconds. Repeat the lesion process on the other side of the brain for each rat. Clean the skull, seal the skull holes with bone wax, dust the skull with Furacin powder and then close the scalp wound using several 9 mm wound clips.

For the 4 sham surgery control rats, mount each rat in the stereotaxic frame, clean and incise the scalp, drill the skull holes and lower the electrode to the proper height on each side of the brain. Clean the skull, seal the skull holes with bone wax and then dust the skull with Furacin powder and close the scalp using 9 mm wound clips. As always, give each rat adequate postoperative recovery care. After each rat has recovered from anesthesia, give continuous access to food and water for 2 or 3 days to allow for recovery.

The scheme of the various procedures are outlined in Table E12.1. Over an 11 day test period, weigh each rat daily. You should use some caution when attempting to remove each lesioned rat from the home cage. Record any attempts on the part of the rat to bite your hand. You may, by the way, wish to use heavy leather gloves during this portion of the exercise. My experience with these gloves (similar to those used to handle certain strains of monkeys), however, is that their bulkiness guarantees that you will be bitten. They do, however, offer some psychological comfort.

Exercise 12: Septum and Emotionality

Table E12.1. Summary of the Behavioral Tests of Exercise 12.

Day(s):	Behavioral Testing Procedures:
1-11	Daily Measurement of Body Weight
1, 6, 8	Measurements of 24 hour Water Intake
2, 4, 9	Measurement of 24 hour Saccharin Intake
3, 5, 7	Measurement of 24 hour Quinine Intake
10	Open Field Test
11	Social Cohesiveness Test

Fluid Intake. Remove the typical water bottle from the home cage and replace it with a calibrated drinking tube. For each rat on Days 1-9 following recovery from surgery, record 24 hour fluid intake with each rat offered either tap water, 0.025% quinine or 0.13% saccharin as indicated in Table E12.1. Always read the fluid level at the bottom of the meniscus. Correct each reading for spillage by attaching a bottle to an empty cage to estimate the amount of spillage associated with cage movement.

Open field test. On Day 10, place each rat into the center of an open field. This apparatus consists of a box (76 x 76 x 25 cm) with a black interior and outfitted with a wire-mesh lid. The floor of the box should be painted with a series of white lines that form a grid (25 squares that are each approximately 3 x 3 cm). For each rat, note the number of grid crossings during a 60 second period. Use a clean damp sponge to wipe the interior of the open field between successive tests.

Social Cohesiveness test. Prepare a standard polyethylene rodent cage with a sawdust bedding floor and a wire lid. On Day 11, pairs of rats will be placed into the cage (one at each end) and you will record the cumulative number of seconds of contact between the rats during a 300 second interval. Contact here refers to any contact between the pair of rats whether grooming, agonistic or clinging contact. Because you will want to compare the average amount of contact exhibited by the various combinations of pairs, be prepared to carry out the following combinations (the control rats are represented by the letters a, b, c and d whereas the septal rats are represented by the letters e, f, g, and h):

Exercise 12: Septum and Emotionality

I. CONTROL WITH CONTROL (6 possible pairings: ab,ac,ad,bc,bd and cd)

II. CONTROL WITH SEPTAL (16 possible pairings: ae,af,ag,ah,be,bf,bg,bh,ce,cf,cg,ch, de,df,dg, and, of course, dh)

III. SEPTAL WITH SEPTAL (6 possible pairings: ef,eg,eh,fg,fh,gh)

If you are not interested in the possible effect of pairing each control with each of the septal rats, then delete the middle sequence of tests. You would of course, randomize the order that these pairings were carried out.

At the end of the social cohesiveness tests, deeply anesthetize each lesioned rat with 60 mg/ml/kg (ip) sodium pentobarbital, perfuse with 0.9% saline and then fix the brain with 10% formalin. Remove the brain and store in 10% formalin for 48 hours. Section the brain through the septal region and describe the location and extent of the lesion damage, using the procedures of Chapter 5.

Data Summary and Interpretation

Describe the location and extent of the lesions. Data summaries should be computed for those lesioned rats that exhibit lesions that focus on the lateral and/or medial septal nuclei. For each group, calculate the average amount of tap water consumed, the average amount of saccharin solution consumed and the average amount of quinine consumed (collapse across the 3 access periods for each group for each solution). Present these data in a table comparable to that of Table E12.2. In addition, calculate the average open field activity for each group and present in Table E12.2. Then calculate the average contact time for each type of pairing (control/control and septal/septal; control/septal is optional) and present as in Table E12.3.

Discussion points that you should address in your experiment summary include the following:

a. Was there any evidence that the septal rats lost body weight during the 11 day period after recovery from surgery? As you handled the septal rats during the 11 day period, did any of the rats attempt to bite you?. If so, did this effect abate as you continued to handle the septal rats? The latter outcome, termed the handling effect, has frequently been reported in the literature (Thorne et al., 1983).

b. Did the septal rats exhibit hyperdipsia when offered tap water or a saccharin solution? Did septal rats exhibit lower fluid intake of a quinine solution? Here the comparisons are with the fluid intake of the sham-surgery group. If so, you may wish to compare your data with that of Beatty and Schwartzbaum (1968).

Exercise 12: Septum and Emotionality

c. Was there any tendency for the septal rats to exhibit freezing in the open field test? That is, did the septal rats remain motionless, and therefore cross fewer of the grid squares on the floor of the open field cage?

d. If you compare the average contact time on Day 11 between pairs of septal rats with that of pairs of control rats, was there any tendency for the septal pairs to maintain contact for a greater proportion of the time relative to the contact times of control pairs? Meyer et al.,(1978) observed that rats with large lesions of the septal nuclei were in contact with each other for 78% of a 300 second test interval. You should compare the locus of your lesions and your data with that of Meyer et al. (1978). You should also address the issue of whether the septal pairs are indeed "clinging" to each other or whether the rats are engaging in other behaviors (for example, one septal rat grooming another septal rat).

e. Finally, was there any commonality to the effect of septal lesions on behavior? That is, was there a common quality to any observed changes in behavior or are there a multitude of disparate behavioral changes observed after septal lesions? For a potential source for the latter view, see Grossman (1976).

REFERENCES AND SUGGESTED READINGS

Beatty, W.W. and J.S. Schwartzbaum. (1967). Enhanced reactivity to quinine and saccharin solutions following septal lesions. Psychonomic Science, 8, 483-484.

Brady, J.V. and W.H.A. Nauta. (1955). Subcortical mechanisms in emotional behavior: The duration of affective changes following septal and habenular lesions in the albino rat. Journal of comparative and physiological Psychology, 48, 71-2-420.

Grossman, S.P. (1976). Behavioral functions of the septum: A reanalysis. In: J. de France (Ed). The Septal Nuclei, pp 361-422, New York: Plenum Press.

Harvey, J.A. and H.F. Hunt. (1965). Effects of septal lesions on thirst in the rat as indicated by water consumption and operant responding for water reward. Journal of comparative and physiological Psychology, 59, 49-56.

Meyer, D.R., R.A. Ruth and D.G. Lavond. (1978). The septal cohesiveness effect: Its robustness and main determinants. Physiology and Behavior, 21, 1027-1029.

Thorne, B.M., K.N. Lin, and M.L. Weaver. (1983). Water intake after septal damage in Long Evans hooded rats and muricide, irritability to handling and open-field activity. Physiological Psychology, 11, 73-77.

Exercise 12: Septum and Emotionality

Table E12.2. Summary table for body weight (g), fluid intake (ml) and open field (# crossings) data for Exercise 12.

Group:	Body Weight Preop.:	Day 11:	Saccharin Intake:	Quinine Intake:	Water Intake:	Open Field Activity:
Control						
Septal						

Table E12.3. Average contact time (secs) for various rat pairs during a 300 sec test.

Group	Control:	Septal:
Control		Optional
Septal	Optional	

Exercise 12: Septum and Emotionality

Stereotaxic Surgery Record Sheet

Student Name: _____

Animal Number:

Strain:

Age:

Sex:

Weight:

   Preoperative:
   Operative:
   Post-operative

Operation Date:

Anesthesia:

  Volume:
  Type:

Atlas Coordinates: AP: H: L:

Instrument Zero: AP: H: L:

Final Coordinates: AP: H: L:

Surgery Comments:
   Type:
   Upper Incisor Bar at: _____ mm
   Intended Structure-
   Stereotaxic Atlas:

Sacrifice date :

Histology Results:

Exercise 12: Septum and Emotionality

Stereotaxic Surgery Record Sheet

Student Name: _____

Animal Number:

Strain:

Age:

Sex:

Weight:

   Preoperative:
   Operative:
   Post-operative

Operation Date:

Anesthesia:

  Volume:
  Type:

Atlas Coordinates: AP: H: L:

Instrument Zero: AP: H: L:

Final Coordinates: AP: H: L:

Surgery Comments:
   Type:
   Upper Incisor Bar at: ____ mm
   Intended Structure-
   Stereotaxic Atlas:

Sacrifice date :

Histology Results:

Exercise 12: Septum and Emotionality

Stereotaxic Surgery Record Sheet

Student Name: _____

Animal Number:

Strain:

Age:

Sex:

Weight:

   Preoperative:
   Operative:
   Post-operative

Operation Date:

Anesthesia:

   Volume:
   Type:

Atlas Coordinates: AP: H: L:

Instrument Zero: AP: H: L:

Final Coordinates: AP: H: L:

Surgery Comments:
   Type:
   Upper Incisor Bar at: _____ mm
   Intended Structure-
   Stereotaxic Atlas:

Sacrifice date :

Histology Results:

Exercise 12: Septum and Emotionality

Stereotaxic Surgery Record Sheet

Student Name: _____

Animal Number:

Strain:

Age:

Sex:

Weight:

    Preoperative:
    Operative:
    Post-operative

Operation Date:

Anesthesia:

    Volume:
    Type:

Atlas Coordinates: AP: H: L:

Instrument Zero: AP: H: L:

Final Coordinates: AP: H: L:

Surgery Comments:
    Type:
    Upper Incisor Bar at: _____ mm
    Intended Structure-
    Stereotaxic Atlas:

Sacrifice date :

Histology Results:

Exercise 13
Rewarding Brain Stimulation

Background and Problem

In 1954, James Olds and Peter Milner reported that rats would emit operant responses that produced a brief pulse of electrical current at the tip of an electrode implanted within the rat's brain. The brain stimulation was clearly of a rewarding nature as numerous studies by Olds (1956, 1973) subsequently demonstrated that rats would forgo food, traverse shock grids and emit a variety of operant responses in order to obtain electrical stimulation of the brain (ESB) (see Figure E13.1). The brain region that is most likely to support electrical stimulation of the brain is along the medial forebrain bundle at the level of the lateral hypothalamus. Interestingly, this area is also associated with stimulation-bound feeding: that is, rats given a 20-30 second train of ESB are likely to consume pellets of food during the stimulation. Obesity can be induced by chronic ESB stimulation (Hoebel, 1975). The events that led to the discovery of rewarding brain stimulation are summarized by Milner (1989).

Figure E13.1. An apparatus for testing electrical stimulation of the brain (ESB). A leash is attached to the rat's head which leads to a commutator at the top of the cage which is connected to programming equipment and an electronic stimulator (not shown).

Exercise 13: Rewarding Brain Stimulation

The purpose of this exercise is to introduce this fascinating motivational phenomenon. You will implant a single bipolar electrode within the lateral hypothalamus and then train the rat to press for ESB. In addition, you will determine the relation between stimulation intensity (current) and rate of responding for ESB and then test the rat for stimulation-bound feeding. For further reading, you should read the excellent summaries provided by Olds (1973), M. Olds and Fobes (1981) and Valenstein (1973).

Materials
  Bipolar electrode (Plastics One MS303-1)
  Electrode connector cable (Plastics One MS306)
  Stereotaxic instrument with electrode carrier
  Ear plugs for stereotaxic ear bars
  Scalpel (#10) with handle (#3)
  Surgical scissors
  Hemostatic forceps
  Atropine sulfate (1.0 mg/ml)
  42 mg/ml sodium pentobarbital
  Watchglass and metal spatula
  Jewelers screws
  Dental acrylic powder and liquid
  9 mm wound clips with applicator
  Vaseline or heavy mineral oil, cotton balls
  Tape
  Electronic stimulator
  Mercury commutator and stimulation leash
  Operant chamber with lever
  Programming equipment: switches, relays, timer and counters hand-held switch
      used to shape the rat

Procedure
    In this exercise, separate periods will be required to surgically implant the electrode into the lateral hypothalamus using the procedures described in Chapter 4. Allow your rat about 5 days to recover during which it is weighed daily and handled.

    On the day of testing, you will first connect the rat to the stimulation cable and then conduct a series of stimulations. To connect a rat to the commutator, place your left thumb and forefinger around the rat's neck. Bring the rat's head to and restrained against your chest. Now use your right hand to insert the dual prongs of the stimulator cable into the receptacles of the electrode. Turn the plastic locking ring down onto the electrode shaft. Place the rat into the test chamber and connect the female end of the stimulator cable to the male end of the commutator. After connecting the rat to the cable and the chamber, allow the rat to explore the chamber for 5 minutes prior to beginning stimulation tests.

Exercise 13: Rewarding Brain Stimulation

Prior to beginning the stimulation tests sequence, consult with your instructor to become familiar with the operating characteristics of the stimulator you will use. Most modern electronic stimulators are capable of generating large quantities of current that are sufficient to lesion the rat brain and provoke motor seizures. Therefore, always begin any stimulation test sequence at very low levels of current (around 40 microamps) and gradually increase current intensity to, but not beyond, 160 microamps. You should be aware that electrical stimuli can be described in terms of voltage (the potential difference between two points) and current (the amount of charge passed per unit time). In ESB work, current is a better descriptor of stimulation. Ohms law describes the relation between current (I), voltage (E) and Resistance (R):

$$I = E/R$$

where I is in Amperes, E is in volts and R is in ohms. To obtain relatively constant current, it is worthwhile to have a large amount (>70000 Ohms) of resistance in the stimulation circuit: thus as the resistance of the rat brain (approx 12000-15000 Ohms) changes over time, the current intensity will remain approximately the same (this occurs because the rat's resistance is small relative to the large external resistance that is placed in series with the voltage source). Many stimulators are designed to deliver constant current output.

To begin the test session, set current intensity at 40 microamps (uA) and deliver a few "free" shots of stimulation to the rat's brain. Carefully observe the reaction of the rat to each stimulation burst. Rats that eventually become good self-stimulators often exhibit the following signs during free stimulation: vigorous sniffing, increases in locomotion and chewing of the cage floor and lever. If the rat squeals and urinates and/or defecates during stimulation, discontinue the testing and wait 5 minutes to remove the rat from the chamber: such a rat is likely to have a stimulating electrode located within a pain site. If each rat shows no obvious behavioral effect at 40 uA, then increase the current intensity in 20 uA steps until an effect is noted or you have reached 160 uA. Do not deliver a rapid series of stimuli as these can provoke motor seizures. Clinical signs of a motor seizure include repetitive, convulsive movements of the head and forepaws and a loss of posture as the rat falls to the cage floor. If a motor seizure occurs, you should be aware that any noise or movement on your part can prolong such a seizure. Therefore, turn off the chamber lights and be very quiet for 10-15 minutes before removing the animal from the chamber.

Once you have determined that the rat reacts with sniffing and chewing to brief pulses of stimulation, you may begin the shaping procedure. The technique of shaping involves breaking the desired response (here, pressing a lever) down into smaller components that can be successively rewarded. The following describes the sequence of responses that you must reward in order to shape the rat to press a lever for ESB:

Exercise 13: Rewarding Brain Stimulation

Steps in the shaping process:
 a. rat faces the general direction of the lever
 b. rat sits at least 10 cm from the lever
 c. rat sits at least 5 cm from the lever
 d. rat must now approach the lever
 e. rat must touch the lever with one or more paws
 f. now the rat must press the bar for ESB

Remember that you are making a contingency between one of the above responses and your delivering a shot of ESB. Do not be "tenderhearted" and give the rat numerous free shots in hopes of getting the rat to move toward the lever: the only behavior that you are reinforcing in such a situation is the rat sitting there...

After the rat has begun to easily press the lever to obtain ESB, allow it to respond for ESB for 15 minutes and then return it to the home cage. On the second day, you should determine the stimulation intensity-response curve for each rat. That is, you should determine the effect of varying stimulation intensity on the rate of bar pressing for ESB. Each stimulation intensity will be given for 5 minutes during which you will record the total number of ESB responses. Because rats typically require "priming" at the beginning of the test session, give each rat a few "free" shots at an intensity of 40-60 uA. Randomly select a series of current intensities that vary by 20 uA (e.g. 40, 80, 60, 140, 120, 100 and 160 uA) up to 160 uA. Use a different series for each rat. From this series, you should ascertain the minimal and maximum current intensities for each rat. The minimum is that intensity at which responding drops off to zero and the maximal is that intensity that produces no further enhancement in rate of responding.

Rats with electrodes within the lateral hypothalamus often show another interesting phenomenon in which prolonged stimulation (approximately 30 seconds) will induce gnawing of wood chips or feeding or drinking. This behavior is "stimulation-bound" in that the behavior onset and offset coincides with the onset and offset of the electrical stimulation. To verify whether your rat shows "stimulation-bound" behavior, place the rat into the test chamber and connect it to the stimulation leash. Food pellets should be scattered on the floor. A drinking tube should be available through one wall and you should provide wood chips on the cage floor. Disable the lever so that lever depression will not produce ESB. Now manually deliver ESB at 100 uA for 30 seconds and observe the behavior of the rat. If the rat fails to show stimulation-bound behavior (rat does not eat, drink or gnaw the wood chips), try the procedure again several times at 100 uA and then repeat the test series at 16O uA. At the end of the 160 uA test series, inject each rat with 60 mg/ml/kg (ip) sodium pentobarbital and perfuse the heart with 0.9% saline followed by 10% formalin. Remove the brain and store for 48 hours in 10% formalin prior to sectioning the brain to determine the location of the electrode tip (see procedures in Chapter 5).

Exercise 13: Rewarding Brain Stimulation

Data Summary and Interpretation

You should calculate the average number of responses per 5 minute interval as a function of current intensity and graph these data using the axes provided in Figure E13.2. In your summary of the experiment, you should address the following issues:

a. Describe the reaction of your rat to the "free" shots of ESB. What was the minimal amount of current required to support ESB? What was the current intensity that produced a maximal amount of responding? Did your rat show any evidence of motor seizures during the stimulation series? You may wish to compare your results with those of Olds (1958).

b. When given a 30 second train of ESB, did the rat show evidence of stimulation-bound feeding, drinking or gnawing? If the rat showed these behaviors, was the behavior consistent? That is, did the rat only eat or only drink or was there a tendency for the rat to shift from feeding to gnawing wood to drinking?. Compare your data with those of Valenstein (1973).

c. Describe the location of the electrode tip within the brain. If your rat failed to exhibit both ESB and stimulation-bound behavior, was the electrode located outside the lateral hypothalamus?

REFERENCES AND SUGGESTED READINGS

Hoebel, B.G. (1975). Brain stimulation reward and aversion in relation to behavior. In: A.Wauquier and E.T. Rolls (Eds) Brain Stimulation Reward, New York: Elsevier/North Holland, Inc.)

Milner, P. The discovery of self-stimulation and other stories. Neuroscience and Biobehavioral Reviews, 13, 61-67.

Olds, J. (1956). Pleasure centers in the brain. Scientific American.

Olds, J. (1958). Effects of hunger and male sex hormone on self-stimulation of the brain. Journal of comparative and physiological Psychology, 51, 302-324.

Olds, J. (1973). Drives and Reinforcements, New York: Raven Press.

Olds, M.E. and J.L. Fobes (1981). The central basis of motivation: Intracranial self-stimulation studies. Annual Reviews of Psychology, 32, 523-574.

Olds, J. and P. Milner (1954). Positive reinforcement produced by electrical stimulation of septal area and other regions of rat brain. Journal of comparative and physiological Psychology, 47, 419-427.

Exercise 13: Rewarding Brain Stimulation

Pellegrino, L.J., A.S. Pellegrino and A.J. Cushman. (1979). <u>A Stereotaxic Atlas of the Rat Brain</u>, New York: Appleton-Century-Crofts.

Valenstein, E.S. (1973). History of brain stimulation: Investigations into the physiology of motivation. In: E.S. Valenstein (Ed), <u>Brain Stimulation and Motivation</u>, Glenview, Illinois: Scott, Foresman and Company.

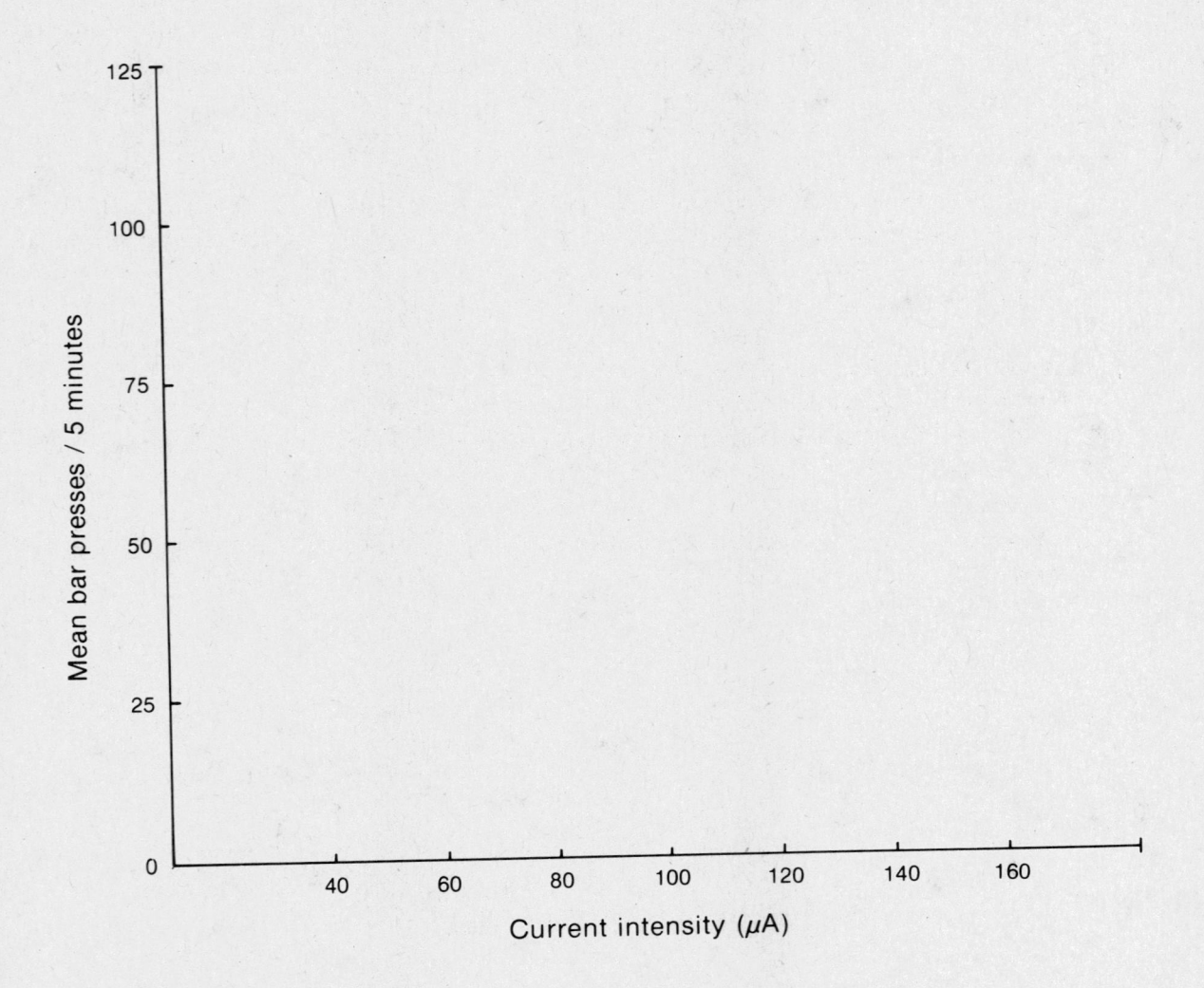

Figure E13.2. Graphic axes used to depict the effect of varying current intensity (microamperes) of ESB on number of lever presses per 5 minute period.

Exercise 13: Rewarding Brain Stimulation

Stereotaxic Surgery Record Sheet

Student Name: _____

Animal Number:

Strain:

Age:

Sex:

Weight:

    Preoperative:
    Operative:
    Post-operative

Operation Date:

Anesthesia:

    Volume:
    Type:

Atlas Coordinates: AP: H: L:

Instrument Zero: AP: H: L:

Final Coordinates: AP: H: L:

Surgery Comments:
    Type:
    Upper Incisor Bar at: _____ mm
    Intended Structure-
    Stereotaxic Atlas:

Sacrifice date :

Histology Results:

Exercise 13: Rewarding Brain Stimulation

Stereotaxic Surgery Record Sheet

Student Name: _____

Animal Number:

Strain:

Age:

Sex:

Weight:

    Preoperative:
    Operative:
    Post-operative

Operation Date:

Anesthesia:

  Volume:
  Type:

Atlas Coordinates: AP: H: L:

Instrument Zero: AP: H: L:

Final Coordinates: AP: H: L:

Surgery Comments:
   Type:
   Upper Incisor Bar at: _____ mm
   Intended Structure-
   Stereotaxic Atlas:

Sacrifice date :

Histology Results:

Exercise 14
Peripheral Catecholamines and Memory

Background and Problem

Memory processes are thought to involve encoding of stimuli events and progressive consolidation into permanent memory. Catecholaminergic mechanisms have been implicated as critical for the retention of learning (Kety, 1970). Catecholamine agonists such as epinephrine and amphetamine facilitate learning and memory whereas antagonists of the beta-adrenergic receptor such as propranolol impair memory (Hunter et al., 1977; Gold and Van Buskirk, 1978; Martinez et al., 1980). Systemic injections of epinephrine facilitate memory but this effect is likely to be due to an action of epinephrine on ascending pathways which eventually cause the release of norepinephrine within the amygdala (McGaugh, 1983; McGaugh, 1990).

This exercise will serve to demonstrate the measurement of learning and memory in the rat and the role of peripheral catecholamines in memory. You will train and test rats in a step-through passive avoidance task. In this task, the rat enters a dark compartment, is briefly shocked and is then returned to the home cage. On a retention test 24 hours later, you will measure the latency of the rat to re-enter the dark compartment. In this paradigm, good learning and memory is indicated by very long latencies (> 300 seconds) to reenter the dark compartment on the test day while amnesia or retention problems are indicated by short latencies. To assess the role of catecholaminergic activity on memory, you will inject, just after training, either saline, epinephrine (3.0 ug/kg), or propranolol (1.0 mg/ml/kg). Rats treated with epinephrine, a sympathomimetic agonist, should exhibit facilitated retention of the shock experience whereas propranolol, a beta-adrenergic antagonist, should attenuate retention.

Materials
1 cc syringes with 27-gauge (0.5 inch) needles
0.9% saline
3.0 mg/ml epinephrine (Sigma Chemical)
1.0 mg/ml dl-propranolol hydrochloride (Sigma Chemical)
stop watch or electronic clock
Passive avoidance apparatus (see description below)

Procedures

The apparatus and procedures of this exercise are similar to those described by Martinez et al. (1980). Briefly, the passive avoidance apparatus consists of a Plexiglass start chamber illuminated by an overhead 7 watt bulb and separated from a dark shock compartment by a guillotine door. Each chamber should be equipped with a hinged lid. The chambers should be made as different as possible by lighting (white vs dark), wall covering (white vertical stripes can be placed on the walls of the light start compartment) and flooring (the dark chamber must have a floor constructed of metal bars through which shock can be delivered whereas the light compartment floor may be

Exercise 14: Catecholamines and Memory

constructed of wood). No lighting should be provided for the shock compartment so as to take advantage of the tendency of rats to spontaneously enter a dark area.

A minimum of 3 rats are required for each of the drug conditions, for a minimum total of 9 rats (sex, age and weight should be comparable). Randomly assign the rats to the 3 treatment conditions. On the training day, place each rat into the start chamber, facing away from the guillotine door and then time the latency of each rat to enter the dark compartment. Depending on the level of light within the start chamber (greater intensities produce faster step-through latencies), each rat should enter the dark compartment within 10 seconds. Upon entry, close the guillotine door (to prevent the rat from reentering the lighted start chamber) and manually deliver 1.0 mA of shock for 1 second to the floor of the dark chamber. If a rat does not enter the chamber within 90 seconds, terminate the trial: such a rat should be replaced. After shock training, remove each rat from the dark chamber and inject (ip) each with either 1.0 ml/kg 0.9% saline, 3.0 mg/ml/kg epinephrine or 1.0 mg/ml/kg propranolol and then return each rat to the home cage. Because alarm odors can be transmitted via urine, be certain that you carefully clean each chamber with a clean sponge between shock training trials. On the test day (24 hours after training), again place each rat into the start chamber, facing away from the open guillotine door, and record the latency to enter the dark chamber. After a rat enters the dark chamber, close the guillotine door but do not deliver shock. After a brief period, remove the rat from the dark chamber and return it to the home cage. If any rat does not step through to the dark compartment within 600 seconds, terminate the trial and record a latency of 600 seconds. Again, be certain that you carefully clean each chamber between retention tests.

Data Summary and Interpretation

Collate the latency to step through on the training day and the test day for each of the three drug groups. Calculate the average step-through latency on the training day and the test day for each group and then use bar graphs to depict these values using the axes provided in Figure E14.1.

Several issues will be addressed in your lab writeup of this experiment. Were there any differences between the groups with regard to step-through latency on the training day? If there were differences between the groups, how would you explain these? Describe the performance of the saline-injected control rats on the test day. Did these rats exhibit step-through latencies that exceeded their training step-through latencies? Ordinarily, this paradigm will produce test step-through latencies on the order of 300-500 seconds. Did the post-trial drug treatments have any effect on retention of the aversive experience given just prior to drug treatment? If so, are these consistent with the data reported by McGaugh (1983) and Martinez et al. (1980)?

Exercise 14: Catecholamines and Memory

REFERENCES AND SUGGESTED READINGS

Kety, S.S. (1970). The biogenic amines in the central nervous system: Their possible role in arousal, emotion and learning. In: F.O. Schmidtt (Ed). The Neurosciences, Second Study Program, New York: Rockefeller University Press.

Gold, P.E. and R. Vanbuskirk. (1978). Post-training brain norepinephrine concentrations: Correlation with retention performance of avoidance training and with peripheral epinephrine modulation of memory processing. Behavioral Biology, 23, 509-520.

Hunter, B., S.F. Zornetzer, M.E. Jarvik and J.L. McGaugh. (1977). Modulation of learning and memory: Effects of drugs influencing neurotransmitters. In: L.L. Iversen, S.D. Iversen and S.H. Snyder (Eds). Handbook of Pharmacology, 8, 531-537, New York: Plenum Press.

Martinez, J.L., Jr., B J. Vasquez, H. Rigter, R.B. Messing, R.A. Jensen, K.C. Liang and J.L. McGaugh. (1980). Attenuation of amphetamine-induced enhancement of learning by adrenal demedullation. Brain Research, 195, 433-443.

McGaugh, J.L. (1983). Remembering the presence of the past. American Psychologist, February, 161-174.

McGaugh, J.L. (1990). Significance and remembrance: the role of neuromodulatory systems. Psychological Science, 1, 15-25.

Exercise 14: Catecholamines and Memory

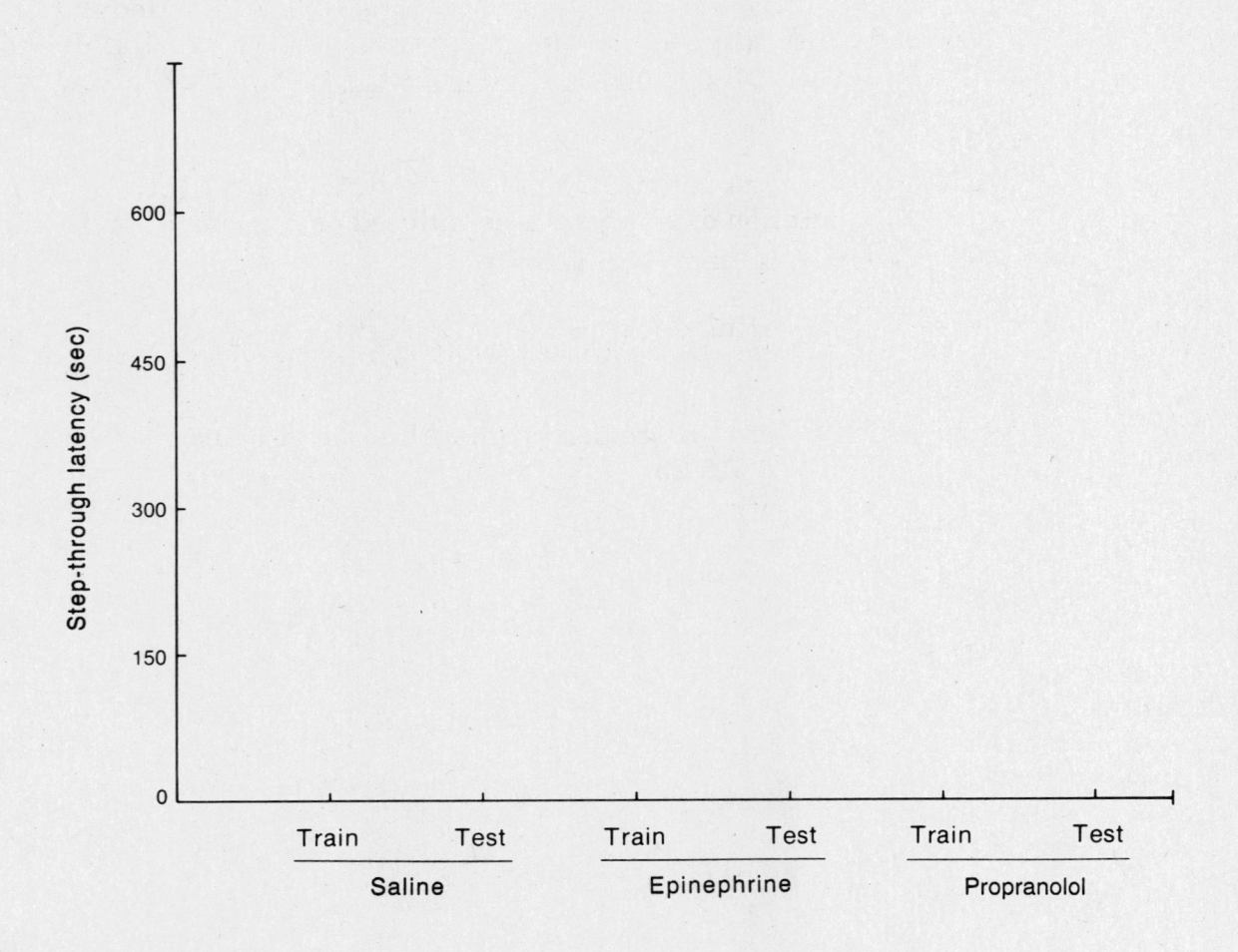

Figure E14.1. Graphic axes used to depict the effects of either saline, epinephrine or propranolol on a step-through passive avoidance response.

Appendix A
Commercial Sources for Equipment and Materials

Acrylic Cement (fluid and powder)
  IDE Interstate
  Plastics One
  Stoelting Corp

Animal Caging
  Ancare Corp
  Fischer Scientific
  Nalge Co

Animal Suppliers (Rats)
  Charles Rivers Labs
  Harlan Sprague-Dawley
  Taconic Farms
  Zivic-Miller

Behavioral Test Equipment (chambers, shockers, recorders, clocks, feeders)
  Columbus Instruments
  Coulbourn Instruments
  Gerbrands Corp
  Harvard Apparatus
  Lafayette Instruments
  Med Associates
  Stoelting Co

Cannulae
  Brain Research Instruments
  Harvard Apparatus
  IITC Life Science Instruments
  Plastics One
  Popper and Sons
  Small Parts Inc (tubing to make cannulae)

Chemicals
  Aldrich Chemical Co
  J.T. Baker
  Cal Biochemical
  Sigma Chemical

Appendix A: Equipment and Materials

Connectors (electrode, commutators)
  Amphenol
  Harvard Apparatus
  Plastics One
  Stoelting

Dissecting Instruments
  Biomedical Research Instruments
  Fine Science Tools Inc
  Roboz Surgical Instrument
  Stoelting Co

Drugs (also see Appendix B)
  Ciba Geigy
  Lilly and Company
  McNeil Consumer Products
  Parke-Davis
  Pittman-Moore
  Sigma Chemical Company
  Smith, Kline and French
  Upjohn Company

Electrodes (wire and materials)
  Brain Research Instruments
  California Fire Wire
  Harvard Apparatus
  Plastics One
  Roboz Surgical Instrument Co

Electronic Stimulators
  Grass Instruments
  Harvard Apparatus
  Stoelting Co

Freezing Microtomes
  Fischer Scientific
  Hacker Instruments
  Carl Zeiss Inc

Histology Supplies (stains, medium, slides)
  Carolina Biological
  Eastman Kodak
  Fischer Scientific
  Sigma Chemical Company

Appendix A: Equipment and Materials

Lesion Makers
  David Kopf
  Grass Instruments
  Stoelting Co

Microsyringes
  Hamilton Inc

Osmotic Minipumps
  Alza Corporation

Stereotaxic drills and burs
  Harvard Apparatus
  Small Parts Inc
  Stoelting

Stereotaxic Instruments (student)
  Brain Research Instruments
  David Kopf
  Stoelting Co

Surgical Instruments (scalpels, blades, hemostats, wound clips)
  Brain Research Instruments
  Clay Adams
  Fischer Scientific
  Fine Science Tools
  Roboz Surgical

Equipment and Material Sources

Aldrich Chemical Co
PO Box 355
Milwaukee, WI 53201
414-273-3850

Alza Corp
950 Page Mill Rd.
PO Box 10950
Palo Alto, CA 94303
800-692-2990

Amphenol Corp
2122 York Rd.
Oak Brook, IL 60521
312-966-2300

Ancare Corp
PO Box 661
North Bellmore, NY 11710
516-781-0755

J.T. Baker Chemical Co
222 Red School Lane
Phillipsburg, NJ 08865
800-582-2537

Biomedical Research Instruments
12264 Wilkins Avenue
Rockville, MD 20852
800-327-9498

Appendix A: Equipment and Materials

Brain Research Instrument Co
207 Hartley Ave.
Princeton, NJ 08540
609-921-6612

Calbiochem
10933 N. Torrey Pines Rd.
P.O. Box 12087
San Diego, CA 92039-2087
800-854-3417

California Fine Wire
PO Box 446
Grover Beach, CA 93483
805-489-5144

Carolina Biological Supply Co
2700 York Rd.
Burlington, NC 27215
919-584-0381

Charles Rivers Labs
251 Ballardvale St
Wilmington, MA 01887
508-658-6000

Clay Adams
299 Webro Rd.
Parsippany, NJ 07054

Columbus Instruments
950 N. Hague Avenue
Columbus, OH 43204
800-669-5011

Coulbourn Instruments Inc
William Penn Business Center
7462 Penn Drive,
Allentown, PA 18106
800-424-3771

David Kopf Instruments
7324 Elmo St.
Tujunga, CA 91042
818-352-3274

Eastman-Kodak
343 State St B-701
Rochester, NY 14652-3512
800-225-5352

Fine Science Tools
373-G Vintage Park Drive
Foster City, CA 94404
800-521-2109

Fisher Scientific Co., Allied Corp.
711 Forbes Avenue
Pittsburgh, PA 15219
412-562-8300

Gerbrands Corp
8 Beck Rd.
Arlington, MA 02i74
617-648-6415

Grass Instrument Co
101 Old Colony Avenue
Quincy, MA 02169
617-773-0002

Hacker Instruments
PO Box 10033
17 Sherwood Lane
Fairfield, NJ 07004
201-226-8450

Hamilton Co
PO Box 10030
4970 Energy Way
Reno, NV 89502
800-646-5950

Harlan Sprague Dawley, Inc
Laboratory Animals
PO Box 29176
Indianapolis, IN 46229
317-894-7521

Appendix A: Equipment and Materials

Harvard Apparatus Co, Inc
22 Pleasant St.
S. Natick, MA 01760
800-272-2775

ICN Nutritional Biochemicals
26201 Miles Rd.
Cleveland, OH 44128 216-831-3000

IITC Life Science Instruments
23924 Victory Blvd
Woodland Hills, CA 92367
818-710-1556

Lafayette Instrument Co
PO Box 5729
3700 Sagamore Parkway
Lafayette, IN 47903
800-428-7545

Med Associates
Box 47
East Fairfield, VT 05448
317-447-2216

Nalge Co
75 Panorama Creek
PO Box 20365
Rochester, NY 14602
716-586-8800

Plastics One
PO Box 12004
Roanoke, VA 24022
703-772-7950

Popper and Sons
300 Denton Avenue
New Hyde Park, NY
516-248-0300

Roboz Surgical Instrument Co
9210 Corporate Boulevard, Suite 220
Rockville, MD 20850
800-424-2984

Sigma Chemical Co
PO Box 14508
St Louis, HO 63178 314-771-5765

Small Parts, Inc
13980 NW 58th Ct.,
P.O. Box 4650
Miami Lakes, FL 33014-0650
800-423-9009

Stoelting Co
620 Wheat Lane
Wood Dale IL 60191
708-860-9700

Taconic Farms
Hover Rd, Box 273
Germantown, NY 12526
518-437-6208

Timco Breeding Labs
305 Almeda Genoa Rd.
Houston, Texas 77407
713-433-5681

Ward's Natural Science
P.O. Box 1712
Rochester, NY 14603
716-467-8400

Carl Zeiss Inc
One Zeiss Drive
Thornwood, NY 10594
800-233-2343

Zivic-Miller Labs
3848 Heiber Rd
Allison Park, PA 15101
800-422-LABS

Appendix B: Drug Sources

Appendix B
Common Laboratory Drugs and Sources

(Any drug denoted by a * is controlled by the Federal government; use in the lab requires a drug handlers license or a prescription)

LABORATORY DRUGS

Amphetamine Sulfate *
    Sigma Chemical
    Smith, Kline and French

Angiotensin II
    Sigma Chemical
    RBI

Apomorphine *
    Sigma Chemical

Atropine Sulfate
    Sigma Chemical
    IDE Interstate
    RBI

Carbachol (Carbamylcholine chloride)
    Sigma Chemical

Chloral Hydrate *
    Parke-Davis
    Sigma Chemical

Epinephrine
    Parke-Davis
    RBI
    Sigma Chemical

Estrogen
    Savage Labs
    Schering Corporation

Haloperidol
    McNeil Consumer Products
    RBI
    Sigma

4-Hydroxyamphetamine (Paredrine)
    Smith, Kline and French

6-Hydroxydopamine
    RBI
    Sigma Chemical

Isoproterenol
    Abbot Labs
    RBI
    Sigma Chemical

Sodium Pentobarbital
    Sigma
    IDE Interstate

Appendix B: Drug Sources

DRUG SOURCES

Abbott Laboratories
North Chicago, IL 60064
800-441-4987

Ayerst Laboratories
685 Third Avenue
New York, NY 10017
215-688-4400

Ciba-Geigy Corp
556 Morriss Avenue
Summitt, NJ 07901
201-277-5000

Eli Lilly and Company
Lilly Corporate Center
Indianapolis, IN 46285
317-276-3714

IDE Interstate
1500 New Horizons Blvd
Amityville, NY 11701
800-666-8100

McNeil Consumer Products
Fort Washington, PA 19034
215-233-7000

Parke-Davis
201 Tabor Road
Morriss Plains, NJ 07950
201-540-2000

Pittman-Moore
P.O. Box 1656
Indianapolis, IN 46206

Research Biochemicals Incorporated
One Strathmore Road
Natick, MA 01760-2418
800-736-3690

Savage Laboratories
60 Bayliss Road
Melville, NY
800-231-0206

Schering Corporation
Galloping Hill Road
Kenilworth, NJ 07033
201-298-4000

Sigma Chemical
P.O. Box 14508
St Louis, MO 63178
800-325-3010

SmithKline-Beecham
One Franklin Plaza
P.O. Box 7929
Philadelphia, PA 19101
215-751-4000

Wyeth Labs
P.O. Box 8299
Philadelphia, PA 19101
215-688-4400

Appendix C
Stereotaxic Atlas

The following stereotaxic plates are reproduced with permission from G. Paxinos and C. Watson (1986), <u>The Rat Brain in Stereotaxic Coordinates</u>, second edition, New York: Academic Press.

Appendix C: Stereotaxic Atlas

Figure 13

2n	optic nerve	Fr2	frontal cortex, area 2	Pir	piriform cortex
aca	anterior commissure, anterior	FStr	fundus striati	RF	rhinal fissure
AcbC	accumbens nu, core	gcc	genu corpus callosum	SHi	septohippocampal nu
AcbSh	accumbens nu, shell	GI	granular insular cortex	Tu	olfactory tubercle
AI	agranular insular Cx.	ICj	islands of Calleja	VDB	nu vertical limb diagonal band
cg	cingulum	ICjM	islands of Calleja, major island	VP	ventral pallidum
Cg1	cingulate cortex, area 1	IG	indusium griseum		
Cg2	cingulate cortex, area 2	lo	lateral olfactory tract		
Cl	claustrum	LSD	lateral septal nu, dorsal		
CPu	caudate putamen	LSI	lateral septal nu, intermediate		
DEn	dorsal endopiriform nu	LSV	lateral septal nu, ventral		
DI	dysgranular insular cortex	LV	lateral ventricle		
ec	external capsule	mfba	medial forebrain bundle, a		
FL	forelimb area of cortex	MS	medial septal nu		
Fr1	frontal cortex, area 1	Par1	parietal cortex, area 1		

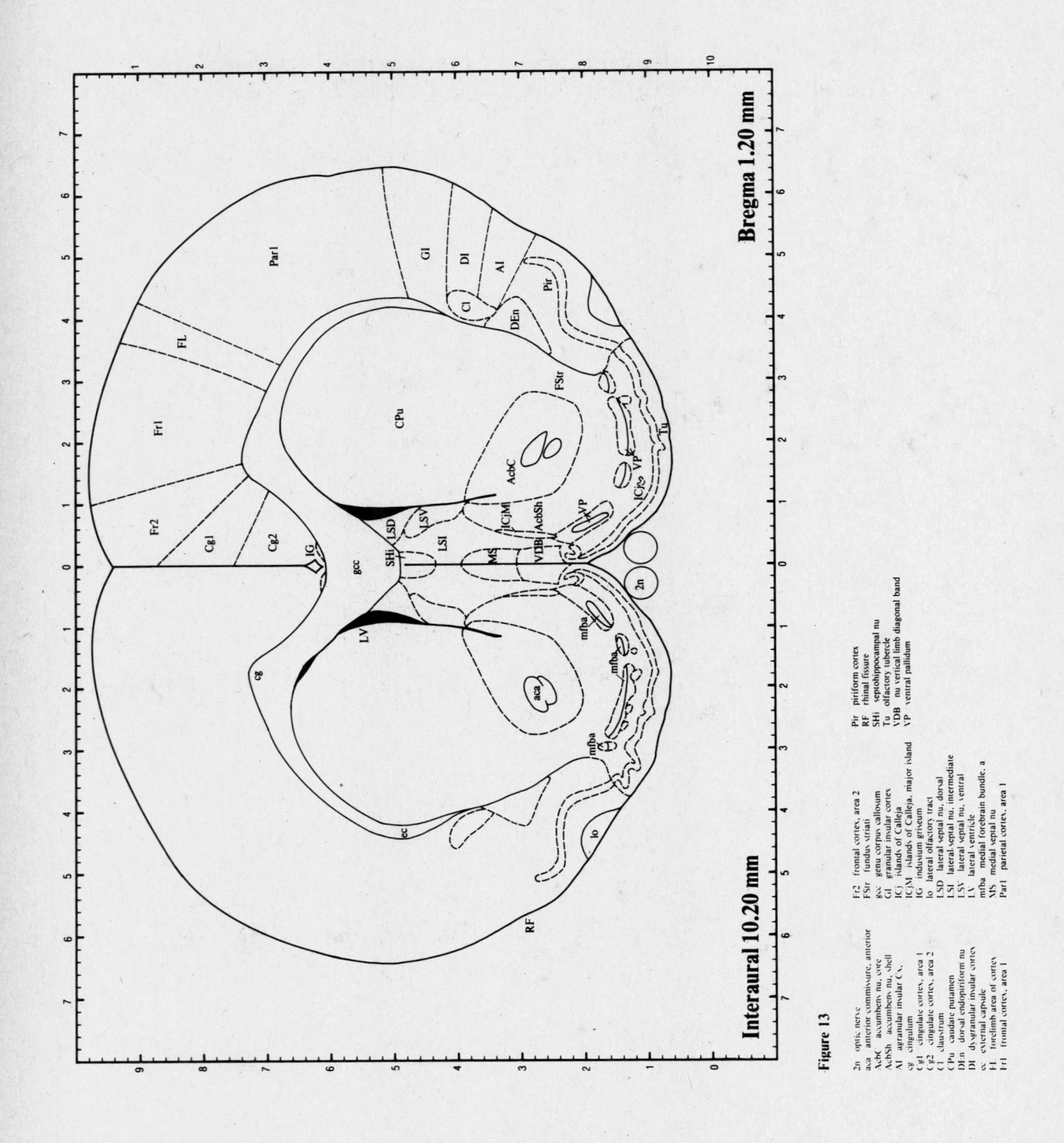

Interaural 10.20 mm   Bregma 1.20 mm

Appendix C: Stereotaxic Atlas

Figure 25

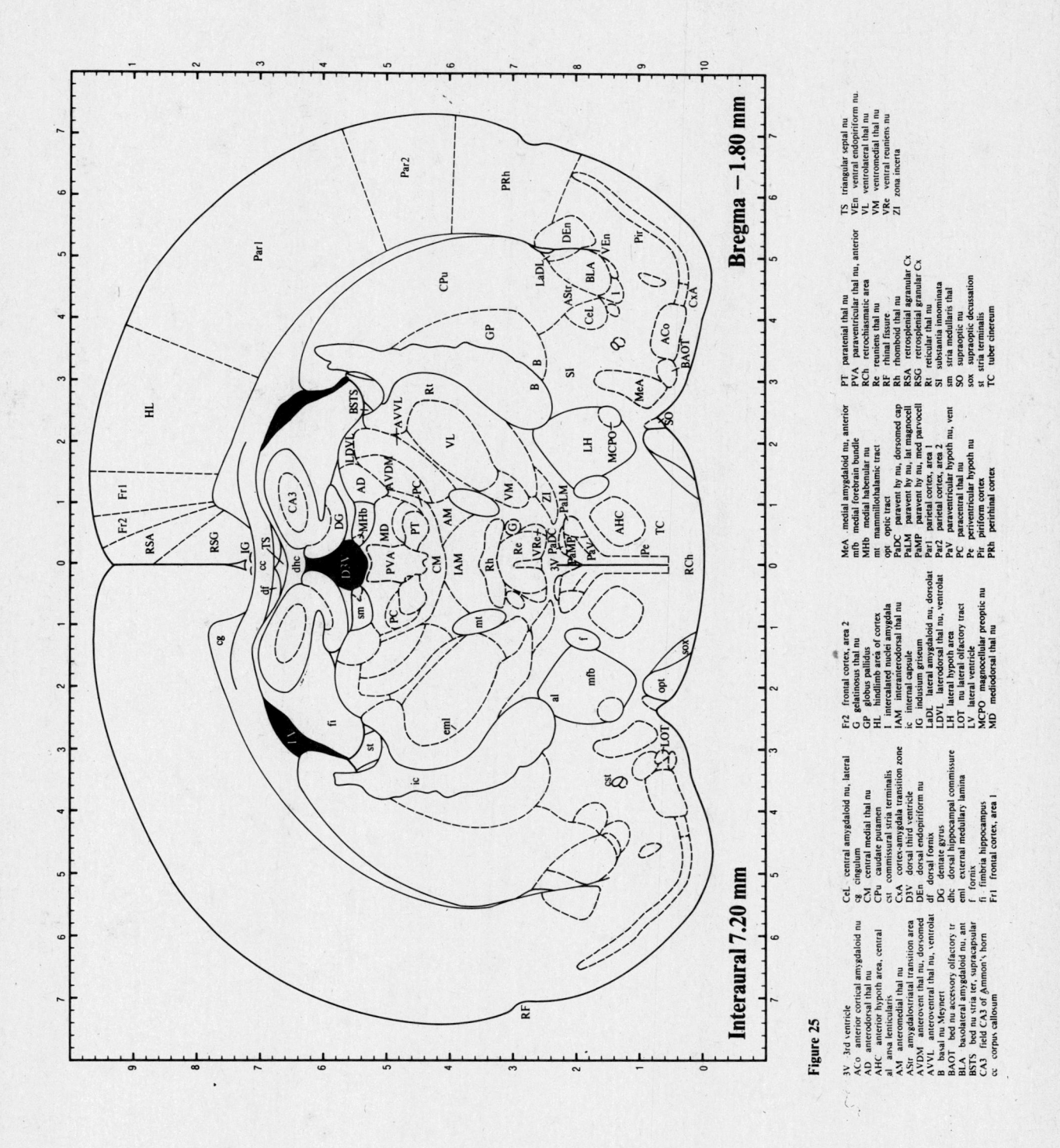

Interaural 7.20 mm   Bregma −1.80 mm

Appendix C: Stereotaxic Atlas

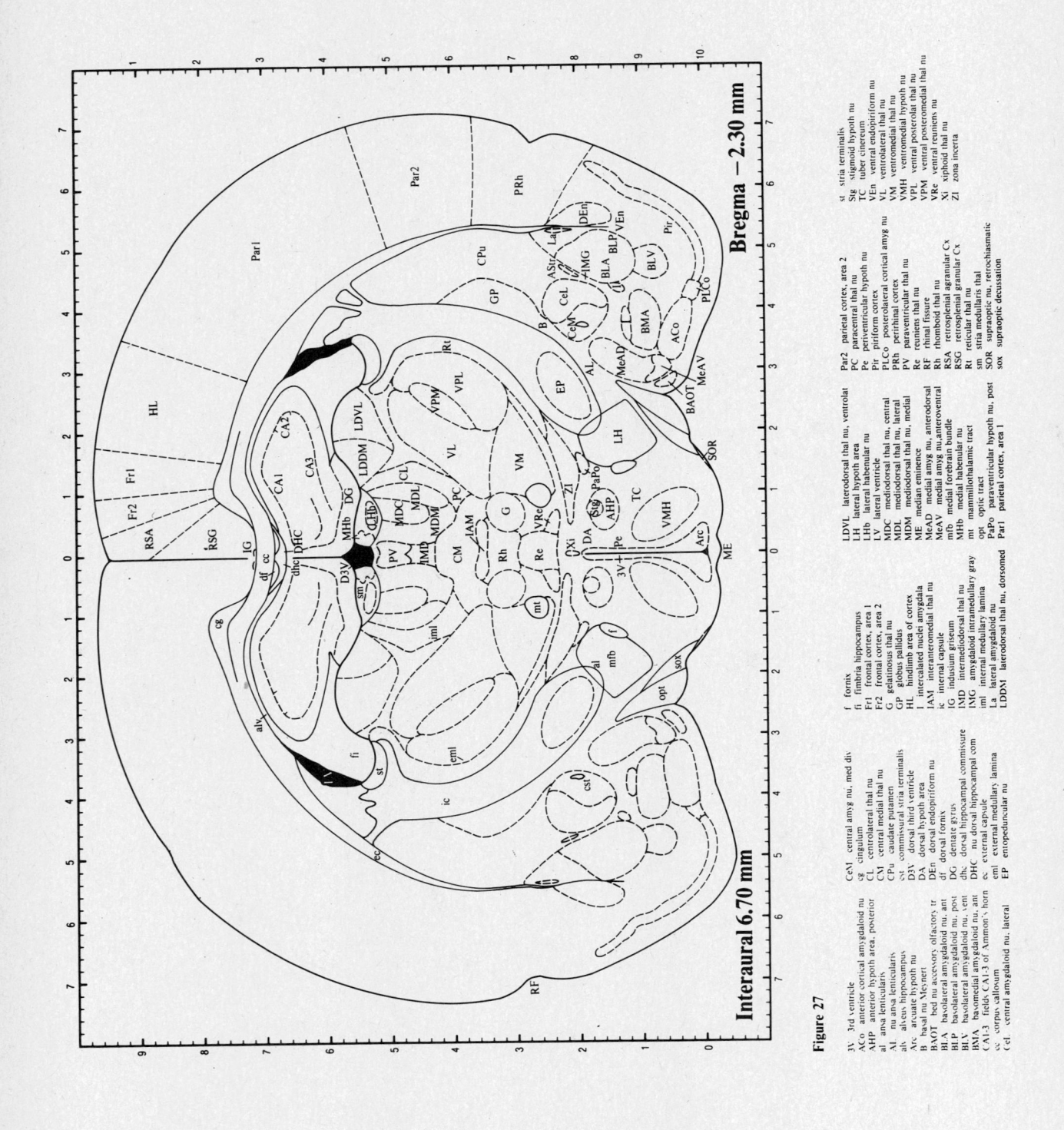

Figure 27

Appendix C: Stereotaxic Atlas

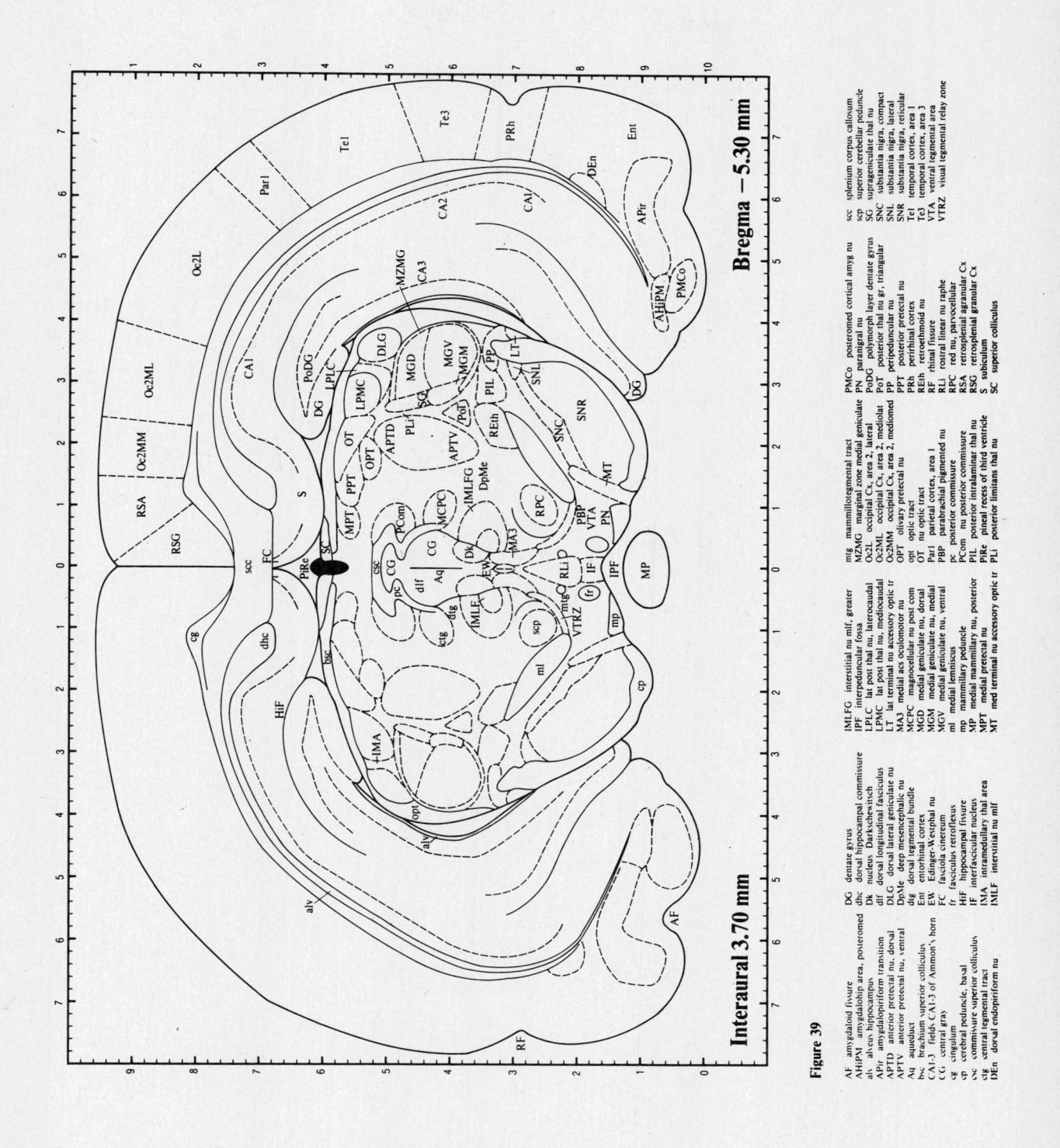

Figure 39

Appendix C: Stereotaxic Atlas

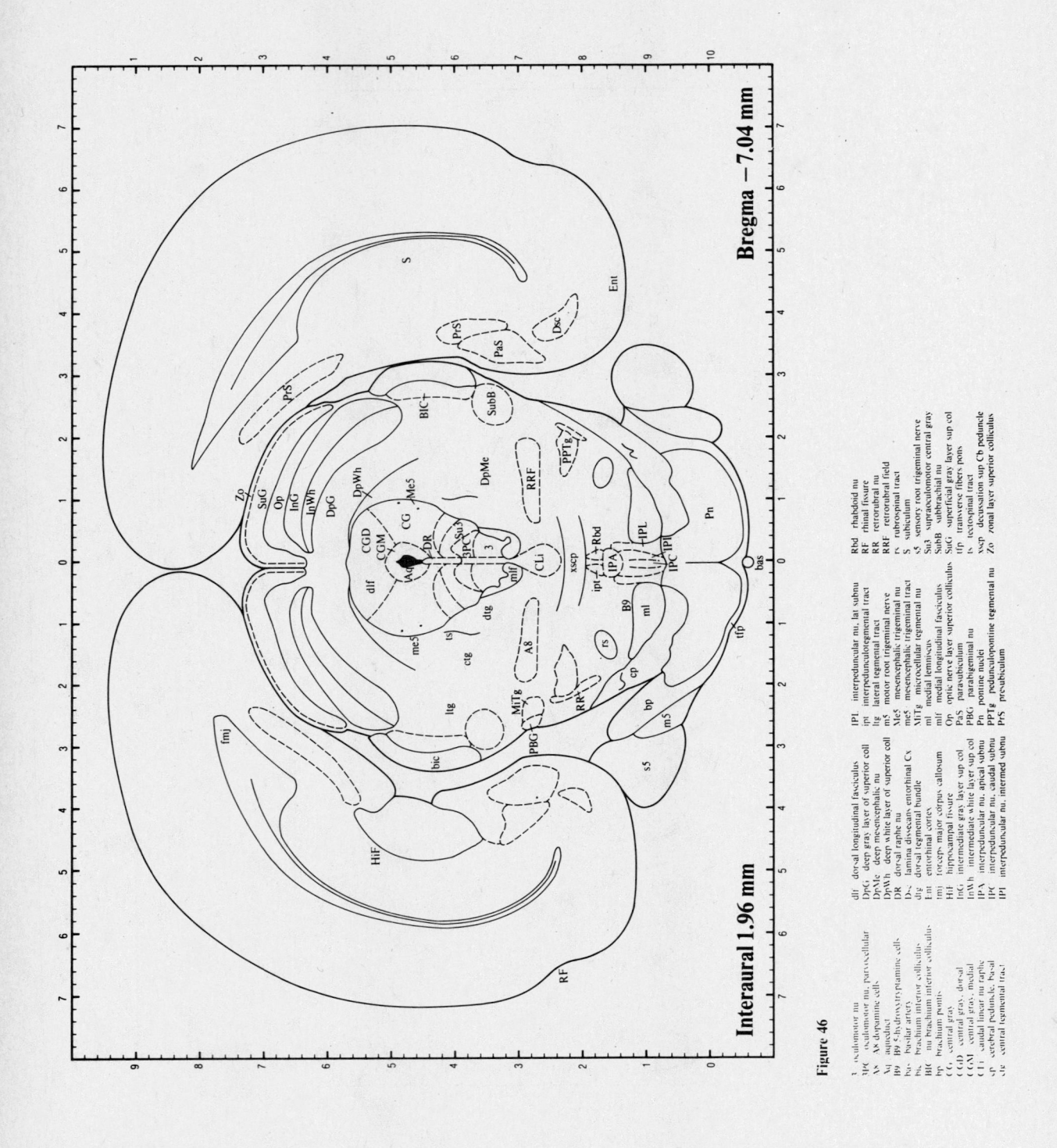

Figure 46

Appendix C: Stereotaxic Atlas

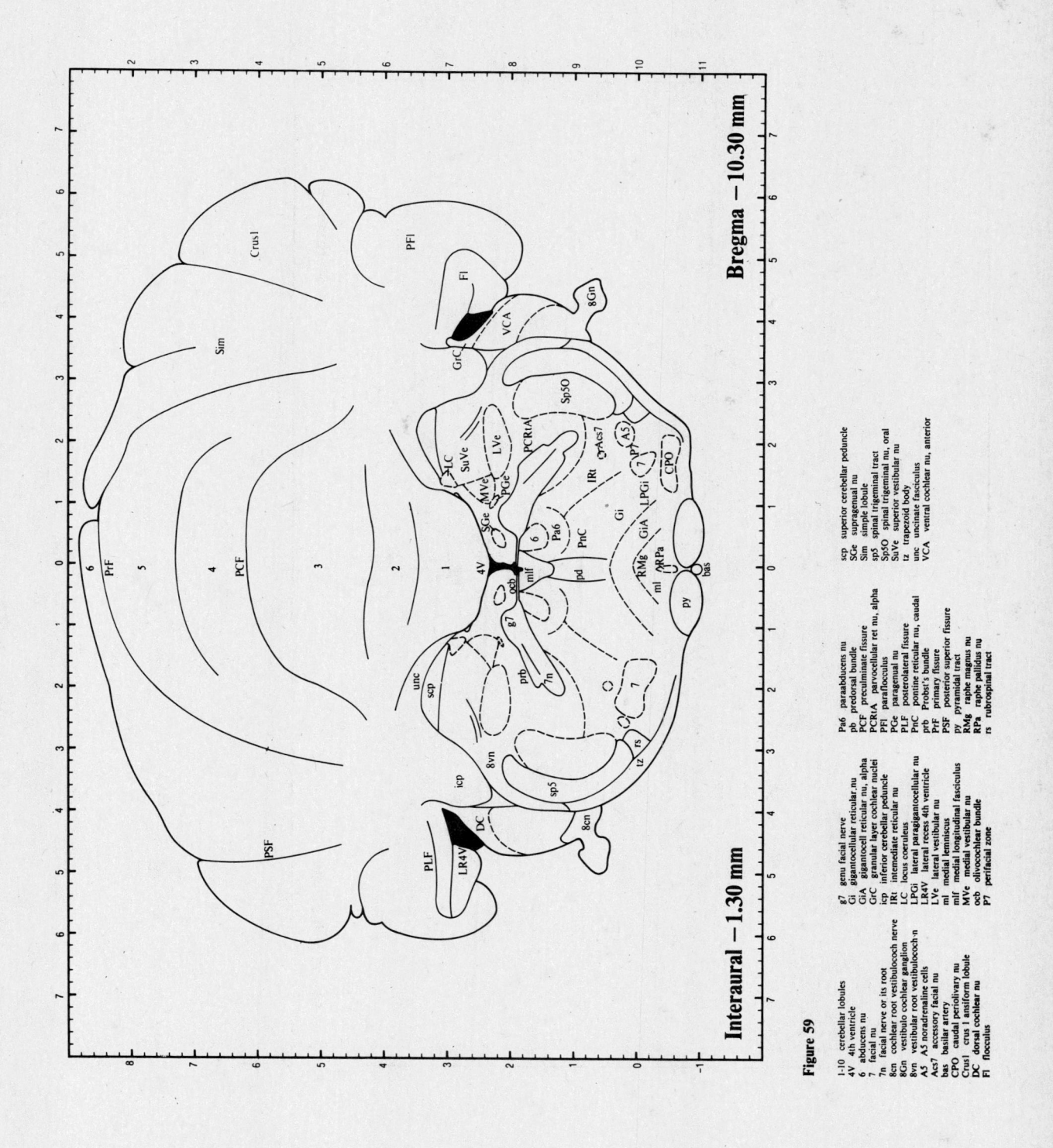

Figure 59

Appendix C: Stereotaxic Atlas

Interaural – 4.80 mm   **Bregma – 13.80 mm**

Figure 73

1-10	cerebellar lobules	dsc	dorsal spinocerebellar tract	PM	paramedian lobule
10	dorsal motor nu vagus	Ge5	gelatinous layer caudal sp trigem	PMn	paramedian reticular nu
12	hypoglossal nu	Gr	gracile nu	PPF	prepyramidal fissure
12n	root of hypoglossal nerve	ia	internal arcuate fibers	py	pyramidal tract
A1	A1 noradrenaline cells	IOA	inferior olive, subnu A med nu	Ro	nu Roller
Amb	ambiguus nu	IOB	inferior olive, subnu B med nu	ROb	raphe obscurus nu
AP	area postrema	IOBe	inferior olive, beta subnu	RPa	raphe pallidus nu
APMF	ansoparamedian fissure	IOC	inferior olive, subnu C med nu	RVL	rostroventrolateral reticular nu
C1	C1 adrenaline cells	IOD	inferior olive, dorsal nu	SF	secondary fissure
CC	central canal	IOK	inferior olive, cap kooy med nu	Sol	nu solitary tract
Cop	copula pyramis	LRt	lateral reticular nu	sol	solitary tract
Crus-2	crus 2 ansiform lobule	LRtPC	lat reticular nu, parvocellular	SolC	nu solitary tract, commissural
cu	cuneate fasciculus	MdD	medullary reticular field, dorsal	sp5	spinal trigeminal tract
Cu	cuneate nu	MdV	medullary reticular nu, ventral	SpSC	spinal trigeminal nu, caudal
CVL	caudoventrolateral reticular nu	mlf	medial longitudinal fasciculus	Sp5I	spinal trigem nu, interpolar

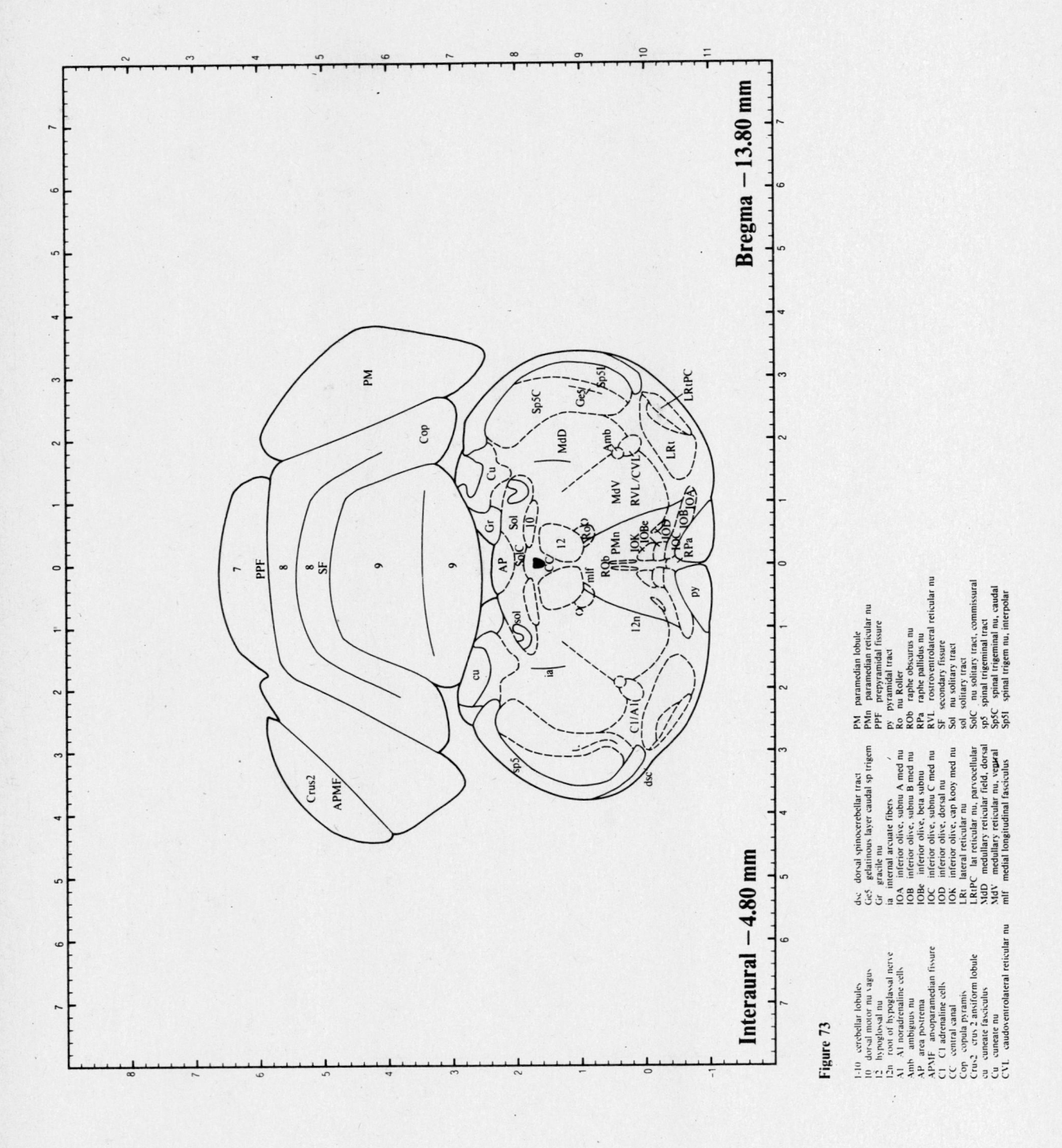

204